GOD
and the
ANCIENT
CHINESE

Samuel Wang
and
Ethel R. Nelson

Read Books Publisher
Dunlap, TN

All Scripture quotations in this books are from the New King James Version of the Holy Bible (unless otherwise designated). NKJV copyright © 1979, 1980, 1982 by Thomas Nelson, Inc., Used by permission.

Copyright © 1998 by Samuel Wang

Second printing 2002

Published by Read Books Publisher
HCR 65, Box 580
Dunlap, TN 37327

All rights reserved. No part of this publication may be reproduced, stored in a retrieval system, or transmitted, in any form or by any means, electronic, mechanical, photcopying, recording, or otherwise, without the prior written permission of Read Books Publisher.

ISBN 0-937869-02-3

Library of Congress Catalog Card Number: 99-70410

Dedication

To the Holy Man who died on the cross, and to the Chinese and the world for whom He died.

ABOUT THE COVER PAINTING

ARTIST: Li Wei San

And someone will say to Him, "What are these wounds in your hands?"
Then He will answer, "Those with which I was wounded in the house of my friends."
(Zechariah 13: 6).

Contents

About the Authors — vii

Introduction — xi

PART I: God Reigned Over China
1. China in Bible Prophecy — 1
2. Discovering Ancient Chinese Prophets — 9
3. Origin and Preservation of Chinese Classics — 21
4. Mencius' Amazing Prophecy — 29
5. The Original God of China — 47

PART II: The Mystery of the Dao
6. Unlocking the Mystery of Dao — 61
7. The Breath of God — 73
8. The Great Plan of Heaven — 81
9. The Master and His Dream — 93

PART III: The Holy Man
10. Behold the Holy Man! — 105
11. Suffering of the Holy Man — 117
12. Poetry of the Creator — 131
13. The Most Excellent Way — 145

PART IV: Sons of the Prince
14. The Way of Man — 161
15. The New Book of Changes — 175
16. Communication with Heaven — 187
17. The Temple of Heaven — 201

PART V: Lost Dao Restored
18. The First Truth and the First Deception — 213
19. The Time Has Come — 227
20. The Course of Heaven — 239
21. The Great Harmony World — 255

Epilogue — 271

References and Notes — 273

Bibliography — 292

Appendix of Quotations in Chinese from the Classics — 294

About the Authors

诗以言志，文以载道。
"Poetry is to express one's will, and writings to convey the Dao [Tao, the truth]."
This is a faithful Chinese saying.

The great Dao of Heaven and the teachings of early Chinese kings and sages were faithfully recorded in ancient Chinese writings over a period of 2,000 years before Christ. Yesteryear's lessons are always today's blessings. Much can be learned, by modern Chinese and Westerners alike, from the way God dealt with the ancient Chinese.

God and the Ancient Chinese is a unique, comparative study of the Chinese classics with the Bible. It is a witness to *"the true Light which gives light to every man who comes into the world,"* (John 1: 9), and to the truth that *"God shows no partiality. But in very nation whoever fears Him and works righteousness is accepted by Him."* (Acts 10: 34, 35). The God of the ancient Chinese is the God of the Bible.

To write such a book is beyond anything I could earlier have imagined. I was born into a farmer's family near the Yangtze River. My father had only six months of education in school. His total learning was from the so-called *Four Books*, a collection of Confucius' and Mencius' teachings, which he had memorized. Ours is a large family—it always takes two tables to have everyone seated at family gatherings. At the time of a family reunion in my parents' home, my father would always recite from these *Four Books*. He especially liked *The Works of Mencius*. This tradition has come down for years, with the same teachings being repeated time and time again—now even the third generation can repeat the stories and sayings. These occasions give special opportunity for the younger generation to be educated in the great traditions of these ancient writings, woven together with our parents' deep love for them. The effect has been tremendous.

But my father no longer had these books in his possession. His only set, which had been well kept in a fine wooden box, was carried away with everything else in the house in a flood before I was born. But we learned that even before he could understand them, he had been required to memorize all the books. That was the practice for teaching young Chinese students in his day. I can never forget the scene when my father saw the gift I brought for his very important 70th birthday. He jumped up from his chair to receive the *Four Books* in a modern edition, tears running down his wrinkled face. For a long time, he stood there speechless, holding the volume as he would the hands of a long lost friend.

In 1994, I went home for another celebration of my father's birthday. Since I had recently accepted Jesus Christ as my best Friend and Saviour, this time I presented my father another book—The Holy Bible. After reading it carefully, he said that the teachings of Jesus were even greater and clearer than those of the *Four Books*. You may have correctly concluded already that both of my parents became the first Christians in their village. They have since turned their home into a house church.

My interest in the Bible was first kindled by attending lectures in social linguistics given by John Evans, an American teacher in my graduate program. Mr. Evans always closed his class by analyzing a Chinese character, and relating the corresponding story recorded in his "favorite Book," a phrase that he used in a communist classroom, indicating the Bible. All the students were amazed to see the integral connection of Chinese characters to the Holy Bible. Later Mr. Evans gave me a copy of *Discovery of Genesis*, the book he used for his character study in the class. That was my first acquaintance with the name of Dr. Ethel Nelson, the other author of the present book. Dr. Nelson's character-study books have planted the seeds of Heaven in the hearts of many modern Chinese, including myself. I realized and accepted for the first time the most obvious and scientific fact: modern Chinese come from the ancient Chinese; and the ancient Chinese came from God, not from Peking Man!

If our Chinese characters could entail so much information about God, how much more should the ancient writings, written with these characters, reveal God to us. As you have seen, my interest and love for the Chinese Classics were implanted in my heart when I was very young, and I have always wanted to understand these books which were so dear to my father. Since studying them myself, a new world has opened for me. My parents' ready acceptance of Christianity convinced me more than anything else that there must be a close connection between the teachings of Chinese sages and of Jesus.

Jesus said to the Jews, *"For had you believed Moses, you would believe Me, for he wrote about Me. But if you do not believe his writings, how will you believe My words?" (John 5: 46, 47)*. This should also be true for those who love and believe the ancient Chinese sages, for they also wrote of Him, as you will find out in this book.

All of these happenings led me to the idea of writing this book. It is my special honor and pleasure to work with Dr. Nelson, whose input has helped make this book possible. We both believe that it is divine Providence that led us to collaborate. The Chinese idiom, "to weed through the old and bring forth the new," (推陈出新), holds the same principle as what Jesus said in *Matthew 13: 52: "Therefore every scribe instructed concerning the kingdom of heaven is like a householder who brings out of his treasure things new and old."* Of course, neither of us is a scribe or a scholar of the Chinese Classics in any sense, yet "things new and old" were discovered in our humble effort. It is our wish that, in the light of the Bible, this book will restore the teachings of the ancient kings and sages that have been distorted, and be of some help in kindling the ancient love for God in the hearts of the Chinese.

I especially want to thank Dr. David Lin, who, incidentally, baptized me in a bathtub in Shanghai, and more recently has taken pains to critically review this manuscript and encourage us in pursuing this important study.

Our special thanks are extended to Bob Smith and Wayne Senner for their generous help. My appreciation goes to Dr. and Mrs. Yew Por Ng who brought Dr. Nelson and myself together. Jeff and Christy Reich have given us their support in many ways. The cover painting was produced by the artist, Li Wei San, after several telephone conversations to China, where he lives. Terri Prouty helped design the cover, and assisted with copy editing. My personal thanks goes to Dr. Drew Liu and Dr. Andrew Lai, whose friendship and help have been a living witness to me that we do have a loving Father in Heaven. I am also greatly indebted to Dr. Charles Taylor, Dr. and Mrs. Sukachevin, Traci Lemon, Mr. and Mrs. Shen, Dr. and Mrs. Dai, Dr. Samuel Young, Pastor Joseph Jiao, Dr. Joseph Hwang and all my church family, and all those supporting our study in many ways.

Finally, I want to express our gratitude to last century's missionary, James Legge, whose translation of the Chinese Classics has been a great help in preparing this book. My translation of the Chinese texts may sometimes be quite different from his. I take responsibility for any errors in translation.

        Samuel Wang
        September 28, 1998
        Chinese Ministries International
        P.O. Box 958
        Whitwell, TN 3739
        Email: CMI@fuyin.org

Introduction

It has been my privilege to be acquainted with Samuel Wang and Dr. Ethel Nelson during the years of their sojourn in China. My friendship with Samuel Wang began after he had spent many years as a leading Yoga teacher in China. He had studied under a famous Hindu guru and had translated, published and distributed scores of titles of Yoga scriptures, including *Bhagavad-gita As It Is*, all over China, and had raised up several groups of Yoga enthusiasts among Chinese university students.

He had read the Bible before, but never saw any light in it until he was led to a right understanding of the truth about life and death, of which he and Dr. Nelson have written in depth in this book. It convinced him that the truth he had been searching for is in the Bible. He repudiated all religious errors built on reincarnation, the so-called "spiritual evolution," and false gods, and dedicated himself to studying and preaching Jesus Christ, the Son of God, as revealed in the Bible. This led him to many new discoveries in the Chinese Classics, in which he had been trained from childhood.

Dr. Nelson was a medical missionary to Thailand for twenty years, and was later led to the study of Chinese philology and etymology. Her study first appeared in *The Discovery of Genesis*, written with Pastor C. H. Kang. Her latest book is *God's Promise to the Chinese*. Both books deal with the comparison of Chinese characters and the Bible.

The authors of this book are of widely differing backgrounds, but have a like faith in the Holy Scriptures, and share the same conviction that there existed a close communion between God and the ancient Chinese, as evinced in certain ancient Chinese writings, as well as in the Chinese characters.

The research done by Samuel Wang and Ethel Nelson in their particular fields has borne fruit in this book, which is now published separately in Chinese and English. While both present the same substance, neither one is a translation of the other. In either book, the reader will find a wealth of material to demonstrate that God loves the "heathen" as well as those who have a knowledge of Bible truth. Said Peter the apostle, *"In truth I perceive that God shows no partiality. But in every nation whoever fears Him and works righteousness is accepted by Him." Acts 10: 34, 35 (NKJV).*

The authors have pooled their efforts in digging out Bible truths that had been buried in the works of ancient Chinese sages, who, Samuel believes, were raised up by God to educate and uplift the Chinese people.

China stands out as the only Oriental nation whose origins date back to the time when Egypt, Assyria and Babylon flourished far to her west. Today those ancient peoples have long become extinct. Their hieroglyphs and cuneiform writings are dead languages known to only a few scholars, while the Chinese race and culture continue to thrive, now in her fifth millennium, and a positive factor in the modern world.

Samuel Wang and Dr. Nelson believe that China's vitality is due mainly to the saving influence of the teachings of noble ethical principles which were taught and perpetuated in the ancient Chinese classics, but are missing in the literature of other ancient races other than the Jews. This is the leading thought in the chapters of this book. Samuel Wang goes so far as to believe that God raised up prophets in China in the same manner as He called the prophets of ancient Israel, though perhaps, not speaking through them so directly.

Much has been written on Chinese culture, and yet more on biblical studies, but few scholars have attempted a systematic comparison of ancient Chinese ethical writings with biblical theology. Linguistic differences have made it difficult to arrive at a common terminology, yet discerning minds can see a similarity of Chinese moral concepts with divine ideals revealed in the Bible. Now we have grounds to believe that these two streams of thought came from the same source. The present work strives to bridge over this terminological gulf to discover that common source. And the authors imagine that this treatise might be regarded as an initial attempt at a systematic theology of the Chinese Classics.

Samuel Wang observes that the ancient Chinese had long looked for the appearance of the Prince, the King, the Holy Man, the Incarnated Dao, the Faithful, the Son of Heaven, coming from above to teach, to bring peace and love to the world and establish the Great Harmony. This book explains that all these longings and prophecies were fulfilled in the Man who died on the cross. Here the lesser light in ancient Chinese writings met the Great Light, *"the true Light which gives light to every man coming into the world" (John 1: 9)*. Jesus Christ is the One to whom the Chinese Classics point and testify! The Bible is truly the Book from the God of Heaven!

More than a century of archeological discoveries have confirmed the historical accuracy of the Bible. For not a shred of real evidence turned up by the spade has yet disproved any biblical record. The findings of our two authors have added more facts from a different angle to strengthen this observation. One example is the year 1766 B.C. Genesis 41: 57 says that the seven-year famine in Joseph's time was "in all the world," not in Egypt alone. Taking the year 2348 B.C as the year of Noah's Flood according to James Ussher's chronology, and then adding up the ages of the patriarchs recorded in Genesis 10 through 46, we come to 1766 B.C. as the year Jacob entered Egypt at the age of 130. That was the second year of the seven-year famine. Now, 1766 B.C. happens to be the first year of the Chinese Shang dynasty (1766 - 1123 B.C.). A reference from *Lu's Spring and Autumn* says that a five-year famine occurred in the beginning of the reign of King Tang, the first monarch of that dynasty. Later writers have corrected this statement by citing earlier records to show that the famine actually lasted seven years, beginning two years before the change of the dynasty. 1766 B.C. is right on target! This is but one of the remarkable harmonies between Chinese history and the Bible record. It is another hard evidence that proves the accuracy of the Bible record.

After reading this book, I can say that every thoughtful reader will be benefited not only intellectually, but spiritually. To one who believes the Bible, the fresh evidence will strengthen his faith. To one not familiar with the Bible, many facts will convince him of its unique value—that it is indeed the word of God.

> David Lin,
> Retired pastor of the Mu En Tang church,
> Shanghai, China.

1

China in Bible Prophecy

One fifth of the world's population today is Chinese. China, occupying the third largest area on earth, has always fascinated modern western minds because of its more than 4,000 years of undivided history and culture. The great ancient insights and wisdom manifested by Confucius (孔子, 551 - 479 B.C.) and Lao Zi (老子, c. 570 B.C.) are spiritual treasures of the world. In the darkness of today's lax morality, the light from these ancient jewels are still shining. If the Bible is a book for all peoples, it seems only reasonable to find China at least mentioned in the Bible! Does the Bible speak of China? In searching for an answer to this intriguing question, let us start our quest by delving into a bit of China's ancient history.

For millennia, China has called herself 神州, "the land of God." It would appear that the Hand of Omnipotence was leading this ancient civilization. In the annals of Chinese history, we do not find a single instance of God's anger being poured out upon a Chinese city because of moral depravity, as happened to Sodom, Gomorrah, or Pompeii. Ancient Chinese art has never featured pornography or naked female sculptures—like that uncovered in Near and Middle East excavations.[1]

When it comes to China, however, you might agree that, for most people in the world today, the familiar image that comes to mind is not Confucius or high moral standards, but the Great Wall! Construction of the Great Wall was intensified by the first Chinese emperor, Qin Shi Huangdi (秦始皇, 259 - 210 B.C.).

The Chinese nation, earlier known as the "Middle Kingdom," (中国) dates back to 2205 B.C. with its first dynasty, the Xia (夏), established by King Yu (禹). Even today in China, King Yu is still well-remembered as "the great Yu." He was favored by ShangDi [上帝, the God of Heaven] who instructed him in the nine methods which enabled him to solve the problem of draining a huge flood that prevented further development and habitation of their land.[2] King Yu was also renowned as a virtuous and exemplary ruler, providing a fit pattern for later rulers to emulate.

Following the Xia were the Shang (商) and Zhou (周) dynasties. Each of these kingdoms ruled over many states, some of these states having more extensive land and greater power than the royal dynasty itself. We will learn that most of the many kings of these first three dynasties served as Heaven-appointed agents, ministering by love rather than by force.

During the later Zhou dynasty, the rulers of the eastern states fought one another for the control of all China. In 221 B.C., the Qin State defeated all its rivals and established China's first empire controlled by a strong self-imposed emperor, Qin Shi Huangdi. Thus China entered its fourth dynasty, the Qin, (秦, 221 - 206 B.C.).

To keep out invaders, Qin Shi Huangdi ordered the construction, repair and strengthening of the Great Wall, which, with its eventual completion, stretches about 4,000 miles. It was built with the blood and tears shed by thousands of slave workers under ruthless oppression, and was finished several centuries after the Qin dynasty. The Great Wall, the greatest human project in the history of mankind, has a sad history. Many of the 300,000 workers, who suffered from a most inhumane and cold-blooded treatment, lie entombed within its massive structure. Even though the Great Wall today is a symbol of unity and peace for the Chinese, no one can forget the high price paid to keep out potential foreign aggressors. Now, more than 2,200 years after Qin Shi Huangdi, the Great Wall has gradually become a landmark of unity for Chinese all over the world, and an identifying symbol of China. The name of "China" in all foreign languages of the world finds its root in the Qin [Chin] Dynasty.

Back to our opening question: does the Bible, which is meant for all people of the world, have anything to say about the land of China? The Holy Bible, inspired by the Holy Spirit of God and written by more than 40 authors over a period of 1,600 years, faithfully records the words of the God of the universe. It is a treasure mine of priceless truth. It is the great standard of right and wrong, clearly defining sin and holiness. Of all the books that have flooded the world, however valuable, the Bible is the most deserving of our closest study and attention.

The Bible opens the history of past ages. Without it we should have been left to fables and speculation regarding occurrences in past eras. This sacred volume gives not only an accurate history of the creation of this world, a history of our human race, but also the world's only authentic account of the origin of nations. It contains instruction concerning the wonders of the universe, and reveals God as the Author of the heavens and the earth. The Scriptures unfold a simple and complete system of theology and philosophy. Without the Bible, we are soon enveloped by false theories, superstition, and spiritual darkness.

Although unappreciated by many in today's secular world, the Bible is, in fact, the foundation of all true knowledge, for it is the revelation of God to man. Throughout the ages God's divine hand has preserved its purity. The many mysteries found in the Bible are perhaps the strongest evidence of its divine inspiration. One of these mysteries is Bible prophecy—foretelling persons or events in the future. In the entire Bible there are thousands of prophecies. By now, most of them have been exactly fulfilled in time and place as predicted. The rise and fall of nations have been foretold in the Bible long before they happened. Some prophecies are yet to be fulfilled in due time. This is entirely beyond human comprehension!

Jesus clearly revealed God's purpose for giving prophecies when He said:

> *"And now I have told you before it comes,*
> *that when it does come to pass, you may believe."*
> *(John 14: 29).*

One of the most powerful, yet often neglected, Bible prophecies that might bring conviction to the Chinese, as well as the world, is the prophecy of China written by Isaiah (c. 720 - 680 B.C.).

The ancient Dead Sea Scrolls,[3] found in 1947, include the book of Isaiah, and once again confirm that today's Bible is accurate and reliable. This verse in Isaiah is thought to refer to China:

> *Surely these shall come from afar;*
> *Look, those from the north and the west;*
> *And these from the <u>land of Sinim</u>.*
> *(Isaiah 49: 12).*

You may wonder what the word "Sinim" means. Where is this land of Sinim, mentioned by Isaiah before his service was terminated in 680 B.C.?[4] According to *Strong's Concordance*, "Sinim is a distant Oriental region."[5] *Young's Concordance* reports, "Sinim is a people in the far east; the Chinese?"[6]

However, the meaning is still not quite clear. Let us now check an English dictionary for help: "'Sino' indicates Chinese; for example, Sinophile. [French, from Late Latin Sinae, the Chinese, from Greek Sinai, from Arabic Sin; China, from Chinese (Mandarin) Ch'in [Qin], dynastic name of the country.]"[7]

Now it is clear that the Hebrew word "Sinim" means China, as can be seen, for example, in the word "sinology"—a study of things Chinese. As we mentioned earlier, all Chinese roots meet in the Qin dynasty. However, the Hebrew alphabet does not have the equivalent of "ch" in English and "Q" in Chinese. Thus Qin has been phonetically translated as "Sinim."

China in Bible Prophecy

In Isaiah's day, the state of Qin (770-256 B.C.) was only one of hundreds of states under Zhou. It was located in the present Gansu (甘肃) Province through which trade with the West was conducted. How is it that Isaiah chose Qin to indicate the Middle Kingdom? What was so special about Qin?

Rang Kung (襄公) was appointed as the first Duke of Qin (770 B.C.), then a small, aristocratic house. Under his administration, the state of Qin emerged as one of the 14 major states under the Zhou dynasty.[8] It was 500 years after Isaiah that Qin Shi Huangdi defeated all the other competitive states and established the Qin dynasty. From then on, Qin represented the Middle Kingdom [China].

Simply put, the God of Isaiah, with divine foreknowledge, saw all the stages in the development of Qin—from a small, dependent, aristocratic house to becoming the famous Qin empire. God knew that the Duke of Qin would become ever stronger, equal with those of the other 13 states. Furthermore, He foresaw that after another 500 years, the Dukedom of Qin would still exist, defeat all the other states, and unite them as one empire, even choosing "Qin" as the name for the new empire!

Some attempt has been made to identify Sinim as Syene [Aswan] in upper Egypt. Yet a closer look at what Isaiah said precludes this opinion. Listen to what he said:

> *Indeed He says,*
> *"It is too small a thing that You*
>   *should be My Servant*
> *To raise up the tribes of Jacob,*
> *And to restore the preserved ones of Israel;*
> *I will also give You as <u>a light to the Gentiles</u>,*
> *That You should be <u>My salvation</u>*
>   *<u>to the ends of the earth</u>."*
>   *(Isaiah 49: 6).*

God proclaimed here that the mission of His Servant [Jesus Christ] was not limited to the salvation of the Jewish nation and its colonies [like Aswan] alone, but is also extended to all Gentiles throughout the world. In fact, when Jesus affirmed the faith shown by the Roman centurion [a Gentile] He said,

> "And I say to you that many will come <u>from east and west</u>, and sit down with Abraham, Isaac, and Jacob in the kingdom of heaven." (Matthew 8:11).

Jesus used the expression, "from the east and west," to represent all the Gentiles. Isaiah used the term, "those from the north and the west and these from the land of Sinim," in the same sense. "These from the land of Sinim" should naturally be a large group of people among the Gentiles. Only China, not the small city Aswan, could fit this verse well. Also, compare Jeremiah 44:1: *"The word that came to Jeremiah concerning <u>all the Jews who dwell in the land of Egypt</u>, who dwell at Migdol, at Tahpanhes, at Noph, and in the country of Pathros, ..."* Here Jeremiah, in his time, failed to even mention Aswan as a place where Jews were living in Egypt!

Isaiah's prophecy about China did not stop with the Qin dynasty, but rather it extended into the future. Over the 2,600 years since Isaiah, many countries have come and gone, but the land of Sinim [Qin] still stands firm as the land of China.

The most exciting phases of this prophecy relative to "Sinim" will surely continue to be fulfilled. Reading earlier verses in this 49th Chapter of Isaiah, we find these words:

> *"That You [Jesus Christ] may say to the*
> * prisoners, 'Go forth,'*
> *To <u>those who are in darkness</u>,*
> * 'Show yourselves....'*
> *For He who has mercy on*
> * them will lead them,*
> *Even by the springs of water*
> * He will guide them....*
> *Surely these shall come from afar;*
> *Look! Those from the north*

> *and the west,*
> *And these from the land of Sinim."*
> *(Isaiah 49: 9, 10, 12).*

Isaiah's foretelling of a final gathering of God's faithful among those "in darkness" must indicate a multitude of peoples—even from China. Most of the people living in China, since Isaiah's day, have been "in darkness" concerning the Savior of the world, Jesus Christ. Yet here is a specific prophesy and a promise to bring "prisoners of darkness" in the land of Sinim to the light of salvation, freedom and mercy.

We mentioned earlier that the Great Wall has forever been associated with the land of China—ever since the establishment of the Qin dynasty. The existence of the Great Wall is reminiscent of its first builder and planner. Hundreds of emperors have ruled and died in the long history of China. Most of them are forgotten. But the name of Qin Shi Huangdi stands out! (We will learn more of him later.)

The same prophet Isaiah foretold that the God of Israel paid the greatest price of all in sending His Son, Jesus Christ, to rescue fallen humanity! Jesus Christ came to earth, was nailed to a wooden cross, and died that all mankind might be rescued from sin. He would bear the nail print scars in the palms of His hands forever.

Does the God of Israel know and care about the land of Sinim [China]? Listen to what He says right after the prophecy of China in this book:

> *"Can a woman forget*
>   *her nursing child,*
> *And not have compassion*
>   *on the son of her womb?*
> *Surely they may forget,*
>   *Yet I will not forget you.*
> <u>*See, I have inscribed you*</u>
>   <u>*on the palms of My hands*</u>;

Your walls are continually before Me."
(Isaiah 49: 15 - 16).

The land of Sinim is still there. The massive Walls are still before the people of China and before the God of Israel. God has not forgotten the people of China, for He says, *"See, I have inscribed you on the palms of My hands."* Jesus also died for the people of China who must now come out of darkness. We must learn why it was necessary for this Holy Man, the suffering Servant, to die. Just as the Great Wall cannot be separated from the land of Sinim, so the Great Wall of defense from evil and sin, built at the cost of Jesus Christ's blood on Calvary, cannot be separated from the God of Israel!

One might ask if, since the God of heaven was so interested in Sinim as to speak through His prophet Isaiah regarding this distant nation, is there a possibility that God could have spoken directly to the people of China in past ages? Could He actually have raised up "prophets" for Himself in this ancient land? If so, could these ancient Chinese wise men yet speak to the people of China today?

2

Discovering Ancient Chinese Prophets

> *... the living God, who made heaven, the earth, the sea, and all things that are in them, ...in bygone generations allowed all nations to walk in their own ways. Nevertheless He did not leave Himself without witness....*
> *(Acts 14: 15 - 17).*

As the sun has never stopped giving light to the earth from the beginning, so it has been with the *"Sun of Righteousness." (Malachi 4: 2).*

> *That was the true Light which gives light*
> <u>*to every man coming into the world*</u>.
> *(John 1: 9).*

The controversy between good and evil, light and darkness, truth and deception has been in constant conflict since man's fall. The True Light has been *"given to every man coming into the world."* There was never a moment when man was left in total darkness on the earth.

> *And the Scripture, foreseeing that God would justify <u>the Gentiles (nations)</u> by faith, preached the*

gospel to Abraham beforehand, saying, "In you all the nations shall be blessed." (Galatians 3: 8).

It was God's will that *"He chose us in Him before the foundation of the world, that we should be holy and without blame before Him in love." (Ephesians 1: 4)*. <u>It was God who preached the gospel beforehand to the nations</u>. How? Through His prophets: *"God, who at various times and in different ways spoke in time past to the fathers by the prophets." (Hebrews 1: 1)*.

Has the gospel of peace ever been preached to other countries besides Israel in ancient times? Was it possible that the message has been preached to ancient China?

The apostle Paul said,

> *So then faith comes by hearing,*
> *and hearing by the word of God.*
> *But I say, have they not heard? Yes indeed:*
> *"Their sound has gone out <u>to all the earth</u>,*
> *And their words to the<u> ends of the world</u>."*
> *(Romans 10: 17, 18).*

As Paul pointed out, if *"their sound has gone to all the earth, and their words to the ends of the world,"* then there should have been voices of truth in the land of Sinim [China] in ancient times. The Bible calls the coming Messiah *"the Desire of All Nations." (Haggai* 2: 7). This indicates a desire for Him had been planted in all nations from the beginning.

Who could these voices be in ancient China? Were there "prophets" through whom God could speak? If so, who might the Chinese prophets have been?

To answer these questions, let us first define a "prophet."

The dictionary definition is: "One who utters divinely inspired revelations; one gifted with more than ordinary spiritual and moral insight; one who foretells future events; an effective or leading spokesman for a cause, doctrine, or group."[1]

The Chinese, on the other hand, have their own unique definition of a *prophet* 先知, which means *the first* 先 *to know, understand* 知. The ancient Chinese wise man, Mencius (孟子, 372 - 289 B.C.), recorded the definition of Yi Yin (伊尹), a sage of early 1700 B.C., often quoted also by Confucius. According to Yi Yin:

> **Heaven's [God's 天] plan for the education and cultivation of mankind is this: that they who are *first informed* should instruct those who are later to be informed, and they whose *understanding is given first* should instruct those whose understanding comes after them. I am one of Heaven's [God's] people who have been *first informed;*—I will take these principles and instruct the people in them.[2]**

The Bible definition of a prophet is similar, for God reveals His plans first to His prophet [God's spokesman], before taking action:

> *Surely the Lord GOD does nothing,*
> *Unless He reveals His secret*
> *to His servants the prophets. (Amos 3: 7).*

The Chinese prophet therefore not only received the message from the God of Heaven, but was also ordained as a teacher for his people, just as the *Shu Jing* (*Book of History*) records:

> **Heaven gives birth to kings;**
> **Heaven gives birth to teachers.**
> **The kings and teachers are assistants of Heaven**
> **To teach the people the love of Heaven.[3]**

While the name of "Heaven" is repeatedly used in the Chinese Classics, a clearer picture of this Deity is found in the Holy Bible. The God of the Bible is actually three divine Beings who act and think as One. These are God the Father, God the Son, and God the Holy Spirit. Each Member of the Godhead has a different role in relation to mankind. For example, the role of the Son was for Him to come to earth as a human. Therefore, *"when the fullness of time had come, God sent forth His Son, born of a woman," "taking the form of a bondservant, and coming in the likeness of men." (Galatians 4: 4; Philippians 2: 7).* He was born in Judea (now Israel) in 4 B.C. His name is JESUS, which means, *"for He will save His people from their sins." (Matthew 1: 21).* There are many prophetic references in the Hebrew Scriptures to the coming and mission of this divine Holy Man.

For example, note the 49th Chapter of Isaiah (already cited in Chapter 1), where God foretells of His Servant [Jesus Christ] to come:

> *"I will also give You [His Servant]*
> *as a light to the Gentiles,*
> *That You should be My salvation*
> *to the ends of the earth. . . .*
> *That You may say to the prisoners, 'Go forth,'*
> *To those who are in darkness,*
> *'Show yourselves. . .'*
> *For He who has mercy on them*
> *will lead them. . . ."*
> *(Isaiah 49: 6, 9, 10).*

Has this "light" ever come to ancient China? Has God shown Himself to the Chinese who have been "in darkness?" God has never forgotten the great land of China, nor the rest of the Chinese people scattered over the earth. Who could be God's Light-bearers to this ancient land? A clear clue can be found in the analysis of the commonly-used Chinese words *to understand, know* 知道. This literally means "to understand the *Dao*" [the Word, the Way] 道. (A detailed discussion of the *Dao* will be found in Chapter 6.)

Now let us analyze completely the character *to understand* 知. This reveals an *arrow* 矢 with a speaking *mouth* 口, indicating that real knowledge and understanding are like an arrow coming from God's mouth. When the prophet hears and understands God's word, he feels his heart being cut as by an arrow. Note again the 49th Chapter of Isaiah:

> *He made my mouth like a sharpened sword;*
> *in the shadow of his hand He hid Me;*
> *he made me into a polished <u>arrow</u>;*
> *and concealed me in his quiver.*
> *(Isaiah 49: 2, NIV).*

The arrow in God's quiver represents the Holy Spirit's moving on the prophet's mind.

> *For prophecy never came by the will of man,*
> *but <u>holy men of God spoke as they were moved</u>*
> *<u>by the Holy Spirit</u>. (2 Peter 1: 21).*

> *For the Word of God is living and powerful, and sharper than any two-edged sword, piercing even to the division of soul and spirit, and of joints and marrow, and is a discerner of the thoughts and intents of the heart. (Hebrews 4: 12).*

In this second verse, we find the mouth of God's Servant compared to a sword. *Ephesians 6: 17* says that *"the word of God"* is the *"sword of the Spirit."* The word of God was *"moved by the Holy Spirit."* When the *arrow* 矢 from God's *mouth* 口 pierced the prophet's heart, he began to know or *understand* 知.

Thus we may learn that Chinese sages, who lived righteous lives, were "moved by the Holy Spirit," (the third member of the Godhead) being "informed first" of the *Dao* [the Way], and it was their obligation to pass their knowledge on to others. This is not to say that everything these sages wrote was inspired, but certainly when prefaced by *"Heaven* [God 天] *said,"* or *"Shangdi* [God, the Heavenly Ruler 上帝] *said,"*—this was an indication of a prophetic message.

We have learned what a prophet is, and how it came to be that China has had prophets. Next, who were these prophets? Nearly everyone has heard of Confucius (孔子, 551 - 479 B.C.). Mostly he is known for his wise sayings.

He often referred to himself as an editor, for he collected and arranged ancient Chinese writings. However, his disciples and followers were so inspired by his words that they, in time, thought of him as a holy man. Today, Confucianism is one of several religious persuasions not only in China, but also in Korea, Singapore and Malaysia.

A contemporary of Confucius was Lao Zi (老子, c. 570 B.C.), today known as the founder of Daoism, "the Way," another great religious movement of China. Though events in his life are not clearly recorded, he left behind a short, yet wonderful book, *Dao De Jing*. Its only 5,000 words embrace almost every imaginable subject. Perhaps he has been misunderstood for thousands of years. Light hidden in his book has been covered by a mystical veil, and now the time has come to let it shine out!

Then there was Mencius (孟子, c. 372 - 289 B.C.), a philosopher and teacher who lived about a hundred years after Confucius and Lao Zi. He also left a religious legacy. There were a number of even earlier ancient Chinese prophets: two (Yao and Shun) being rulers in the so-called "legendary period." Before Confucius, the teachings of the ancient prophets were called "the Way of Yao and Shun." King Wen and the Duke of Zhou were also in the list of ancient Chinese prophets. Han Yu (韩愈, 768 - 824 A.D.), one of China's greatest poets and writers, wrote in his famous article, "On the Dao" [Way]:

> **What I call the Dao [Way] is this: Yao (尧) taught it to Shun (舜); Shun taught Yu (禹); Yu taught Tang (汤); Tang taught the Duke of Zhou (周公); The Duke of Zhou taught Confucius; Confucius taught Mencius. When Mencius died, the Dao [Way] is no longer taught in full any more.[4]**

Thus we find that the ancient Chinese were teaching the same *Dao* 道 throughout the years from Yao until Mencius. After Mencius, no other Chinese tried to establish a new independent religious system. (Buddhism is not of Chinese origin, but was imported from India). Now what remains to be discovered is the true interpretation of these men's venerable writings. One would fail to arrive at the right understanding without going back into ancient Chinese history.

The Chinese have kept accurate records since their first recorded Xia dynasty in 2205 B.C. Why were there no dynastic records prior to 2205 B.C.? Could it be that this was truly the beginning of the Chinese people as a nation? Is there another world record to shed light on this puzzle?

There is only one complete record in existence which chronicles earth history from its very creation, and that is the Hebrew Scriptures, preserved today as the Holy Bible. The first book (Genesis) of this inspired epic was written down, under the guidance of inspiration, by the prophet Moses in about 1500 B.C. It tells how, in the beginning, God created our earth, its plant life and bodies of water; its solar system; and all animal life—including mankind—in six literal days. *"And on the seventh day God ended His work which He had done, and He rested on the seventh day from all His work which He had done." (Genesis 2: 2).* Thus the weekly cycle was initiated, worldwide, for all time.

God created the first man, Adam, and his mate Eve, in His own image and likeness. They were perfect and holy. God placed them in the lovely Garden of Eden where there were two special trees: the Tree of Life and the Tree of the Knowledge of Good and Evil. Before they could receive God's full measure of blessing, their loyalty to Him must be proven. So God warned the first couple not to eat of the Tree of Knowledge or they would die. This was not because the fruit was poisonous, for God had said that everything which He had created was *"very good." (Genesis 1: 31).* But He reserved this tree as His own. When they saw the tree it would remind them of God's Creatorship, Ownership and Sovereignty. It was a reminder to be loyal to their great Benefactor.

It was God's mandate that mankind should know only the true and good. God did not want Adam and Eve to become acquainted with evil, with sin, with disappointment, pain, grief, and death. In love, God intended to withhold all of this from them, seeking only their good. On the other hand, God's enemy, Satan, a fallen angel, intended to ruin them. One day Eve met God's enemy, who, talking through a serpent, tempted her to eat the forbidden fruit. She then took some of the fruit to Adam and he ate also. Thus they disobeyed God's one test of loyalty and thereby became sinners. The beautiful new earth underwent dreadful changes as a result of this one act. (More details will be discussed in Chapter 8.)

Would God immediately strike them dead? No. Instead, this wonderful, loving Creator-God was merciful in providing a means of rescue. The three Holy Persons of the Godhead formulated their plan that God the Son would remove His glorious crown and step down from His throne in heaven. He would be born as a human babe in a stable surrounded by dumb animals, live and teach righteous living, and even in young adulthood suffer a cruel death so that *"whoever believes in Him should not perish but have everlasting life." (John 3: 16)*. A second chance with probational life was given to man that he might once again choose between good and evil, between truth and error, between God and Satan, between life and death.

Ten generations of mankind followed the creation of Adam and Eve, and as men multiplied on the earth, so did wickedness. According to the Bible, in the calculated year of 2348 B.C., God sent a world-wide flood to cleanse the earth of depravity. The waters covered every high mountain and destroyed all life, including mankind, except for faithful Noah, his wife, three sons and their wives—just eight people. God had instructed Noah to build a great ship in which, not only this family, but also, under God's direction, pairs of all animals, were preserved. The Chinese have memorialized this event in their character meaning *boat* 船 which shows a *vessel* 舟 with *eight* 八 *people (mouths)* 口.[5]

Interestingly, one of the oldest Chinese legends concerns a man named Nu-wa (女娲, note the phonetic similarity to Noah). "They told of Nu-wa, the progenitor of mankind, and Shen Nong (神农), and Fu Xi (伏羲) patriarchs whose names coincide with 'Shem' and the 'phe-th' in 'Japheth.' ('Ja' was lost in transmission because the Hebrew 'Yodh' is a weak consonant. The Chinese 'Xi' is pronounced 'hsi,' corresponding to the Hebrew 'th,' which Askenazic Jews pronounce like 's,' vocalizing 'Japheth' as 'Yaphess'). These were two of Noah's three sons. Why Ham's name was not preserved, we are not sure. His disrespect for his father may be one reason why his name was stricken from the honor roll of China's patriarchs."[6]

Legend tells us that Shen Nong invented agricultural tools and experimented with hundreds of herbs to determine which had healing properties. He is believed to be the "Father of Chinese medicine."[7] Fu Xi, by tradition believed to be the son of Nu-wa, taught how to catch fish with nets (fish would be the only available flesh food after the Flood). He is also credited with being the first author of the *Yi Jing,* the oldest written record of the Chinese.[8]

Scripture tells us that after the waters of the flood receded and Noah's family emerged from the ark, God instructed Noah to build an altar and sacrifice clean animals upon it in thanksgiving for the family's salvation. A beautiful rainbow appeared in the sky and God promised that He would never again destroy the earth with a flood. The Chinese legend relates that Nu-wa fused together five-colored rocks to patch up the heavens, which coincides with the scenario of Noah offering burnt sacrifices on a stone altar against a background rainbow spanning the heavens. (Genesis 8: 20; 9: 17).[9]

According to the Biblical record, after only three generations, just 101 years following the flood, another great debacle took place. Mankind had not only multiplied greatly during this period, but also became wicked again, defying God by building a great tower. God acted. This time He confused the common language and thus scattered over the earth various people groups who now had new and differing tongues.

> *But the LORD came down to see the city and the tower which the sons of men had built. And the LORD said, "Indeed the people are one and they all have one language, and this is what they begin to do; now nothing that they propose to do will be withheld from them. Come, let Us go down and there <u>confuse their language</u>, that they may not understand one another's speech."*
>
> *So the LORD <u>scattered them abroad from there over the face of all the earth</u>, and they ceased building the city. (Genesis 11: 5 - 8).*

This event took place about 2247 B.C. It certainly seems likely that at this time the Chinese family, with a new language, migrated from the area of the Tower of Babel in Mesopotamia, traveling eastward to the land of China where God appointed them a new habitation.

> *And He has made from one blood every nation of men to dwell on all the face of the earth, and <u>has determined their preappointed times and the boundaries of their dwellings</u>, so that they should seek the Lord, in the hope that they might grope for Him and find Him, though He is not far from each one of us. (Acts 17: 26, 27).*

This great event was also recorded in the ancient Chinese Classics:

The great Heaven gave this Middle Kingdom with its people and territories to the former kings.[10]

Not long thereafter, in 2205 B.C., China's first dynasty, the Xia, was founded. Referring now to ancient Chinese writings, we find mention of a "Legendary Period of Five Rulers." The last two rulers of this "Legendary Period," Yao and Shun, appear to have lived in the post-Flood period and were possibly leaders of the Chinese migration. Of Shun it is recorded that **"he sacrificed to Shangdi."**[11] *Shangdi* (上帝) is the earliest Chinese name for God. His attributes of creatorship are identical to those of the Hebrew

God, *Shaddai,* the "Almighty One." Note the similarity in the name "Shangdai," as it is pronounced in the Cantonese dialect, with "Shaddai."[12] Is this just a coincidence?

Both rulers, Yao and Shun of this ancient legendary period, are referred to as being "virtuous." They, together with Yi Yin, are perhaps the earliest of China's sages, and are rather frequently quoted by later sages. We will find that their teachings of righteousness are similar to biblical teachings. Furthermore, when we find that some prophecies of the ancient Chinese sages are nearly as accurate as those of the Bible, we will become convinced that these are from the *"true light which gives light to every man coming into the world." (John 1: 9).*

The ancient Chinese prophets, as voices for Heaven, left precious writings with God-given teachings. A controversy between Christ and Satan can be followed throughout Chinese history. One focus of the controversy between good and evil was the preservation or destruction of these writings. During a "dark age," an attempt was made to eradicate these books with their heavenly light by burning them, or by forbidding their reading. But darkness could not obscure light shining from the Sun of Righteousness! New light of truth has ever shone upon searching hearts in the land of Sinim.

The Bible says that *"The path of the just is like the shining sun, That shines ever brighter unto the perfect day." (Proverbs 4: 18).* As true light shines from the ancient Chinese prophets, this small light from them will point to the great shining Light—which is the Good News of the Bible—the Gospel from Heaven!

3

Origin and Preservation of the Chinese Classics

Like the Bible, the Chinese Classics have been preserved rather miraculously for millennia. Also like the Bible, these writings have multiple authors. It may come as a surprise to the Westerner that many of the Chinese authors point to *Heaven* [God] 天 as the inspiration for various of their writings. For thousands of years the sole purpose of this literature was to convey truth, or the *Dao* 道 [*Tao,* The Way and the Word].

In 1856 James Legge, a minister and missionary to China from the Nonconformist Church of England, began his 20-year, self-imposed task of translating the Chinese Classics. He was the first professor of the Chinese Department at Oxford University. As Legge viewed the 4,000-year existence of China, he declared: "It is clear that there must be amongst the people certain moral and social principles of the greatest virtue and power.... In no country is the admiration of scholastic excellence so developed as in China, no kingdom in the world where learning is so highly reverenced."[1]

The so-called Chinese Classics include nine books: *"The Four Books"* (《四书》) and the *"Five Jing"* (《五经》). In Chinese, *"Jing"* means *"Eternal Truth."* For the traditional Chinese, these books have held the same place as the Bible does for Christians. Having come down through the centuries, they have shaped Chinese culture and history, and are deeply rooted in the mentality and conscience of the common people. Even the invading conquerors, the Mongols and Manchus, unconditionally surrendered and adapted themselves to the Chinese way, in an "ideal Chinese victory"—virtue over force, and culture over the uncivilized. In this sense, the Chinese culture has never been broken.

The greatest disaster which the Chinese writings sustained was the order of Emperor Qin Shi Huangdi, founder of the Qin dynasty (255 - 209 B.C.) and unifier of China, to burn the ancient Books. In the 34th year of his reign (213 B.C.), Qin gave a feast in his palace where 70 Great Scholars appeared and wished him long life. But then there arose a dispute and the emperor turned to his prime minister, Li Si (李斯) for his opinion. It was the prime minister's devastating words which sealed the doom of the scholars.

Li Si began, "The scholars do not learn what belongs to the present day, but study antiquity. They go on to condemn the present time, leading the masses of the people astray, and to disorder. Your Majesty has consolidated the empire, and distinguished black from white. They still honor their peculiar learning, and combine together. They teach men what is contrary to your laws. If these things are not prohibited, Your Majesty's authority will decline. I pray that all the Records in charge of the Historiographers be burned, excepting those of this Qin dynasty, and that all who may dare to speak about these books be put to death—along with their relatives. Whoever shall not have burned their Books within thirty days after the issuing of the ordinance, should be branded and sent to labor on the Wall for four years."[2] Sadly, Li Si's harsh and unjust pronouncement became an imperial edict.

About 460 scholars were all buried alive in pits. The emperor's own son, Fu-su (扶苏), remonstrated with him, saying that such measures against those who repeated the words of Confucius and sought to imitate him would alienate all the people. This offended his father so much that the prince was sent away from the Imperial court to be with the general who was superintending the building of the Great Wall. The life of Qin Shi Huangdi lasted only three years after his edict took effect. He died in 210 B.C.[2]

This emperor was one of the most famous in the annals of Chinese history, for he accomplished much good, as well as evil. During the first 25 years of his reign, he conquered all of the separate warring states and unified China, as mentioned in the first chapter, declaring himself the "first universal emperor." From his dynastic name, Qin [Chin], comes the appellation of "China." Because of the threat of a Mongol invasion, he initiated the tremendous task of building the Great Wall. He built roads and a vast canal system. He even had Li Si standardize the style of their character-writing. But he also allowed the corruption and change of the ancient Border Sacrifice, and erected an additional four altars to the white, green, yellow, and red *"Dis"* [Heavenly Rulers].[3]

Qin Shi Huangdi was buried beneath a great artificial mound, 500 feet wide. The complex of subterranean passages was filled with untold treasures, even yet unexcavated. Ten thousand workmen employed in its construction were entombed with him.[4,5] In 1974, excavation of this mammoth 2,200-year-old burying ground at Xian was begun, and today is still being explored by Chinese archaeologists. Thousands of life-sized pottery soldiers and horses guard the resting emperor. Building on this immense mausoleum began when the king ascended the throne at the age of 13 and continued for 36 years, utilizing the services of some 700,000 slave artisans.[6]

Fortunately, in spite of the emperor's decree in 213 B.C., there was not complete destruction of the priceless books of antiquity. Scholars of the following Han dynasty set about to recover them from many reliable sources.

"The Four Books"

These are: *The Confucian Analects, The Great Learning, The Doctrine of the Mean* [Balance], and *The Works of Mencius.*

1. ***The Confucian Analects*** 《论语》: called *Lun Yu* in Chinese, record Confucius' discussions of various issues when asked (*Lun*), and his talks or teachings without being asked (*Yu*). The writings were compiled at least 40 years after Confucius' death. It is one of the earliest biographical pieces of literature in the world. From the time of recovery of the books during the Han Dynasty (206 - 8 B.C.), *Lun Yu* has been the most important textbook of Chinese students. Children are required to memorize the whole, long text before receiving an explanation by the teacher.

The *Lun Yu* consists of 20 chapters with 15,917 words altogether. It is a brief and simple recording of Confucius' talks and those among his disciples. Its depth and influence are beyond estimation. Only here one finds the most reliable life story of the Master. One copy of the *Analects*, along with other ancient texts, were discovered about 150 B.C. in the wall of Confucius' house when it was torn down. The book had evidently been secreted in the wall during the great burning of books in the Qin dynasty.

2. ***The Great Learning*** 《大学》 was originally Chapter 43 of the *Li Ji,* or *Record of Rites.* (《礼记》) Its authorship is in doubt. An ancient tradition attributes it to Zi Si, the grandson of Confucius. Zi Si was afraid lest the lessons of the former sages should become obscure, and the principles of the ancient sovereigns and kings be forgotten. He therefore made *The Great Learning* as the warp of them, and *The Doctrine of the Mean* as the woof. This book is a genuine monument of the Confucian school. There are not many words in it from the sage himself, but it is a faithful reflection of his teachings, written by his followers and not far removed from him by lapse of time.

The object of *The Great Learning* is to cite the duty of those who govern (probably the Sovereign) to observe the duty delegated by *Heaven, God* 天; to show virtue; to love the people and perform with the highest excellence. There are seven steps to attainment: investigation, knowledge, sincere thoughts, rectified heart, personal cultivation, regulated family, all of which ends with a tranquil kingdom.[7]

H. G. Wells, the famous English historian, listed *The Great Learning* with ten of the greatest books in the world.

3. ***The Doctrine of the Mean*** 《中庸》 is thought to have been recorded by Confucius' grandson, Zi Si (子思, 483 - 402 B.C.) who, as a boy, spent time with his grandfather. The story is told that one day the lad, upon hearing the sage sighing, asked, "Is your grief because your descendants fail to cultivate themselves and are unworthy, or is it because you are vexed because you fall short of the ways of Yao and Shun [early Chinese rulers and moral leaders]?" Confucius recognized in the wisdom of the boy someone who would carry on his undertakings. Although Zi Si did not reach the capacity of thought or administration that Confucius did, nevertheless he was considered a great philosopher and "Transmitter of the Sage."[8] He actually qualifies as a prophet, as previously defined (pp. 10, 11).

4. ***The Works of Mencius*** 《孟子》 is a book written by Mencius, himself, and his students to magnify the teachings of Confucius and attack heretical teachings of his time. The importance of this book is seen from the fact that Mencius is regarded as the second sage after Confucius himself. The illustrious "inheritance" of Mencius is seen in this quotation from Han Yu (768 - 824 A.D.), **"Yao handed the scheme of doctrine down to Shun; Shun handed it to Yu; Yu to Tang; Tang to Wen, Wu, and the Duke of Zhou; Wen, Wu, and the Duke of Zhou to Confucius; and Confucius to Mencius, on whose death there was no further transmission of it."**[9] Here, actually, we find listed the spiritual lineage of the Chinese sages!

"The Five Jing"

These are: *Yi Jing* [*I King*, "The Book of Changes"]; *The Shu Jing* [*The Shoo King*, "The Book of Documents"]; *The Shi Jing* [*The She King*, "The Book of Songs"]; *Li Ji* ["The Book of Rites"]; and *Chun Qiu* ["Autumn and Spring"].

1. **The *Yi Jing*** 《易经》 is considered the greatest among the five *Jing*. The *Yi Jing* is the essence and foundation of the five *Jing*. It was written to encourage man to explore truth and understand one's own need in order to fulfill the commandments of Heaven. Its instruction is similar to that found in the Bible. The *Yi Jing* endeavors to help man establish a correct concept of life; it points the way to come into harmony with Heaven; and teaches how one may lead a life pleasing to Heaven.

The *Yi Jing*, like the rest of the *Five Jing*, was not written by a single person, but was written by four sages, including Confucius (and his students), over a period of 2,000 years. In this respect it is similar to the Holy Bible which also had multiple authors writing over a period of 1,600 years. The first writer of the *Yi Jing* is believed to be Fu Xi, possibly Noah's son, Japheth (see p. 17). This was written hundreds of years before Moses wrote the first books of the Bible. The *Yi Jing* is the only one of the *Five Jing* which was not burned by Emperor Qin Shi Huangdi. Therefore it is truly the only complete Chinese *Jing* coming down from antiquity.

2. **The *Shu Jing*** 《書經》 contains historical documents. The term *shu* 書 literally means *a writing instrument* 聿 *speaks* 曰. The book is an unconnected collection of historical governmental memorials, extending over a space of about 1,700 years, compiled by Confucius.

It is one of the earliest books in Chinese and at one time consisted of 100 short chapters. However, the original book was lost in the great burning of the Classics under the Emperor Qin Shi Huangdi. During the next dynasty, the Han, great effort was made to find and restore the lost books. The *Shu Jing* of today consists of 28 chapters which are considered reliable history of China and her leaders' intimate relationship with Shangdi and Heaven, God.

3. **The *Shi Jing* 《诗经》** is a collection of 305 poems compiled by Confucius, originating from fifteen different states in ancient China. It is the world's oldest poetry anthology. It provides a rich collection of authentic social and religious situations of ancient China. These poems have been recited over the centuries on various occasions. Like Christian hymns which extol God as Creator and Jesus Christ as Savior, many Chinese prayers and praises are lifted to Heaven, or Shangdi 上帝. In the words of Confucius, *The Book of Songs* is to purify one's mind and thought.

4. ***Li Ji*** 《礼记》 is the book that records Confucius' teachings, having been written by his disciples. There is no accurate word which translates the Chinese word, *"Li."* It might be defined as the "sum of the law, the ceremonies and all regulations according to the spirit of the law." The *"Li"* rules one "from the inside" rather than by external regulations. It contains the highest, most honorable principles guiding and governing a nation, a family and a man. The present edition consists of 49 chapters.

5. **The *Chun Qiu* 《春秋》,** *Autumn and Spring,* is the only book fully written by Confucius himself. It is the history of the state of Lu (722 - 481 B.C.) where the Master was born. Mencius (c. 373 - 289 B.C.) wrote, **"Confucius said, 'Yes! It is the Spring and Autumn which will make men know me, and it is the Spring and Autumn which will make men condemn me.'"** In this book, Confucius faithfully recorded the events of his time and uplifted the mandate of Heaven. A careful reader will understand that he was not just recording things for recording's sake, but rather to teach the righteousness of Heaven. The kings, having received their appointments from Heaven, should therefore have been the ones to guide the country in the way of Heaven. But since they failed to do so, Confucius, in his book, pointed out their evil deeds. There were those who thought

Confucius had gone beyond his responsibilities, and condemned him for doing so. When the book was completed the social effect was startling. **"And rebellious ministers and villainous sons were struck with terror;"**[10] for they were afraid to have this blot on their names recorded in a historical book. In a sense, this book might be compared with the "Chronicles" and "Kings" of the Bible.

Three other books are often considered Classics:

The Book of Filial Piety 《孝经》, often regarded as the sixth *Jing*, was taught by Confucius and written by his grandson. The *Four Books* and *Five Jing* are better known by the scholars, whereas this book is used by every family to teach their children the principles of family and social relations. It consists of only 1,800 words, but its influence is possibly the greatest among the Classics.

Lao Zi's ***Dao De Jing*** 《道德经》 is a short book of only 5,000 words. It is the most translated of the Chinese Classics. Perhaps it is one of the greatest books in the world, as well as possibly the most misunderstood book, having been given a false mystical application.

Finally, we will quote quite extensively from **Mo Zi** 《墨子》, who is thought to have lived in the era between Confucius and Mencius. Practically nothing is known about the life of this venerable wise man, but his writings have survived and become famous, and are the foundation of the Mohist teachings.

As we become familiar with various quotations from these ancient sources, long-buried hidden treasures will dazzle our eyes and the voices of these Chinese prophets will echo in our ears!

4

Mencius' Amazing Prophecy

Mencius was the last of the great sages. Recall (p. 25) the statement:

> Yao handed the Dao [the enigmatic teachings of the prophets] to Shun; Shun handed it to Yu; Yu to Tang; Tang to Wen, Wu, and the duke of Zhou; Wen, Wu, and the duke of Zhou to Confucius; and Confucius to Mencius, on whose death there was no further transmission of it.

The sages here mentioned will, later in this chapter, be further identified, as they are cited in an amazing prophecy uttered by Mencius. But first, let us look into the background of Mencius (373 - c. 289 B.C.) himself. Most of what is known of the life of Mencius has been passed down by legend— that his father died when the child was young, and that his mother played an important role in shaping the future of this great man.

One story relates how Mencius' mother, Zhang (仉), moved no less than three times during his childhood, and with good reason. She was determined that the child be reared in a favorable environment for purity and study. At first they lived in a neighborhood near a cemetery. The child, Mencius, witnessing funeral processions, soon imitated the mourners in his play. His mother was perturbed. He was making light of death, not taking it seriously. They moved, but their next home was surrounded by merchants. Mencius' playmates naturally imitated their fathers, "doing business" with each other. Mother Zhang did not want her son to grow up with predominant thoughts of profit-making. They moved again.

Their next home proved to be just the right place. Each morning the neighborhood children could be heard loudly reciting their reading assignments. To Zhang this was an indication that families paid good attention to their children's education. This was where she decided to settle.

But there was still a problem. When Mencius was young, he was rather lazy and disliked his studies. Wanting only the best for her son, what was the mother to do now? She decided on a unique plan. In ancient China, before the modern loom was invented, all cloth was woven by hand and it took months to produce a sizable piece of cloth. As Mencius was still paying little attention to his studies, in despair one day, his mother threw her shuttle to the ground and cut the cloth she had been working on for many days. In shock, Mencius asked, "Why, Mother, did you do this?"

She replied that her cutting the valuable cloth was nothing compared to his ruining his young life by inattention to his studies. This impressive demonstration so touched Mencius that he realized, for the first time, how really important it was to change his careless attitude. Henceforth, he became an avid student.

In time, Mencius was privileged to study with a disciple of Zi Si, the grandson of Confucius. From this teacher he learned the precepts and doctrine of the great sage who had preceded him by a little more than one hundred years. Like Confucius, Mencius became a famous educator with many students. He and his students traveled together extensively throughout the country. Most of the time, although the band of scholars was well received, their Heaven-oriented important doctrines were politely declined by the people.

Mencius lived to about the age of eighty-three, leaving his writings—a seven-chapter book—for future generations to ponder, and for many to follow. He was China's last great sage and in his book entitled, *The Works of Mencius*, we will find a number of statements inspired by Heaven 天.

Mencius' 2000-Year "King" Prophecy

On several occasions Mencius spoke of the sacred doctrines which had been handed down since the time of Yao and Shun, two of the rulers in the "legendary period" [prior to 2205 B.C.]. In round numbers he gave the time taken for the passage of the *Dao* doctrines from one group of ancient sages to another:

> Mencius said, "From Yao and Shun down to Tang [first emperor of the second dynasty—the Shang] were 500 years <u>and more</u>."[1]

When Shun became old, he passed his rulership to Yu, who became the first emperor of the first dynasty [Xia] c. 2205 B.C. According to dynastic records, the first ruler of the Shang dynasty, Tang, died in 1753 B.C. Five hundred years prior to this would be 2253 B.C.— a date that would fit quite well with the role Yao and Shun had likely played in the earliest history of China. With the Tower of Babel incident being c. 2247 B.C., this date of 2253 B.C. ["and more"—earlier] would make Yao and Shun the leaders at the time of the Chinese migration from Mesopotamia to China.

Continuing from Mencius:

> "As to Yu [first king of the Xia first dynasty] and Ao Tao (皋陶), they saw those earlier sages [Shun and Yao] and so knew their doctrines, while Tang heard their doctrines as transmitted, and so knew them."[2]

One can see that Mencius was painting a picture of the continuous line of "sacred doctrine"—either transmitted by word-of-mouth or in written form from China's sages. King Tang is the next sage in line. We find that Tang, a good and honorable man, became the first king of the Shang dynasty. His reign began in 1766 B.C., and ended in 1753 B.C. upon his death. Mencius continues:

> "From Tang to King Wen were 500 years <u>and more</u>. As to Yi Yin [who will be quoted again later] and Lai Zhu (莱朱), they saw Tang and knew his doctrines, while King Wen heard them as transmitted, and so knew them."[3]

Here was another 500-year <u>and more</u> prophecy. But who was King Wen? This name we do not find in the dynastic record, so we might ask, was "Wen" this man's true name? No, King Wen's real name was Chang. But this name is also not found in the dynastic records! He was actually a duke serving under the last Shang dynasty king. Chinese history books record that Chang [King Wen] was born with special wisdom and power.

When Chang was grown, his father gave him the sovereignty to rule over Zhou, a satellite state in subjection to the Shang dynasty. He was given the title of "Chief of the West," and faithfully governed and showed great respect for the elderly. Therefore, the Chief of the West won the hearts of his people. Even some of the main ministers of the Shang Dynasty came to join him.[4] Many songs in the *Book of Poetry* record that he was chosen by God for his perfect obedience to Him, and his great love for his people.

The last king of Shang, however, was envious of this Chief's fame and good merit, and arrested him. It was during this seven-year arrest that he wrote his portion of the *Yi Jing*, which is still in existence today. After his friends bribed the king, the Chief was released. The Chief [King Wen] died ten years before his son, King Wu, overcame the Shang dynasty and established the Zhou dynasty in 1122 B.C. The title of "King Wen" was given posthumously by his son, King Wu, for his father had paved the way for the establishment of the Zhou dynasty.

King Wen died in 1132 B.C. at the age of 97. Therefore, this "500-years-and-more" time period from Tang to Wen extends from the death of Tang (1753 B.C.) to the birth of King Wen (c. 1229 B.C.) or 524 years!

Finally, we may calculate the last of Mencius' remarkable prophecies regarding the transmission of the ancient sages' doctrines:

> "**From King Wen to Confucius were 500 years and more. As to Tai-Gong Wang (太公望) and San Yi-sheng (散宜生), they saw Wen, and so knew his doctrines, while Confucius heard them as transmitted, and so knew them.**"[5]

It is with great care that Mencius reassures the reader that the original virtuous doctrines of Yao and Shun have been perfectly preserved and transmitted to Confucius. From the last date, 1132 B.C. (date of King Wen's death) to the time of Confucius' birth in 551 B.C. is 581 years. Note that these are *approximations,* and each time Mencius clearly states 500 years AND MORE.

All of this documentation was historical record before the time of Mencius. So how does Mencius' amazing prophecy come about? Mencius must have known from the *Yi Jing* that **"Heaven is constantly in motion,"**[6] which means that since heaven and earth are moved by the hands of God, the God of Heaven will never fail in doing His will. Seeing an unchanging God moving the universe, Mencius confidently prophesied:

> "If that was the case of time then, it should be the same now. <u>The King should arise in the course of five hundred years</u>, and during that time there should be men illustrious in their generation."[7]

Mencius was saying here that if the God of Heaven never failed in the past to raise up someone to transmit His Dao, God would surely send another transmitter to teach His Way in the future. Note, however, that this time Mencius said there would come a "King in the course of 500 years"—to his mind, not a transmitter, but THE DAO. He therefore used the date of Confucius' death to continue the unbroken line of transmitted Dao. Even though Mencius considered Confucius the greatest sage of China, he expected this King to be even greater than Confucius!

If we count forward 500 years from the time of Confucius' death in 479 B.C., we reach the year 22 A.D. (adding one year for the lack of a 0 year in the transition from B.C. to A.D.). In China, the last emperor of the Western Han dynasty was reigning in 22 A.D. He was not great, nor was there any other king who could transmit the Dao [Way of God] better than Confucius had, much less this particular king of China.

Does this mean that Mencius' prophecy had failed? If not, who could the "King" be, and where might He be found? If not in the history of China, where then? Was there another prophecy about a coming King, who would appear elsewhere in the world around the same time? (Study the Chinese history chart on the following page for a visual reference.)

Concerning this King, even Confucius had something to say:

> **The Master said, "If truly a King were to arise, it would still <u>require thirty years for His love to be manifested</u>."[8]**

Why would the King have to wait for thirty years to demonstrate His great Love? What was the meaning of Confucius' puzzling words? Perhaps we can find a clue in the prophecy of a Hebrew prophet living at the same time as Confucius.

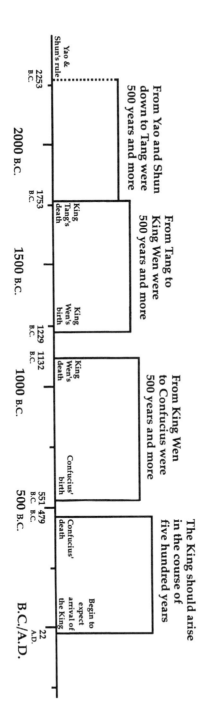

Biblical Prophecy Of Jesus Christ

The Hebrew Scriptures is a sacred Book full of prophecies, most of which are not only remarkably detailed, but have already been fulfilled in history. One ancient Hebrew prophet, Daniel, was actually a contemporary of Confucius, being born about 587 B.C., at a momentous time in the kingdom of Judah's [Israel's] history. This small kingdom, with its capital city of Jerusalem, was being besieged by the Babylonians. In 605 B.C., when Daniel was about 18 years old, he was taken captive to Babylon. Sadly, the last four kings of Judea had been wicked, having abandoned their Creator-God to worship idols. Therefore God allowed King Nebuchadnezzar of Babylon to overrun their country.

A hundred years before this time, one of Israel's prophets, Isaiah, had given the ruling king at that time this warning: *"And they [Babylonians] shall take away some of your sons who will descend from you, whom you will beget; and they shall be eunuchs in the palace of the king of Babylon." (Isaiah 39: 7)*. Daniel was one of those princes of Judah.

Although a foreigner in Babylon, Daniel endeared himself to Nebuchadnezzar by interpreting the king's dreams through insights given by God. Daniel was recognized not only as a prophet of the God of heaven, but as a wise man whom the king elevated to the position of prime minister over the entire kingdom. Daniel was well aware that Judah would remain a captive of Babylon for 70 years, according to the prior prophecy of Jeremiah: *"And this whole land shall be a desolation and an astonishment, and these nations shall serve the king of Babylon seventy years." (Jeremiah 25: 11)*.

After King Nebuchadnezzar died, his grandson, Belshazzar succeeded him to the throne of Babylon. But he was wicked, and as Daniel had prophesied the very night Belshazzar was deposed, Babylon would fall to the Medes and Persians. Daniel himself, after an exemplary and fruitful life, was by this time quite aged. In the first year of Darius the Mede, who had been made king over the Medo-Persian realm, Daniel, knowing that the 70-year Judean captivity was nearly over, prayed earnestly to his God:

> *"O Lord, great and awesome God, who keeps His covenant and mercy with those who love Him, and with those who keep His commandments. . . .O Lord, according to all Your righteousness, I pray, let Your anger and Your fury be turned away from Your city Jerusalem, Your holy mountain; because of our sins, and for the iniquities of our fathers, Jerusalem and Your people are a reproach to all those around us. . . .O Lord, hear! O Lord, forgive! O Lord, listen and act! . . ."*
> *(Daniel 9: 4, 16, 19).*

In response to Daniel's urgent prayer, God sent from heaven the angel Gabriel who told the prophet, *"O Daniel, I have now come forth to give you skill to understand. . . .you are greatly beloved; therefore consider the matter, and understand the vision." (Daniel 9: 22, 23).* Gabriel continued *(Daniel 9: 24):*

> *"Seventy weeks are determined*
> *for your people and for your holy city,*
> *To finish the transgression,*
> *to make an end of sins,*
> *To make reconciliation for iniquity,*
> *to bring in everlasting righteousness,*
> *To seal up vision and prophecy,*
> *and to anoint the Most Holy."*

Daniel must have trembled in anticipation. What did Gabriel mean? The Jews "and the holy city of Jerusalem would be given seventy weeks to make an end of sins. . .to bring in everlasting righteousness. . .to anoint the Most Holy?" Was this a promise of the long-awaited Holy One—the Messiah [anointed One]? Gabriel continued speaking to Daniel:

> "Know therefore and understand,
> That from the going forth of the command
> To restore and build Jerusalem
>   until Messiah the Prince,
> There shall be seven weeks and sixty-two weeks;
> The street shall be built again and the wall,
> Even in troublesome times."
>   (Daniel 9: 25).

Yes! Gabriel was giving a prophecy of the coming long-awaited Messiah! The Holy One had been first promised so many years before to Adam and Eve in the Garden of Eden after their disobedient act of eating the forbidden fruit. But when would He come? Daniel must have eagerly awaited the rest of Gabriel's message:

> "And after sixty-two weeks Messiah shall be cut off,
>   but not for Himself;
> And the people of the prince who is to come
>   shall destroy the city and the sanctuary.
> The end of it shall be with a flood, and till the end of
>   the war desolations are determined."
>   (Daniel 9: 26).

Surely Daniel wondered, "What does it mean, 'Messiah shall be cut off, but not for Himself'? The destruction of the city of Jerusalem and the sanctuary was easily understood. But how could it happen again? Had not Jerusalem already been destroyed by the Babylonians? Must it be rebuilt and destroyed again? However, Gabriel's message was not yet ended. He continued:

> "Then He shall confirm a covenant
>   with many for one week;
> But in the middle of the week He shall
>   bring an end to sacrifice and offering.
> And on the wing of abominations shall be
>   one who makes desolate,

> *Even until the consummation, which is determined,*
> *Is poured out on the desolate." (Daniel 9: 27).*

Here was a prophecy covering so many future years that it was impossible for Daniel to understand it completely. He doubtless grasped its great importance, for the message concerned the Messiah. The prophecy obviously had reference to times in the future. It is now our privilege, with retrospective eyes, to analyze this communication to Daniel from the God of heaven, Himself.

Since this was clearly a "time prophecy," one must first look for a meaning of the "seventy weeks." Prophetic time is measured as *"a year for a day" (Numbers 14: 34; Ezekiel 4: 6).* This Bible principle was espoused by Sir Isaac Newton who wrote, "In Daniel's Prophecies days are put for years."[9] Therefore, seventy weeks in prophetic time are equal to 490 years. Next, we must look for an opening date of the 490 years. It's right there in *Daniel 9: 25: "Know therefore and understand, that from the going forth of the command to restore and build Jerusalem. . . ."* In Daniel's day Jerusalem was lying in ruins. Here was a promise of restoration. There would be a command to restore and rebuild the city. We find this fulfilled by a Persian king, Artaxerxes, who would give the order. This is recorded in *Ezra 7: 12, 13:*

> *"Artaxerxes, king of kings,*
> *To Ezra the priest, a scribe of*
>   *the Law of the God of heaven:*
> *Perfect peace, and so forth.*
> *I issue a decree that all those*
>   *of the people of Israel and*
>   *the priests and Levites in my*
>   *realm, who volunteer to go*
>   *up to Jerusalem, may go with you."*

The date of this decree, 457 B.C., is well fixed in history.[10] Artaxerxes not only allowed the people of Israel (Judah) to return to Jerusalem, but also in the decree stated that the gold and silver taken from Jerusalem should be returned; the sanctuary (House of God) be built; and some of the money be spent for *"bulls, rams, and lambs, with their grain offerings and their drink offerings"* which should be offered *"on the altar of the house of your God in Jerusalem." (Ezra 7: 18).*

Now look at Daniel 9: 25 again. From this date of 457 B.C. *"Until Messiah the Prince, there shall be seven weeks and sixty-two weeks; the street shall be built again, and the wall."* In prophecy, as previously explained, it is understood that a day equals a year.[9] Therefore, seven weeks—49 years. The walls and streets of Jerusalem *were* rebuilt in 49 years, by 408 B.C.

Now we must add to the first 49 years an additional 434 years (62 weeks) to find the time of the anointing of the Messiah (total of 483 years) dating from 457 B.C. This gives the date 27 A.D. (adding an extra year for the lack of a 0 year when entering the new millennium—B.C. to A.D.). What happened in 27 A.D.?

Let us pause here for a moment and summarize what we have learned thus far. According to Daniel's prophecy, "Messiah the Prince" was to come in the year 27 A.D. The term "Messiah" simply means the "anointed One," and "the Prince" is synonymous with the "King." We must simply learn who "Messiah the Prince" is. Let us turn again to the Bible.

We read, *"God <u>anointed</u> Jesus of Nazareth with the Holy Spirit and with power." (Acts 10: 38).* How did this happen and when?

> *When all the people were baptized, it came to pass that Jesus also was baptized; and while He prayed, the heaven was opened. And the Holy Spirit descended in bodily form like a dove upon Him, and a voice came from heaven which said, "You are My beloved Son; in You I am well pleased." Now Jesus Himself began His ministry at about thirty years of age. . . . (Luke 3: 21 - 23).*

Jesus was anointed not only by the water of baptism, but by the descent of the Holy Spirit upon Him, and the audible pronouncement from the Father-God in heaven of His Sonship. At 30, candidates for the priesthood were anointed in Judah. It was in the year 27 A.D. that Jesus was baptized, when 30 years old. He was actually born in 4 B.C. (according to our present calendar reckoning). Thus Jesus was anointed for His wonderful mission on earth. He fulfilled exactly the prophecy given to Daniel. The decree issued by Artaxerxes in 457 B.C. with the 483-year span reached till His baptism (anointing) in 27 A.D.

But this is not all! Read again *Daniel 9: 27: "He shall confirm a covenant with many for one week (seven years); but in the middle of the week He shall bring an end to sacrifice and offering."* What event ended forever the sacrifice of bulls and rams? It was the death of Jesus, the *"Lamb of God who takes away the sin of the world." (John 1: 29)*. There was no more need for these sacrifices which were a "type" pointing to the great sacrifice of Jesus upon the cross of Calvary. This last "week" of the seventy-week (490 year) prophecy represents the final seven years, from 27 A.D. to 34 A.D. The *"middle of the week,"* when the sacrifices ceased (after three-and-a-half years), fell in 31 A.D. This was the year of Jesus' crucifixion and death.

What was the covenant that Jesus would confirm for one week (seven years) after the beginning of His ministry in 27 A.D.? God had said that he would give the Jews seventy weeks (490 years) from the command to rebuild Jerusalem. This time period ended in 34 A.D., and a telling event occurred in that very year. The faithful deacon, Stephen, was brought before an official council in Jerusalem, presided over by the high priest. There Stephen bravely recited Israel's history of rebellion against God. Stephen ended his discourse by accusing these high religious officials of rejecting the *"Just One, of whom you now have become the betrayers and murderers."*

The religious leaders, thus condemned, *"When they heard these things they were cut to the heart, and they gnashed at him with their teeth. . . . Then they cried out with a loud voice, stopped their ears, and ran at him with one accord, and they cast him out of the city and stoned him." (Acts 7: 52, 54, 57, 58).* This was the final rejection by Israel's leaders of their Messiah. The people of Israel were no longer God's chosen people to spread a knowledge of Him throughout the earth. How longsuffering and patient God had been with His chosen people, Israel!

Jesus, during the days of His earthly ministry, was once approached by His disciple, Peter, who asked, *"Lord, how often shall my brother sin against me, and I forgive him? Up to seven times?" Jesus said to him, "I do not say to you, up to seven times, but up to seventy times seven." (Matthew 18: 21, 22).* Jesus truly fulfilled His promise in giving the Jews a final 490 years of probation!

This whole important prophecy predicted to the *very year* the advent of Jesus in human form. This wonderful prophecy might be better understood by studying the chart on the following page.

The King—Jesus Christ

This prophecy of Daniel, given more than five hundred years before Jesus was born, is one of the most legitimate proofs of Christianity. Its accurate fulfillment in the life and death of Jesus Christ, confirmed the Messiah, who had been awaited for ages.

And to think that Mencius also made a similar prophecy—that after 22 A.D., a King would come! Mencius had a reason to look for a coming King, for this had been an expectation from antiquity. Mencius said:

> **It is said in the Book of History [*Shu Jing*] "We have waited for our Prince. When our Prince comes, we may escape from the punishments under which we suffer."**[11]

Mencius' Amazing Prophecy

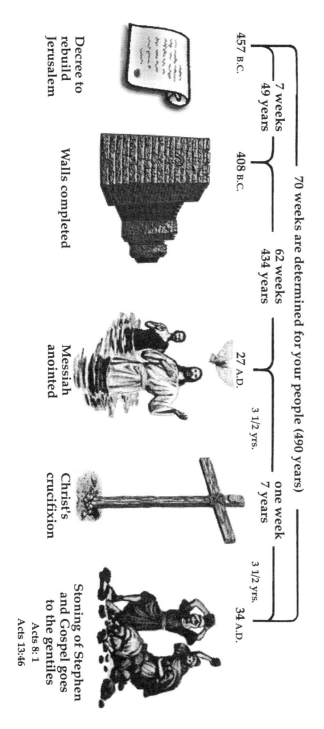

Daniel's Prophecy of 70 weeks (Daniel 9: 24-27)

Ancient Israel had also been waiting for a King for centuries.

> *Lift up your heads, O you gates!*
> *And lift up, you everlasting doors!*
> *And the King of glory shall come in.*
> *Who is this King of glory?*
> *The LORD of hosts, He is the King of glory.*
> *(Psalm 24: 9, 10).*

Where would He be crowned? What would be His kingdom? Five hundred years before the birth of Jesus, the prophet Zechariah foretold the coming of the King to Israel:

> *Rejoice greatly, O daughter of Zion!*
> *Shout, O daughter of Jerusalem!*
> *Behold, your King is coming to you;*
> *He is just and having salvation,*
> *Lowly and riding on a donkey,*
> *A colt, the foal of a donkey.*
> *(Zechariah 9: 9).*

This prophecy was fulfilled when Jesus made His triumphal entry into Jerusalem on the first day of the last week before His crucifixion. Jesus, following the Jewish custom for royalty, rode into Jerusalem on a donkey. A multitude hailed Him as the Messiah, throwing palm branches on the road before Him. Following in the crowd were those He had healed—trophies of His labor of love. "Captives" whom He had rescued from the Devil praised God for their deliverance from darkness. *"Blessed is the king who comes in the name of the LORD! Peace in heaven and glory in the highest!" (Luke 19: 38),* they shouted.

To everyone's surprise and disappointment, Jesus did not claim the throne of David [Israel's most famous king]. Instead, four days later, He was arrested and tried by Pilate, the Roman governor, who asked,

> *"Are you the king of the Jews?"*
> *Jesus answered, "My kingdom is not of this world. If My kingdom were of this world, My servants would fight, so that I should not be delivered to the Jews, but now My kingdom is not from here."*
> *Pilate therefore said to Him, "Are You a king then?"*
> *Jesus answered, "You say rightly that I am a king. For his cause I was born, and for this cause I have come into the world, that I should bear witness to the truth. Everyone who is of the truth hears My voice."*
> *Pilate said to Him, "What is truth?" And when he had said this, he went out again to the Jews, and said to them, "I find no fault in Him at all."*
> *(John 18: 33, 36 - 38).*

The fact is that Jesus' kingdom is a Kingdom of Truth and Love. It was on the cross where Jesus was crowned with a coronet of thorns as the King. He is *"the Desire of All Nations." (Haggai 2: 7)*. Through the prophecy of Mencius, God left rich evidence for the Chinese to recognize the King when He came.

Both the ancient prophets of Israel and China pointed to Jesus as the King. Mencius' prophecy did not fail, but gave a second evidence of the coming Savior. Is it just coincidence that the amazing prophecies of Daniel and Mencius reached the same conclusion? Surely the God of the Bible and the God of ancient China are One and the same! Let us proceed to learn more of the Chinese concepts of God, and make comparisons with the God of ancient Israel.

5

The Original God of China

Before going any further, we must learn more about the original God of China. When the great Chinese family migrated from the Tower of Babel area in Mesopotamia to the Middle Kingdom about 2247 B.C., we find that they were worshipers of the Creator-God—the God of Noah and his son, Shem (see p. 17). As you recall the last two rulers of the "Legendary Period of Five Rulers," we find the names of Yao and Shun. This is what Confucius said of Yao, the righteous Chinese sage-king:

> The Master said, "Great indeed was Yao as a king! How majestic was he! **It is only Heaven [God] that is grand**, and only Yao corresponded to it. How vast and deep was his obedience! The people could find no name for it."[1]

It is also recorded of King Shun that **"He sacrificed to Shangdi (上帝)."**[2]

So we find in these two brief statements that the rulers Yao and Shun were righteous worshipers of the God of Heaven. In the previous chapter (p. 31) we discovered that the sacred teachings of Dao came down from

Yao and Shun. The most ancient Chinese book, The *Shu Jing*, also begins with King Yao.

It seems reasonable to believe that Yao and Shun were the founding fathers of the Chinese Middle Kingdom. The *Shu Jing* records that:

> "The great Heaven [皇天] gave this Middle Kingdom with its people and territories to the former kings."[3]

And so the ancient Chinese fervently believed that the God of Heaven Himself had provided righteous kings for their beautiful new land, which was also a gift from God. All of these early kings thus received their appointment from Heaven. In the Bible it is said that every nation was confined to a certain territory by God. According to the Apostle Paul, *"[God] has made from one blood every nation of men to dwell on all the face of the earth, and has determined their preappointed times and the boundaries of their dwellings, so that they should seek the Lord, in the hope that they might grope for Him and find Him. . . ." (Acts 17: 26, 27)*.

God gave to the peoples of all nations the freedom of choice. *"The living God, . . .in bygone generations allowed all nations to walk in their own ways." (Acts 14: 15, 16)*. When the early Chinese were obedient to the will of Heaven, blessings were bestowed upon them; when disobedient, calamity resulted and their kingdoms were removed and given to more virtuous successors. During this long early period, the rulers of China elected to follow the leadership of God, as they recognized His Sovereignty.

According to Chinese history, the last kings of the first three dynasties [the Xia, Shang and Zhou] all veered from the right path, and God raised up other rulers to defeat them and take away not only their kingships, but also their dynasties.

> The way of Heaven is to bless the good and to punish the bad. It sent down calamities on the House of Xia, to make manifest its crimes.⁴

Tang, a righteous opponent of the last Xia king understood the situation and "punished" the king, overthrowing his government, and setting up the new Shang dynasty. Said Tang:

> The sovereign of Xia is an offender, and, as I fear God, I dare not but punish him.
>
> Now you are saying, "What are the crimes of Xia to us?" The king of Xia does nothing but exhaust the strength of his people, and exercise oppression in the cities of Xia. His people have all become idle in his service, and will not assist him. They are saying, "When will this sun expire? We will all perish with thee." Such is the course of the sovereign of Xia, and now I must go and punish him.
>
> Assist, I pray you, me, the one man, to carry out the <u>punishment appointed by Heaven</u>.⁵

Tang was famous for his virtues. Shi Zi (尸子, 390 - 330 B.C.) recorded that Tang's love and kindness extended even to the realm of animals. It is said that he told workers who made nets for him to knit only three sides and leave one side open. Tang was also remembered as the saviour from the drought which prevailed in the land when he was appointed to fight against Xia and establish the Shang dynasty.

> When Tang fought against drought, . . . He offered himself as the sacrifice and prayed in the forest.⁵ᵃ

This event was also recorded in the historical book, *Lu's Autumn and Spring,* by a contemporary of Confucius.

> When Tang defeated Xia and ruled all under heaven, there were five [seven] years of drought which caused no harvest. Tang offered himself in prayer in the forest. . . .The people were pleased and great rain came down.[5b]

While five years were mentioned in this text, most commentators on *Lu's Spring and Autumn*, from the Han dynasty to the Qin dynasty, including the best known commentator on this historical book, Gao Yao of the Han dynasty, held that the drought was seven years in duration instead of five years. Wang Chong (王充, 27 - 97 A.D.) also wrote of this drought as seven years' duration in his famous book, *On Balance* (《论衡》), reaching this conclusion based on the documents available at his time.

This drought, incidentally, coincides exactly with the seven years of famine suffered in Egypt when Joseph called his father, Jacob, and brothers' families to join him in Egypt where adequate supplies of grain had been stored. This was the year 1766 B.C., the first year of the Shang dynasty. (See the chronological comparison chart on pages 52 and 53.)

> *And the seven years of famine began to come, as Joseph had said. The famine was in all lands, but in all the land of Egypt there was bread . . . <u>The famine was over all the face of the earth</u>. . . .*
>
> *(Genesis 41: 54, 56).*

Careful readers will also be interested in another astonishing, synchronous, historical event: While Moses was called to lead the Israelites out of Egypt, Shangdi chose Pan Gen to lead the ancient Chinese in moving their capital from An to Yin. Why the move? Hear what Pan Gen said to the questioning people:

> **And yet you asked why I was troubling your myriads by removing you here. But Shangdi [God] being about to restore the virtue of my**

> High ancestor (King Tang), and secure the good government of our empire, I, with the sincere respect of my ministers, felt a reverent care for the lives of the people, and have made a lasting settlement in this new city.[5c]

The same reason for Israel's exodus is given: to restore their ancestral belief in God. Both the Israelites and Chinese took almost the same length of time, and reached the final settlement nearly simultaneously: 1401 B.C.! (See the chronological charts, pages 52 and 53.)

To lead His people away from a corrupt and unclean place has always been God's way of preserving and restoring their faith and trust in Him. We saw this in the migration of people from the tower of Babel to different lands, including China; Israel's exodus from Egypt; Pan Gen's moving of the Shang dynasty—and even centuries later in the event of the Puritans moving to the land of America! This fact tells a plain truth: the God who led the Israelites in their exodus was the same Shangdi who guided the ancient Chinese in the move of their dynasty.

While ancient Chinese kings and their roles were noticed and recorded in all important events, the real King has always been Shangdi, Himself—He reigned over China through these appointed kings. It was God's will and the Chinese people's desire to live in peace and order. When there was no king in Israel, the Bible says, *"everyone did what was right in his own eyes."* *(Judges 21: 25)*. Confusion and disorder were the result, as would be the case in any society. Therefore, God raised up virtuous rulers to insure tranquility, and the reason for King Tang's appointment is given:

> Oh, Heaven gives birth to the people with such desires, that without a ruler they must fall into all disorders; and Heaven again gives birth to the man of intelligence whose business it is to regulate them.[6]

Biblical Chronology

B.C. 2348 Flood

    2346   Gen 11: 10 Shem 100 yrs old, and begot <u>Arphaxad</u> 2 yrs after flood.

    2311   Gen 11: 12 Arphaxad lived 35 yrs and begot <u>Salah.</u>

    2281   Gen 11: 14 Salah lived 30 yrs and begot <u>Eber.</u>

B.C. 2247 Tower of Babel Gen 11: 16 Eber lived 34 yrs and begot Peleg ("Division") Gen 10:25 in his (Peleg's) days the earth was divided; Gen 10: 31, 32 according to their languages…the nations were divided on the earth after the flood.

    2217   Gen 11: 18 Peleg lived 30 years and begot <u>Reu</u>

    2185   Gen 11: 20 Reu lived 32 yrs and begot <u>Serug</u>

    2155   Gen 11: 22 Serug lived 30 yrs and begot <u>Nahor</u>

    2126   Gen 11: 24 Nahor lived 29 years and begot <u>Terah</u>

    2056   Gen 11: 26 Terah lived 70 yrs and begot <u>Abram</u> (Nahor and Haran).

    1956   Gen 21: 5 Abraham was 100 yrs old when his son <u>Isaac</u> was born

    1896   Gen 25: 26 Isaac was 60 yrs old when <u>Jacob</u> was born

Gen 47: 28 Jacob lived in the land of Egypt 17 years.

Jacob lived 147 years. Therefore:

B.C.1766 Gen 43: 1 <u>Jacob went into Egypt when 130 yrs old because of famine in the land of Canaan.</u>

B.C. 1445 Exodus of Israel from Egypt—God called Moses to lead the Israelites out of Egypt, to restore the faith of their fathers. The Ten Commandment Law was given at Mt. Sinai.

B.C. 1406 Arrived at Canaan—After forty years of sojourn in the wilderness, Moses led the Israelites to the border of the Promised Land

B.C. 1400 Final settlement in Canaan—Joshua 14: 7, 10. God chose Joshua to lead Israel in the conquest of Canaan, which took six years to accomplish.

Chinese Chronology

B.C. 2348 The Legendary Period
  Nu Wa, Shen Nong, Fu Xi in Chinese legend
  Five Legendary Kings

B.C. 2247 Migration Period (from the Tower of Babel)
  Migration to the Middle Kingdom under the leadership of Yao and Shun

B.C. 2205 - 1766 The Xia Dynasty

Yu	2205	Mang	2014
Qi	2197	Xie	1996
Taikang	2188	Bu Xiang	1980
Zhongkang	2159	Jiang	1921
Xiang	2146	Jin	1900
Interregnum of forty years		Kong Jia	1879
commencing	2118	Kao	1848
Shao Kang	2079	Fa	1837
Zhu	2057	Jie	1818
Huai	2040		

B.C. 1766 The Shang Dynasty
  Tang   1766   <u>Seven years of drought in China.</u>

B.C. 1401 Chinese Exodus Complete
  Pan Gen, Tang's ninth-removed grandson was called by Shangdi to move the capital from An (Shandong) to Yin (Henan). This took many years to restore the pious belief in Heaven and the pure virtues as manifested by the ancient kings. The dynastic title was changed from Shang to Yin at this time.

In later years, the Duke of Zhou summarized the deposing of both the Xia and Shang dynasties because their kings were disobedient to the God of Heaven:

> I announce and declare to you of the many regions, Heaven had no set purpose to do away with the sovereign of Xia, or with the sovereign of Yin [last emperor of the Shang Dynasty]. But it was the case that your ruler, being in possession of your many regions, abandoned himself to great excess, and reckoned on the favoring decree of Heaven, making trifling excuses for his conduct.[7]

In addition, the mercy and long-suffering of God is shown, and a specific period was given by God for reform and repentance:

> The wise, not thinking, become foolish, and the foolish, by thinking, become wise. <u>Heaven for five years waited kindly, and forbore with the descendant of Tang, to see if he would indeed prove himself the true ruler of the people</u>, but there was nothing in him deserving to be regarded. Heaven then sought among your many regions, making a great impression by its terrors to stir up one who might look reverently to it; but in all your regions, there was not one deserving of its regard. There were, however, our kings of Zhou, who treated well the multitudes of the people, and were able to sustain the burden of virtuous government, and to preside over all services to spirits and to Heaven. Heaven thereupon instructed them, and increased their excellence, made choice of them, and gave them the decree of Yin, to rule over your many regions.[8]

We should not be surprised to learn that the God of heaven takes down and sets up kingdoms, for this is His action recorded in the Bible, as well. Nebuchadnezzar had been appointed by God to punish the wicked nation of

Judah for 70 years (see p. 36). But Nebuchadnezzar, himself, in turn was punished by God, as Daniel explained to Belshazzar, the king's grandson:

> "O king, the Most High God gave Nebuchadnezzar your father [margin: ancestor] a kingdom and majesty, glory and honor. And because of the majesty that He gave him, all peoples, nations, and languages trembled and feared before him....But when his heart was lifted up, and his spirit was hardened in pride, he was deposed from his kingly throne, and they took his glory from him....till he knew that the <u>Most High God rules in the kingdom of men, and appoints over it whomever He chooses.</u>"
> (Daniel 5: 18, 21).

This rule of Heaven was summarized by Mencius in brief, yet clear, words:

> **They who accord with Heaven are preserved, and they who rebel against Heaven perish.**[9]

He continued to say that the thrones were given to the founders of the first three dynasties because of their love for Heaven and the people under Heaven.

> **Mencius said, "It was by love that the three dynasties gained the thrones, and by not being loving that they lost them."**[10]

The sage kings knew that they should obey the way of Heaven, and not fall short of their heavenly trust and appointment.

> **To revere and honor the way of Heaven is the way ever to preserve the favoring regard of Heaven.**[11]

Such was the reverence afforded to the God of Heaven. All the kings knew that they were Heaven's agents and accountable to Him. Even when the king received the throne from his predecessor, yet it was understood that Heaven makes the ultimate appointment. Listen to a dialogue between

Mencius and his student Wan Zhang:

> Wan Zhang said, "Was it the case that Yao gave the throne to Shun?"
> Mencius said, "No. The sovereign cannot give the throne to another."
> "Yes; but Shun had the throne. Who gave it to him?"
> "Heaven gave it to him," was the answer.
> "Heaven gave it to him? —did Heaven confer His appointment on him with specific injunctions?"
> Mencius replied, "No. Heaven does not speak [on this specific matter]. Heaven simply showed His will by his [Shun's] personal conduct and his conduct of affairs."
> "Heaven showed His will by his [Shun's] personal conduct and his conduct of affairs? How was this?"
> Mencius' answer was, "The sovereign can present a man to Heaven, but he cannot make Heaven give that man the throne. A prince can present a man to the sovereign, but he cannot cause the sovereign to make that man a prince. A great officer can present a man to his prince, but he cannot cause the prince to make that man a high-ranking officer. Yao presented Shun to Heaven, and Heaven accepted him. He presented him to the people, and the people accepted him. Therefore I say, Heaven does not speak. Heaven simply indicated His will by his [Shun's] personal conduct and his conduct of affairs."[12]

This is the same principle stated in the Bible:

> *"This decision is by the decree of the watchers,*
> *And the sentence by the word of the holy ones,*
> *In order that the living may know*

That the Most High rules in the kingdom of men,
Gives it to whomever He will,
And sets over it the lowest of men." (Daniel 4: 17).

Was the early Chinese realm therefore close to a TRUE THEOCRACY? Sacrifice to God [Shangdi] was the most important rite for the king to perform. Every day there were two sacrifices: one in the morning, the other in the evening. Said King Wu's son of the Zhou dynasty:

> **It is for me [the youth] only to attend reverently early and late to the sacrifices.[13]**
>
> **I have brought my offerings,**
> **A ram and a bull.**
> **May Heaven accept them![14]**

Instead of having an abstract idea of Deity, the ancient Chinese sages believed in a personal God, Shangdi. They knew that their ears, eyes and mouth were created by God. They knew Shangdi listened, saw, and talked to His people. The ancient kings and their assistants recognized the voice of God speaking to them. A minister of the Ruler Shun said:

> <u>Heaven hears and sees as our people hear and see</u>; Heaven rightly approves and displays its terrors, as our people wisely approve and stand in awe:—such connection there is between the upper and lower worlds. How reverent ought the masters of the earth to be![15]
>
> He [King Wen] received the blessing of God,
> And it was extended to his descendants.
> <u>God said to King Wen,</u>
> "Be not like those who reject this and cling to that; Be not like those who are ruled by their likings and desires;"
> . . .<u>God said to King Wen,</u>
> "I am pleased with your intelligent virtue,

> **Not loudly proclaimed nor portrayed,**
> **Without extravagance or changeableness,**
> **Without consciousness of effort on your part,**
> **In accordance with the pattern of God."[16]**

They had the same reasoning as the Bible:

> *The hearing ear and the seeing eye,*
> *The LORD has made both of them.*
> *(Proverbs 20: 12).*
>
> *Understand you senseless among the people;*
> *He who planted the ear, shall He not hear? . . .*
> *He who instructs the nations, shall He not correct,*
> *He who teaches man knowledge?*
> *The LORD knows the thoughts of man,*
> *that they are futile. (Psalm 94: 8 - 11).*

He even appeared to the ancient prophets in dreams. Said one of the kings:

> **But while I was respectfully and silently thinking**
> **of the right way, I dreamt that Shangdi gave me a**
> **good assistant, who should speak for me.[17]**

Because of the king's dream, search was made for the minister revealed in the dream, and he was found. The office was thereupon given to him. He proved to be a righteous, wise, prudent counselor to the king.

Dreams are one of the ways God reveals His plan or will to His people. In the Bible, for example, God said:

> *"If there is a prophet among you,*
> *I, the LORD, make Myself known to him in a vision;*
> *And I speak to him in a dream." (Numbers 12: 6).*

One may question the possibility of a "heathen" receiving visions from God; yet a most amazing dream or vision revealed in the Bible was given to Nebuchadnezzar, "heathen" king of Babylon, who later became a faithful believer in God (see Daniel, Chapter 2 and 4). In this book we will read concerning visions given to the ancient Chinese prophets. Through dreams and visions the will of God was thus revealed. The ancient Chinese were familiar with the nature of Heaven's decree. This was even specified by a character pictogram, *decree, commandment* 命, which held special meaning.[18]

> There is no mistake about the decree of Heaven.
> The purpose of the divine commandments are
> all to the same good effect.[19]

God's commandments are based on His love. The ancient Chinese believed that Shangdi was a God of love.

> Heaven loves the people, and the sovereign
> should reverence this mind of Heaven.[20]

> There is the great God,
> Does He hate any one?
> God does not hate any man.[21]

The great philosopher Mo Zi (408 - 382 B.C.) further revealed God's love:

> Moreover, I know Heaven loves men dearly not without reason. Heaven ordered the sun, the moon, and the stars to enlighten and guide them. Heaven ordained the four seasons, Spring, Autumn, Winter, and Summer, to regulate them. Heaven sent down snow, frost, rain, and dew to grow the five grains and flax and silk so that the people could use and enjoy them. Heaven established the hills and rivers, ravines and valleys, and arranged many things to minister to man's good or bring him evil. He appointed the dukes and lords to reward the virtuous and punish the wicked, . . .this has been taking place from antiquity to the present. Suppose there is a man who is deeply fond of his son and has used his energy to the limit to work for his benefit, but when the son grows up he returns no

> love to the father. The gentlemen of the world will all call him unloving and miserable. Now Heaven loves the whole world universally. Everything is prepared for the good of man. The work of Heaven extends to even the smallest things that are enjoyed by man. Such benefits may indeed be said to be substantial, yet there is no service in return. And they do not even know this to be unloving. This is why I say the gentlemen of the world understand only trifles but not things of importance. . . .[22]

It is obvious that the ancient Chinese read the book of nature and appreciated God's care and provision for all of man's needs. His gracious dealing and patience with their rulers impressed them with His great love. This understanding of God led them to respond with reverence and obedience.

An amazing fact concerning early China is not only that the God of Heaven directed the founding of the kingdom, but appointed each and every king. Most of the kings themselves were righteous, endeavoring conscientiously to follow God's every command as it was passed down from their earliest kings. And this continued for approximately 2,000 years, until the Qin dynasty! The question arises: did the Chinese at this period in their history actually have a full understanding of God—was He revealed to them in the same way that He was revealed to Israel?

We have learned that the Chinese had prophets with whom God communicated directly. With the burning of the books (pp. 22, 23), some of the teachings of the early kings were lost. Did God leave them in darkness, or did more light come to them? Did the ancients ever receive deep revelation of the Dao—the Way of Truth?

6

Unlocking the Mystery of Dao

> I do not know His name.
> Name Him "Dao"(道) possibly.
> For lack of a better word,
> I call Him "The Almighty." (大)[1]
> Lao Zi

Confucius, the great compiler of all China's early writings, was baffled by Dao and believed it was beyond human understanding. That is also why Confucius did not make any speculations about Dao. One of his disciples said that the Master was entirely free of these four things:

> He had no foregone conclusions,
> No arbitrary predeterminations,
> No obstinacy, And no egoism.[2]

Can man understand the depths of Dao? The greatest mystery in the Bible is God Himself. A well-known thought from the Bible expressly tells of man's inability to search the depths of God. Could Dao have any relevance to God?

> *Can you search out the deep things of God?*
> *Can you find out the limits of the Almighty?*
> *They are higher than heaven—what can you do?*

> *Deeper than Sheol [the grave]—what can you know?*
> *Their measure is longer than the earth*
> *And broader than the sea. (Job 11: 7 - 9).*

The apostle Paul said, in a letter to the church at Corinth, that *"the world through wisdom did not know God." (1 Corinthians 1: 21).* The most difficult and humiliating lesson for man to learn is that man is finite and does not know all and everything of the infinite One! One becomes wise when this is learned. Surely it is God's will that man become acquainted with Him! But if man cannot by himself come to know God, how is he to know God?

From Lao Zi's quotation, **"I do not know His name. Name Him 'Dao' possibly. For lack of a better word, I call Him 'The Almighty,'"** we learn that he saw Someone whom he could not describe properly. Who was He that the wise sage, Lao Zi, could not identify? Could "Dao, the Almighty" be God Himself? Will His name remain a mystery forever?

> *The secret things belong to the LORD our God,*
> *but those things which are revealed*
> *belong to us and to our children forever. . . .*
> *(Deuteronomy 29: 29).*

The good news is that *"those things which are revealed belong to us and to our children forever."* Revelation from God is the only way humans can ever come to know Him. He may speak to the human heart in at least these three possible ways: through the speechless book of nature; through His prophets; and above all, through a member of the human family—Jesus Christ. *"For in Him dwells all the fullness of the Godhead bodily."* *(Colossians 2: 9).*

We find that the greatest mystery of the Bible is the so-called "Godhead," or "Trinity." The term "Trinity" is not a Bible term. This simply means that the God of the Bible is One in will, thought, affection, action and purpose, but exists as three distinct Persons. They are not three divine Beings in one body or one

Unlocking the Mystery of Dao

body with three heads, as pictured in Hinduism or other heathen religions.

There are some Bible verses to indicate that the Godhead are three distinct Persons. *"In the beginning was the Word, and the Word was with God, and the Word was God." (John 1: 1)*. "Word" is speech, and speech implies a speaker and a listener. This verse alone tells us there are at least two Persons of God. Another verse, found in *1 John 4: 8* states that *"God is love."* Love calls for at least two parties: a love-giver and love-receiver, to love and to be loved. These verses show that there is more than a single divine Being in the Godhead. Jesus revealed a Godhead of three Persons: God the Father, God the Son, and God the Holy Spirit.

> *"All authority has been given to Me in heaven and on earth. Go, therefore and make disciples of all the nations, <u>baptizing them in the name of the Father and of the Son and of the Holy Spirit</u>, teaching them to observe all things that I have commanded you; and lo, I am with you always, even to the end of the age." (Matthew 28: 18, 19)*.

From eternity past to eternity future, God is self-existent and self-sufficient. The three Persons of the Godhead enjoy and exchange their pure and holy love in fullness among themselves, far beyond human understanding. Love can only beget love. God did not create angels or humans for lack of someone to love, but in order for His created beings to experience and enjoy the close communion and deep love as shared in the Godhead.

How did the ancient Chinese prophets deal with this mystery? How much did they know about the Godhead, and how much inspiration had they received from Heaven? For now, we will focus on the teachings of one Chinese prophet—Lao Zi.

Lao Zi, whose own life is largely a mystery, according to tradition, lived around 570 B.C. He actually lived at the same time, but was older than Confucius, and was also a contemporary of the Hebrew prophet, Daniel. According to Xi Ma Qian (c. 145 B.C.— ?), a great historian of the Han Dynasty, Lao Zi was born in the state of Zhou. His real name was Li Er, and he served as a curator for the state. It is said that Confucius consulted with him about *Li* (the law, including everything from ceremony to the spirit of law).

Regardless of who Lao Zi was, or what he did in his lifetime, he left one treasure—the 5,000-word *Dao De Jing,* which defines the Great Dao. Although Lao Zi is regarded as the founder of Daoism, he really had nothing to do with many of its religious precepts, as followed today. The problem is that Lao Zi has even been misrepresented as being Dao himself. But Lao Zi acted only as the messenger of Dao!

Lao Zi can be compared with John the Baptist, the "forerunner" of Jesus Christ. John's father, a Jewish priest, had a vision of his unborn son's life role, as well as that of the coming Messiah. When John learned of the part he was destined to play for the Messiah, he spent his early years in the wilderness, drawing closer to God. In time, great crowds of people journeyed to the wilderness to hear him preach, to repent of their sins, and be baptized by him. As increasing numbers of people were listening to John the Baptist, the religious leaders of the Jews became fearful that they would lose followers. So they sent spies to learn what he was preaching in order to bring accusations against him.

> *Now this is the testimony of John, when the Jews sent priests and Levites from Jerusalem to ask him, "Who are you?"*
>
> *He confessed, and did not deny, but confessed, "I am not the Christ."*
>
> *And they asked him, "What then? Are you Elijah?"*
> *[Elijah had been a powerful prophet living about 865 B.C. who was translated into heaven alive.]*
> *He said, "I am not."*
>
> *"Are you the Prophet?" [Indicating the Messiah.]*
> *And he answered, "No."*
>
> *Then they said to him, "Who are you, that we may give an answer to those who sent us? What do you say about yourself?"*

> He said: "*I am 'The voice of one crying in the wilderness: Make straight the way of the L*ORD,*'*" as the prophet Isaiah said.
> Now those who were sent were from the Pharisees. And they asked him, saying, "Why then do you baptize if you are not the Christ, nor Elijah, nor the Prophet?"
> John answered them, saying, "I baptize with water, but there stands One among you whom you do not know. It is He who, coming after me, is preferred before me, whose sandal strap I am not worthy to loose." (John 1: 19 - 27).

John was telling the people that it was not important who he was, but rather it was his message that was important. He was a simple, humble messenger for "the Prophet" [Jesus Christ] to come. Compare now, Lao Zi with John the Baptist. No one knew for sure who Lao Zi was. He did not leave anything personal about himself, yet he certainly did his job as *"the voice of one crying in the wilderness: Make straight the way of the* L*ORD.*" Lao Zi was surely a "forerunner," not a contemporary, of the Great Dao. But, like John the Baptist, he has, by his writings, paved the way in the Chinese heart for the appearance of the Great Dao.

In the opening statement of his great sermon on Dao recorded in *Dao De Jing,* Lao Zi warns that the Dao whom he discusses is not the ordinary or expected Dao. This Dao also has an extraordinary name.

> **Dao can be told but is not the ordinary Dao.**
> **The name [of that Dao] can also be given,**
> **but that is not the ordinary name as well.**[3]

One of the first things Lao Zi wanted his listeners to keep in mind was that Dao looked like Someone's Son. He said:

> **I do not know whose Son He is,**
> **He was before any king [born into the world].**[4]

This Son seemed to exist before any known Chinese king or his progenitor. No such Person had been recorded in any other of the Chinese classical writings. Therefore, we ask, might the Bible shed some light on this Son's identity? Some hundred years prior to Lao Zi, the Hebrew prophet Isaiah foretold the birth of "a Child, a Son."

> *For unto us a Child is born,*
> *Unto us a Son is given;*
> *And the government will be*
> *   upon His shoulder.*
> *And His name will be called*
> *   Wonderful, Counselor, Mighty God,*
> *Everlasting Father, Prince of Peace. (Isaiah 9: 6).*

This "Child" is definitely a "Son" beyond human comprehension, for He was both a "Son" and an "Everlasting Father." Therefore this Son was before any king, for as the "Everlasting Father" He has lived from eternity. But the Child is also a "Mighty God" whose name is "Wonderful, Counselor and Prince of Peace." The Bible confirms that this Son is the Son of God, Jesus Christ. He was the Word who was with God. The Bible says in *John 1: 3:* "*All things were made through Him, and without Him nothing was made that was made.*"

Concerning the creation of the heavens and the earth, the Bible says:

> *In the beginning God created the heavens and the earth. The earth was without form, and void; and darkness was on the face of the deep. And the Spirit of God was hovering over the face of the waters.*
> *   (Genesis 1: 1 - 2).*

The word "God" in these verses is the Hebrew term "Elohim," which is a plural noun, indicating more than one Member of the Godhead, probably God the Father and God the Son. We also find the "Spirit" present—so in the creation of the heavens and our earth, all the Members of the Godhead were represented. What was the role of the Son in the creation?

> *When He [God the Father] prepared*
> *the heavens, I [God the Son] was there, . . .*
> *When He marked out the*
> *foundations of the earth,*
> *Then I was beside Him*
> *as a master craftsman.*
> *(Proverbs 8: 27, 29 - 30).*

So God the Son was actually the engineer of the creation! All things were made through Him. Jesus was the Word. *"And the Word became flesh and dwelt among us."* (John 1 : 14). And Jesus also said: *"I am the Way."* (John 14: 6). So keep in mind that God the Son is both "the Word" and "the Way."

It is interesting to note that the Chinese word "Dao" means both "the word" and "the way," two metaphors of Jesus! Could Jesus be the Dao, the Son, about whom Lao Zi wondered? Was it only the Son that Lao Zi saw, or were there other Persons?

> **Look, it cannot be seen—it is beyond form.**
> **Listen, it cannot be heard—it is beyond sound.**
> **Grasp, it cannot be held—it is intangible.**
> <u>**These three are indefinable:**</u>
> <u>**Therefore they are joined in one.**</u> . . .
> **Stay with the ancient Dao;**
> **Move with the present.**
> **Knowing the ancient beginning is the essence**
>   **of Dao.**[5]

Note here that the "ancient Dao" is described as "Three indefinable joined in One!" If it was "beyond form," "beyond sound" and "intangible," how could Lao Zi see, hear and know it? It seems that Lao Zi had an extraordinary experience!

When the apostle Paul described visions and revelations from the Lord, he said, *"I know a man in Christ who fourteen years ago—whether in the body I do not know, or whether out of the body I do not know, God knows—such a one was caught up to the third heaven."* (2 Corinthians 12: 2, 3). Obviously, the experience Paul described here was beyond finite human senses. He was evidently describing one characteristic of a vision or revelation from God.

In Chapter 5, we mentioned that God made Himself known to His prophets through dreams and visions (see pp. 54, 55). Could this have been Lao Zi's experience as recorded here—a direct revelation received from the "Dao?" Is Lao Zi therefore qualified to be called a prophet?

The distinguishing characteristic between the true Godhead and false gods is that of their Creatorship. We have already seen that Dao includes two metaphors of Jesus Christ. If Creatorship is also an integral element of Dao, we can safely say that Dao is none other than the true Godhead.

Is this Dao of Lao Zi also the Creator of everything? Let us hear more from Lao Zi about the Dao whom he saw in vision.

> **Something mysteriously already made,**
> **Existing [living] before heaven and earth**
> **In the silence and the void,**
> **Standing alone and unchanging,**
> **Ever present in constant [cyclic] motion.**
> **Perhaps He is the source of myriads of things.**
> **I do not know His name.**
> **Call Him Dao,**
> **For lack of a better word,**
> **I call Him "the Almighty."**[6]

It appears that Lao Zi was describing an event similar to that of the creation as recorded in Genesis 1: 1, 2, previously quoted. Involved in creation were the three Persons of the Godhead who have no beginning or ending (**"already made," "existing before heaven and earth"**). Compare **"ever present in constant [cyclic] motion"** with *"And the Spirit of God was hovering over the face of the waters." (Genesis 1: 2)*. Surely the Godhead is **"the source of myriads of things."**

The name of God, like God Himself, is a mystery. When God met Moses at the burning bush in the Sinai desert, He revealed His name.

> *And God said to Moses, "I AM WHO I AM." And He said, "Thus you shall say to the children of Israel, 'I AM has sent me to you.'" Moreover God said to Moses, "Thus you shall say to the children of Israel: 'The LORD God of your fathers, the God of Abraham, the God of Isaac, and the God of Jacob, has sent me to you. This is My name forever, and this is My memorial to all generations.'"*
> *(Exodus 3:14, 15).*

Obviously, Lao Zi did not know all these foreign names, such as Abraham, Isaac, or Jacob, but amazingly he gave the Creator the name of "Dao," meaning the "Word" and the "Way." In addition, he used the name, "the Almighty," the Biblical name reserved for God.

After giving these identifying names, Lao Zi continued to tell his listeners about the Almighty Dao.

> **Man follows the earth,**
> **The earth follows the heavens;**
> **The [physical] heavens follow the Dao,**
> **The Dao follows His own way.**[7]

Carefully compare **"The Dao follows His own way"** with **"*I AM WHO I AM*."** Both indicate there is none higher than themselves. Dao and *I AM* are the highest standard, following their own will and law. Both mean the same: the "Self-existent Law-Maker."

THE DAO IS INDEED THE CREATOR OF EVERYTHING! THE DAO IN THE ANCIENT CHINESE CLASSICS IS THE GODHEAD OF THE BIBLE!

How did the Dao create everything?

> **Heaven and earth have been created**
> **from something.**
> **Something has come from nothing.**[8]

How close this is to the idea expressed by the Apostle Paul in *Hebrews 11: 3!* "*By faith we understand that the worlds were framed by the word of God, so that the things which are seen were not made of things which are visible."* The Creator-God was not using pre-existing material when He created all things. Let us read once again *John 1: 1 - 4,* that Jesus Christ is called the "Word" and that He is Creator.

> *In the beginning was the Word, and the Word was with God, and the Word was God. He was in the beginning with God. All things were made through Him, and without Him nothing was made that was made. In Him was life, and the life was the light of men.*

Yet the most famous, mysterious, and frequently quoted statement of Lao Zi is this:

The Dao exists as one.
One exists as two
Two exists as three.
And three create everything.[9]

What does this mean? Many explanations have been given to this enigma, most of which are not clear and satisfactory to the interpreters themselves. We have to admit that we have also been baffled by this statement of Lao Zi. But with this new understanding of the Dao as the Godhead of the Bible, we believe that these two verses from the Bible may be helpful.

> *"Come near to Me, hear this;*
> *I have not spoken in secret from the beginning;*
> *From the time that it was, I was there.*
> *And now the Lord God and His Spirit*
> *Have sent Me." (Isaiah 48: 16).*

> *For there are three that bear witness in heaven: the Father, the Word, and the Holy Spirit; and these three are one. (1 John 5: 7).*

We ventured to give our interpretation of Lao Zi's mystery in the light of the Bible. As we have already pointed out, the Godhead acts and thinks as One. One of the Godhead of three Persons can represent the other Two, or these Two can represent all Three. The whole Godhead of **"three create everything."**

We, in turn, must confess that we do not have all the answers. To acknowledge that we cannot fully comprehend the great truths of God is only to admit that the finite mind is inadequate to grasp the infinite. Man, with his limited human knowledge, cannot understand the purposes of Omniscience. If man understood all the mysteries of God, there would be no need for discovery of additional truth. We would already have reached the ultimate in knowledge. God, then, would not still be supreme. Therefore, this can never be. In the Godhead are *"all the treasures of wisdom and knowledge." (Colossians 2: 3)*. Even in eternity beyond, we can still search and be learners at the feet of the Dao—yet never fully grasp the infinite wisdom and goodness of God.

God and the Ancient Chinese

7

The Breath of God

> *And the LORD God formed man of the dust of the ground, and <u>breathed into his nostrils the breath of life</u>; and man became a living being.*
> *(Genesis 2: 7).*

When Adam was created, all three Members of the Godhead took part. "God," as previously explained, is *Elohim,* a plural noun, and the "LORD" is *Yahweh,* the self-existent One, the I AM. These names would likely refer to God the Father and God the Son who formed the body of Adam from the dust of the ground. But it was the Holy Spirit, the third Member of the Godhead, who "breathed into his nostrils the breath of life," and enervated the otherwise lifeless body.

> *The Spirit of God has made me,*
> *And the breath of the Almighty*
> *gives me life. (Job 33: 4).*

The "Breath of God" is the Holy Spirit, and how important He is to one's very existence!

> *All the while my breath is in me,*
> *and the Spirit of God is in my nostrils.*
> *(Job 27: 3, KJV).*

Evidently the "breath of life" was a great mystery to the ancient Chinese. Listen to this conversation between Mencius and one of his disciples:

> "**I venture to ask,**" said Gong Sun Chu [student], "**Where, Master, do you excel?**"
> Mencius said, "**I understand words. I am skillful in nourishing my vast, great flowing 'Qi'** [氣, breath, life force]."
> Chu persisted, "**I venture to ask what you mean by your vast, great, flowing 'Qi.'**"
> The reply was, "<u>It is difficult to describe it. This is the vast, great, flowing 'Qi.' It is exceedingly great, and exceedingly strong. **Being nourished by righteousness, and being harmless and undefiled, it fills up all between heaven and earth. This is the 'Qi'**—**this joins righteousness and the 'Dao' [the Way]**. Without these, the 'Qi' withdraws gradually.</u>"[1]

What is this "*Qi,*" which Mencius has had difficulty in describing? Obviously it is not the natural physical breath or air, for it joins "**righteousness and the Dao of Heaven.**" There is only one logical answer to this question. The Qi is the breath of the Almighty—symbolic of the Holy Spirit. So in this statement, Mencius is actually talking about the entire Godhead—(righteousness, Jesus Christ; Dao, God the Father).

On another occasion, the Bible says of Jesus and His disciples, *"He breathed on them, and said to them, 'Receive the Holy Spirit.'" (John 20: 22).* This is additional evidence that the "Breath" (Qi) represents the Holy Spirit.

Because of His great wisdom, Jesus was sought out on many occasions. One particularly memorable visit was as follows:

> *There was a man of the Pharisees named Nicodemus, a ruler of the Jews. This man came to Jesus by night and said to Him, "Rabbi, we know that You are a teacher come from God; for no one can do these signs that You do unless God is with him."*
>
> *Jesus answered and said to him, "Most assuredly, I say to you, <u>unless one is born again, he cannot see the kingdom of God.</u>"*
>
> *Nicodemus said to Him, "How can a man be born when he is old? Can he enter a second time into his mother's womb and be born?"*
>
> *Jesus answered, "Most assuredly, I say to you, <u>unless one is born of water and the Spirit, he cannot enter the kingdom of God</u>. That which is born of the flesh is flesh, and that which is born of the Spirit is spirit. Do not marvel that I said to you, 'You must be born again.' <u>The wind blows where it wishes, and you hear the sound of it, but cannot tell where it comes from and where it goes. So is everyone who is born of the Spirit.</u>" (John 3: 1 - 8).*

So Jesus taught that another symbol for the "breath" of the Holy Spirit is "wind."

Before Jesus returned to heaven, He promised that He would send the Holy Spirit as the "Comforter." So it was that on the day of Pentecost, 50 days after His return to heaven, the disciples were gathered together in one place.

> *Suddenly there came a sound from heaven, as of <u>a rushing mighty wind</u>, and it filled the whole house where they were sitting. Then there appeared to them <u>divided tongues, as of fire</u>, and one sat upon each of them. And <u>they were all filled with the Holy Spirit</u> and began to speak with other tongues, as the Spirit gave them utterance. (Acts 2: 2 - 4).*

Just as the Son and Father are mysteries, so also is the symbolism of the Holy Spirit a mystery. The breath, wind, and fire are all symbols of the Holy

Spirit. Breath, wind and fire all have one characteristic in common: they are all in constant motion. Fire burns to give light and energy; wind brings fresh air; the breath takes in oxygen and gives off carbon dioxide. If the sun stopped giving out energy and light, it would explode. If the wind ceased blowing, there would be no more life. Man, of course, can live only a few minutes without breathing. All life: plant, animal, and man are dependent upon these vital processes. So, also, are we indebted to the energizing work of the Holy Spirit in order to even begin to understand the things of God.

> *But God has revealed them to us through His Spirit. For the Spirit searches all things, yes, the deep things of God. For what man knows the things of a man except the spirit of the man which is in him? Even so, no one knows the things of God except the Spirit of God. (1 Corinthians 2: 10, 11).*

The ancient Chinese seemed to understand that a special enlightenment of Heaven was needed to learn the things of God. Said one of the great scholars, Zhu Xi (朱熹, 1130 - 1200 A.D.):

> **Suppose that Heaven had only now given the Book of Lo (《洛书》), if it did not also give the mind to interpret it, no man would understand it!**[2]

The Bible is the book given by God, and man cannot understand the Bible without the help of the Holy Spirit, for *"the Holy Spirit teaches, comparing spiritual things with spiritual." (1 Corinthians 2: 13).*

> *All Scripture is given by inspiration [breath] of God, and is profitable for doctrine, for reproof, for correction, for instruction in righteousness, that the man of God may be complete, thoroughly equipped for every good work. (2 Timothy 3: 16, 17).*

Mencius is not the only one to mention the "Qi," for in the *Li Ji*, we find this statement:

> **The 'Qi' is the filling of God.**[3]

We have noted previously that the disciples of Jesus were "filled with the Holy Spirit" on the day of Pentecost (Acts 2: 2 - 4). When Zacharias, the father of John the Baptist, was visited by a holy angel before the birth of his son, he was given a message regarding John, *"For he will be great in the sight of the Lord, and shall drink neither wine nor strong drink. <u>He will also be filled with the Holy Spirit, even from his mother's womb</u>. (Luke 1: 15)*. Both the father and mother of John were also *"filled with the Holy Spirit." (Luke 1: 41, 67)*.

Spiritual gifts come with this filling.

> *But the manifestation of the Spirit is given to each one for the profit of all: for to one is given the word of wisdom through the Spirit, to another the word of knowledge through the same Spirit, to another faith by the same Spirit, to another gifts of healings by the same Spirit, to another the working of miracles, to another prophecy, to another discerning of spirits, to another different kinds of tongues, to another the interpretation of tongues. But one and the same Spirit works all these things, distributing to each one individually as He wills.*
> *(1 Corinthians 12: 7 - 11).*

In Jesus, the gifts of the Spirit were fully manifested: healing; raising the dead to life; His many miracles; casting out evil spirits; prophesying of things to come; understanding the languages of all people coming to Him. He was filled with the Holy Spirit.

One work of the Holy Spirit is to give the second birth to those who are striving for the kingdom of God. As shown previously in the dialogue between Jesus and Nicodemus, to be "born again" is not to go back to the mother's womb, rather to have a new mind and new heart. *"A new heart also will I give you, and a new spirit will I put within you: and I will take away the stony heart out of your flesh, and I will give you an heart of flesh. <u>And I will put my Spirit within you, and cause you to walk in my statutes</u>."*

(Ezekiel 36: 26, 27, KJV). Simply put, to be born again is to abandon the old rebellious heart which wars against God, and to acquire an obedient mind, *"because the carnal mind is enmity against God: for it is not subject to the law of God, nor indeed can be." (Romans 8: 7)*. Therefore, those who are obedient to Heaven are the ones with a "born-again mind."

The born-again mind is endowed with spiritual discernment.

> *Now we have received, not the spirit of the world, but the Spirit who is from God, that we might know the things that have been freely given to us by God. These things we also speak, not in words which man's wisdom teaches but which the Holy Spirit teaches, comparing spiritual things with spiritual.*
> *(1 Corinthians 2: 12, 13).*

Many things *"have been freely given to us by God,"* in ancient China. This rich spiritual heritage has not only been hidden in the Chinese Classics, but may also be found in their very character-writing. In the Hebrew Scriptures there are different names for God, which we have already met. As might be expected, the Chinese likewise have multiple names for the Members of the Godhead.

Most frequently noted in the Chinese Classics in reference to God is the term *Heaven, Tian* (天).[4] Surely this character represents the God of Heaven, more often referring to God the Father, as used in the "decree of Heaven" (p. 55). The most ancient designation for the Chinese God to whom the early rulers, such as Shun, sacrificed, was *Shangdi* 上帝 (乑),[5] the *Heavenly Ruler*. Another character referring to God is the word *Beginning* 元 (亐).[6] Jesus, in Revelation 1: 8, declared, *"I AM the Alpha and the Omega, the Beginning and the End...who is and who was and who is to come, the Almighty."* In this one verse, we find three names of God: "I AM," the "Beginning," and the "Almighty."

The character which we term the "God radical" 示 (丁)[7] means to *manifest, show, proclaim, exhibit*. Of Jesus it was written:

> *And without controversy great is*
> *the mystery of godliness:*
> *God was <u>manifested</u> in the flesh,...*
> *(1 Timothy 3: 16).*

The purpose of Jesus' life on earth was to show, demonstrate, manifest what God in Heaven was really like. When this radical 示 is combined with 申, *to bring forth, instruct*, the new character becomes *Shen, God, a Spirit* 示申.[8]

As mentioned in this chapter, there are symbols for the Holy Spirit. Examine the radical character, "*Qi*," meaning breath 氣.[9] A second symbol for the Holy Spirit is the radical 風 meaning not only *breath*, but also *wind*. The character meaning *rain* 雨[10] is yet another symbol for the Holy Spirit. The Hebrew Scriptures symbolize the Holy Spirit by rain:

> *And rejoice in the L<small>ORD</small> your God;*
> *For He has given you the <u>former rain</u> faithfully,*
> *And He will cause the rain to come down for you—*
> *The former rain, and the latter rain in the first*
> *   month.... I will pour out <u>My Spirit</u> in those days.*
> *(Joel 2: 23, 29).*

Why were the symbols of wind and rain given for the Holy Spirit? In nature, all life depends on these two elements. It is the wind which brings the evaporated water into the sky to form the rain clouds. The wind again blows the clouds to where they are needed to provide the rain. Of course without rain, there is no life. Therefore both wind and rain are essential to bring forth and sustain life. Thus we find again the relation of God's Spirit and the life-quickening breath.

Let us now look into yet another mystery recorded in ancient Chinese writings.

> **Heaven commissioned a mystical Bird**
> **   to descend**
> **And give birth to the father of our Shang.** (商)[11]

Chinese scholars have never agreed on the meaning of this "Bird." Some have declared it to be only a mystical bird, for how could a real bird give birth to a man? **"The father of the Shang"** would be the second dynasty's first king, King Tang, a righteous man, and one of the sages in the line of illustrious wise men [see Chapter 4, pp. 31, 32]. The difficulty with this verse is therefore obvious: how does a bird give birth to a most righteous king? The ancient Chinese were not evolutionists, believing that man comes from a lower order of animal. They knew that man was created by the great God of Heaven. What was this mystical bird?

Now is the time to unlock this millennial mystery. As we have learned, the obedient mind and heart are born of the Holy Spirit. We also learned that "wind," "breath," "fire," and "rain" are all symbols of the Holy Spirit. Could there be yet another symbol for the Holy Spirit? Let us turn again to the Bible.

> *When all the people were baptized, it came to pass that Jesus also was baptized; and while He prayed, the heaven was opened. And <u>the Holy Spirit descended in bodily form like a dove upon Him</u>, and a voice came from heaven which said, "You are My beloved Son; in You I am well pleased."*
>   *(Luke 3: 21, 22).*

Yes, the Holy Spirit could appear in the form of a bird! Now come back to the mystical "Bird" which gave birth to **"The father of the Shang,"** namely, King Tang: it would seem, according to the biblical reference, that it was the Holy Spirit that descended upon King Tang in the form of a bird. With the "Bird," a new and obedient heart was borne unto King Tang, enabling him to follow the way of Heaven. Not only Tang, but Yao, Shun, King Wen, Lao Zi, Confucius, Mencius, and other ancient Chinese sages all obediently walked in the Way of Heaven, were all bestowed with a new heart. This heavenly "Bird" is still hovering over "the land of Sinim." As the Holy Spirit is welcomed into the heart, God's great plan for redemption will be realized in all its beauty.

8

The Great Plan of Heaven

> To Yu [禹 early king] Heaven gave "the Great Plan with its nine Divisions," and thereby the proper virtues of the various relations were brought forth in their order.[1]

Yu was founder of the first Chinese dynasty in 2205 B.C. We learned that he was recommended by Shun to Heaven for succession to the throne of the Middle Kingdom (p. 56). With the Great Plan of administration from Heaven, Yu not only successfully controlled the devastating flood in the kingdom (p. 2), but also brought social order. We wonder what Heaven's plan for a world flooded with sin could be. What started the sin problem and how can order be restored?

We have alluded to the fact previously (p. 17) that God has an enemy, a fallen angel. We need to go far back into history to learn the background of this. Satan's original name was Lucifer, meaning "the light-bearer." He had been a mighty angel standing in the very presence of God, but he became not only proud of his position, but jealous of the Son of God, and determined to usurp God's power and throne.

> *How you are fallen from heaven,*
> *O Lucifer, son of the morning!*
> *How you are cut down to the ground,*
> *You who weakened the nations!*
> *For you have said in your heart:*
> *"I will ascend into heaven,*
> *I will exalt my throne above the stars of God;*
> *I will also sit on the mount of the congregation*
> *On the farthest sides of the north;*
> *I will ascend above the heights of the clouds,*
> *I will be like the Most High."*
> *(Isaiah 14: 12 - 14).*

In his rebellion, Lucifer influenced a third of the angels of heaven to join in his revolt against the Godhead of Heaven. We read further:

> *And war broke out in heaven: Michael [God the Son] and his angels fought with the dragon; and the dragon and his angels fought, but they did not prevail, nor was a place found for them in heaven any longer. So the great dragon was cast out, that serpent of old, called the Devil and Satan, who deceives the whole world; he was cast to the earth, and his angels were cast out with him.*
> *(Revelation 12: 7 - 9).*

Thus it was that, when Adam and Eve were created, it was Satan's purpose to cause them to disobey God and thus enlist them in joining, along with his evil angels, in rebellion against the Godhead. Satan not only hated God without reason, but also His righteous law which required obedience so that there might be love and peace among all of God's created beings. It was therefore necessary that God prove the loyalty of Adam and Eve to Himself, rather than to Satan. The test was contained in God's one command, *"Of the tree of the knowledge of good and evil you shall not eat, for in the day that you eat of it you shall surely die." (Genesis 2: 17).*

The Great Plan of Heaven

To disobey God's word, or law, is to commit sin. *"Whoever sins is guilty of breaking God's law, because sin is a breaking of the law." (1 John 3: 4, TEV)*. The result of disobedience would be separation from God, the lifegiver, and this would result in death of the defiant one.

You may review the scenario briefly mentioned (pp. 16, 17), when earth's first woman, Eve, took fruit from the forbidden tree of the knowledge of good and evil and ate, sharing some with her husband, Adam. They had thereby disobeyed God's one command.

God's enemy the Serpent, Satan, on the other hand had promised, *"You will not surely die, for God knows that in the day you eat of it your eyes will be opened, and you will be like God, knowing good and evil." (Genesis 3: 4, 5)*.

But Adam and Eve did not die after eating the forbidden fruit and disobeying God. In fact they lived on for a great number of years after this event. Was Satan right, or God? God had been challenged by His enemy. Why had the death of Adam and Eve not occurred after God promised this result? What is the answer? Let us turn again to the Bible. From the ancient prophet, *Zechariah 6: 12, 13*, we find these mysterious words:

> *Thus says the L<small>ORD</small> of hosts, saying:*
> *"Behold, the Man whose name is the BRANCH!*
> *From His place He shall branch out,*
> *And He shall build the temple of the L<small>ORD</small>,*
> *Yes, He shall build the temple of the L<small>ORD</small>.*
> *He shall bear the glory,*
> *And shall sit and rule on His throne;*
> *So He shall be a priest on His throne;*
> *And the <u>counsel of peace</u>*
> *<u>shall be between them both</u>."*

First, we must identify the BRANCH. From the following words of the prophet Jeremiah, we may identify the "Branch" as a clear prophecy of the coming Son of God, Jesus Christ, in the human lineage of the Judean king, David.

> *"Behold, the days are coming,"*
> *says the LORD,*
> *"That I will raise to David*
> *a Branch of righteousness;*
> *A King shall reign and prosper,*
> *And execute judgment and*
> *righteousness in the earth.*
> *In His days Judah will be saved,*
> *And Israel will dwell safely;*
> *Now this is His name by which He will be called:*
> *THE LORD OUR RIGHTEOUSNESS."*
> *(Jeremiah 23: 5, 6).*

The word "counsel" in the first quotation means "advice, purpose," and by implication, "Plan."[2] The Hebrew word for "peace" here means "peace, friendship; with God especially in a covenant relationship."[2] The "counsel of peace" is therefore the "plan of reconciliation" or the "plan of redemption and salvation." Next in this prophecy, we would want to know who the "both" refers to. It refers to God the Father, and God the Son. These two divine Beings devised the plan of redemption for the sin problem which had arisen on earth.

The unavoidable penalty for the sin of breaking God's law was death. To eradicate sin, life blood had to be shed. God accepted an animal offering only as a promise of a future better Sacrifice. The blood of beasts could not ultimately atone as a sacrifice for breaking God's righteous law.

It is also impossible for sinful man to atone for another man. God had created Adam perfect and sinless, but after his transgression there was no acceptable sacrifice, short of an offering superior to man in his original sinless perfection. In the order of life, heaven's angels are sinless and higher than humans. But God's holy law is of more value than the angels, for since they, too, are created beings, they are also on probation—their existence depends upon obedience to God. What was God's solution to this problem in an otherwise perfect universe?

We find the answer in *John 3:16: "For God so loved the world that He gave His only begotten Son, that whoever believes in Him should not perish but have everlasting life."* Only Jesus Christ, the holy Son, could meet the requirements of God's holy law. His life alone was of sufficient value to rescue fallen man, to elevate him, and to restore him to his original state of perfection.

When was this plan of redemption devised, of which we have just read? After Adam and Eve sinned? No! According to *1 Peter 1: 18 - 20: "Knowing that you were not redeemed with corruptible things. . .but with the precious blood of Christ, as of a lamb without blemish and without spot. <u>He indeed was foreordained before the foundation of the world</u>, but was manifest in these last times for you."*

This wonderful plan for man's salvation was arranged before Adam sinned, and even before man was created! *Revelation 13: 8* confirms that Jesus, the Lamb of God was *"slain from the foundation of the world."* Besides this, Christ died not only for Adam and Eve, but for all humans in all ages!

The salvation of mankind cost the precious life of Jesus, the Holy Man who is equal with God the Father. At the cost of Jesus' infinite sacrifice, all sinners gain the privilege of living a probationary life, dependent upon their ultimate belief in His saving blood. The Bible relates how this plan of redemption was revealed not only to Adam, but to his descendants such as Abraham, Job, Noah, Moses, David, Isaiah, Daniel, and other patriarchs.

But has this wonderful saving plan ever been revealed to the Chinese prophets? It seems impossible that a loving God would not reveal His plan to the ancient believing Chinese. In Chapter 4 we discovered that Mencius was moved to speak an amazing prophecy of the "King" [Jesus Christ]. We cannot expect to discover a systematic description of this saving plan in the Chinese writings, for God has His own way of conveying knowledge to His people about His plan. Even in the Bible, God disclosed His plans to His prophets:

> *Precept upon precept, precept upon precept,*
> *Line upon line, line upon line,*
> *Here a little, there a little. (Isaiah 28: 13).*

Apart from God's consideration of our finite minds and slow understanding, God has many other reasons for the specific ways in which He reveals truth. Although we can find many references, both to the principles and details of God's great plan in the Chinese Classics, we will for now, limit our discoveries to one book—the *Yi Jing*.

The *Yi Jing* (p. 27), as you may recall, was written by a number of authors over a period of 2,000 years. It is the only complete Chinese Jing coming down from antiquity, having survived the great book burning disaster during the Qin dynasty (p. 23). The *Yi Jing* is the foundation of all Chinese Classics. The most diligent Chinese scholars, from mystical antiquity to the present time, have poured over this book. The founders of Chinese philosophy, Confucianism and Daoism, have their common roots here. We are impressed to say that the principles written in the *Yi Jing* are the teachings of the "Holy Man" and the Way to heaven. Confucianism is a reflection of these principles in practice, whereas Lao Zi more directly revealed the Dao [the "Way"] and the "Holy Man."

The Bible, on the other hand, has a complete and clear revelation of God—His plan for mankind, and derived explanations of the only true "Dao," and the revelation of the "Holy Man."

The Bible relates the history of mankind from the time of creation. It also tells us that when Satan, the enemy of God and mankind, is finally eliminated, probationary time for the world will come to an end. We will find that these same principles of this great plan are recorded in the *Yi Jing* as we analyze it for redemption's plan.

1. The Substance of the Plan of Redemption

Deliverance (解, or it may be translated as Redemption or Salvation) is found in Chapter 40 of the *Yi Jing:*

> **Thunder and rain set in:**
> **The image of DELIVERANCE.**
> **Thus the Son of the King pardons offenses**
> **And forgives sins.**[3]

This Salvation chapter tells us at least three truths:

- The reason for man's need of deliverance is his entanglement in "offenses."
- The key for man's salvation is forgiveness of his offenses and sins.
- Only the "Son of the King" can pardon man's sin and bring salvation.

We must ask, who is this "Son of the King" through whom comes the pardon of sins and resultant salvation? Who will be man's Savior?

2. The "Great Holy Man" Is the Savior

At the end of the first chapter of the *Yi Jing*, we read:

> **This is the Person who is called the Great Man: His character matches with Heaven and earth; His light shines like that of the sun and moon; His schedule of action is precisely accurate—like the change of the four seasons; His good or evil fate is in accordance with gods and spirits. When he acts before Heaven 天 , Heaven does not disagree with Him. When He follows Heaven, He adapts Himself to the time of Heaven. If Heaven Himself does not disagree with Him, who else can confront Him—either men, gods, or spirits!**[4]

> **It is only the Holy Man who understands how to press forward and how to draw back. He knows life and death as well, yet does not deviate from the righteous Way. The Holy Man alone can attain this.**[5]

A careful reader may come to the following conclusions or questions:
- The "Great Man and the "Holy Man" are one and the same.
- His character matches that of Heaven [God the Father].
- He shines like the sun and the moon.
- His actions are perfectly timed.
- He alone knows the secret of life and death.
- What was His "evil fate?"
- What were His "prior" actions with which Heaven does not disagree?

If we look back to all the ancient Chinese sages and virtuous kings, we find that none of them took any "prior action," but rather "followed after," and were always obedient to the commands of Heaven. Therefore, these sages did not fit the criteria for the "Holy Man." But Jesus Christ does fit all of these descriptions!

Does the character of Jesus Christ match that of Heaven, God? The Bible says that *"Christ Jesus, who, being in the form of God, did not consider it robbery to be equal with God." (Philippians 2: 6). "For in Him dwells all the fullness of the Godhead bodily." (Colossians 2: 9).*

Were His actions perfectly timed? *"But when the fullness of the time had come, God sent forth His Son [Jesus Christ], born of a woman, born under the law, to redeem those who were under the law, that we might receive the adoption as sons." (Galatians 4: 4).*

These three verses tell us clearly that Jesus was born as the Savior to save mankind from sins. He came to the world according to the time table of God; He was equal with God. Therefore, the first two statements of the *Yi Jing* description of the Holy Man are fulfilled exactly.

In answer to the third question regarding life and death—does Jesus have the answer? We read, *"In Him [Jesus Christ] was life, and the life was the light of men." (John 1: 4).* Jesus said, *(Revelation 1: 17): "Do not* *be afraid; . . . I AM He who lives, and was dead, and behold, I am alive forevermore. Amen. And <u>I have the keys of Hades [the grave] and of Death</u>."* Jesus is the source of life; He died and was resurrected. He, alone, knows the mystery of life and death!

We have already seen that Jesus' "evil fate" was to suffer death—but not for any wrong He had done. Recall that in Chapter 4, (p. 46), Pilate said, *"I find no fault in Him at all." (John 18: 38)*. It is clear that Jesus voluntarily took upon Himself the responsibility to save man and die in man's stead as a sacrifice. Notice again what the *Yi Jing* says of this voluntary step: **"When He acts prior to Heaven, Heaven does not disagree with Him"** God the Father did not ask this Great Man to become the Sacrifice. Instead, the Great Man volunteered to be the sin-bearer in the plan of redemption. Jesus said,

> *"Therefore My Father loves Me, because I lay down My life that I may take it again. No one takes it from Me, but I lay it down of Myself. I have power to lay it down, and I have power to take it again. This command I have received from My Father."*
> *(John 10: 17, 18)*.

After Jesus' offer was accepted by God the Father, Jesus' birth as a human, His baptism (anointing), His public ministry, His death, His resurrection and ascension —all took place according to God's time table.

3. The Plan of Redemption Involved Struggle and Humiliation for the Great Man.

> **Although with struggling and hesitation, His mission and action came out just and right. Stepping down from a noble position, He assumed a low position, thus winning the hearts of all people.**[6]

Jesus came down from His glorious throne in heaven to become a man without honor or position. It was His determination to give His life for mankind to save all persons from their sins, yet, being in human form, He was not without struggles and even hesitation. This was especially true of His awful experience in the Garden of Gethsemane the night before his arrest, trial and crucifixion.

> Then Jesus came with them to a place called Gethsemane, and said to the disciples, "Sit here while I go and pray over there."
> And He took with Him Peter and the two sons of Zebedee, and He began to be sorrowful and deeply distressed. Then He said to them, "<u>My soul is exceedingly sorrowful, even to death</u>. Stay here and watch with Me."
> He went a little farther and fell on His face, <u>and prayed</u>, saying, "O My Father, if it is possible, let this cup pass from Me; nevertheless, not as I will, but as You will."
> Then He came to the disciples and found them asleep, and said to Peter, "What! Could you not watch with Me one hour? Watch and pray, lest you enter into temptation. The spirit indeed is willing, but the flesh is weak."
> Again, <u>a second time, He went away and prayed</u>, saying, "O My Father, if this cup cannot pass away from Me unless I drink it, Your will be done."
> And He came and found them asleep again, for their eyes were heavy. So He left them, went away again, and <u>prayed the third time</u>, saying the same words. (Matthew 26: 36 - 44).

In this Bible passage, we find that Jesus hesitated from His mission three times, asking God the Father to remove the cup of suffering from Him, yet three times He wanted God's will to be done. Jesus was determined, for He had previously concluded, *"And I, if I am lifted up from the earth [crucified], will draw all peoples to Myself." (John 12: 32).*

True to the words in the *Yi Jing*, Jesus died a most humiliating death on the cross. But He also understood **"how to press forward"** and did not **"deviate from the righteous Way."** By doing just this, **"He won the hearts of all people,"** from nations throughout the entire earth.

4. The Teaching of the Holy Man and the Results of the Plan of Redemption Are Found in the Yi Jing.

> **The Holy Man teaches with the Dao [Word] of God (神道), and all under heaven [the entire universe] surrenders to Him.**[7]

The Word of God has power and life. Always Jesus represented God the Father in His teachings. Jesus said, *"I have not spoken on My own authority; but the Father who sent Me gave Me a command, what I should say and what I should speak." (John 12: 49).*

The *Yi Jing* reveals that the result of the Holy Man's teaching is to bring everyone under heaven to surrender to the Holy Man. The literal meaning of the Chinese words, "under Heaven" is broader than just the people of this world. Let us compare what the Bible says:

> *In him we have redemption through His blood, the forgiveness of sins, according to the riches of His grace which He made to abound toward us in all wisdom and prudence, having made known to us the mystery of His will, according to His good pleasure which He purposed in Himself, that in the dispensation of the fullness of the times He might gather together in one all things in Christ, <u>both which are in heaven and which are on earth—in Him.</u>*
> *(Ephesians 1: 7 - 10).*

From this we can understand that the plan of salvation has a broader and deeper purpose than the salvation of man alone. It was not only for the redemption of mankind that Christ came to the earth. The ultimate purpose goes far beyond having earth's people reverence God's word and law. *"For this reason I bow my knees to the Father of our Lord Jesus Christ, from whom <u>the whole family in heaven and earth is named</u>." (Ephesians 3: 14, 15)*. Christ's sacrifice and death was to vindicate God's character before the entire universe—to intelligences of other worlds, as well as the angels of heaven.

Just before His crucifixion, Jesus declared, *"Now is the judgment of this world; now the ruler of this world will be cast out. And I, if I am lifted up from the earth, <u>will draw all peoples to Myself</u>." (John 12: 31, 32)*. Jesus' sacrifice was not only to give humans on earth access to heaven, but to justify, before the whole universe, the Father and Son's dealing with the rebellion of the fallen angel, Satan. With Satan's final just eradication, the devastating results of sin would be revealed and forever eliminated from the universe.

It is true that the *Yi Jing* has only a few words to say about the Great Man's role in the plan of salvation and redemption of man from sin, but these words contain a vast kernel of truth!

9

The Master and His Dream

In the Chinese Classics, "The Master" is a title reserved for Confucius. Above all the ancient sages, he has been honored for his wisdom and exemplary life. It is to Confucius that a great debt is owed in the preservation and teachings regarding the heavenly Dao [the Way]. He was the first and greatest educator in the history of China. He founded the first private university in the world. During his lifetime, he educated more than 3,000 students, of whom 70 were extraordinarily excellent, both in capacity and virtue. These helped shape the great culture of China.

Probably more is known of Confucius than of any other sage. It is said that in his ancestry were kings. He was born to Shu Liang Heh, a famous soldier of great prowess and bravery, in his old age. Heh married young and had nine daughters; then one son by a concubine. Since this one son was crippled, Heh sought, when over seventy, a second wife through Yan's family.

Yan, who had three daughters, said to them, "Here is the commandant of Shu [Heh]. His father and grandfather were only scholars, but he is a descendant of the sage kings. He is a man ten feet tall [much taller than average], and of extraordinary prowess. I am very desirous of his alliance.

Although he is old and austere, you need have no misgivings about him. Which of you three daughters will be willing to become his wife?"

The two elder daughters remained silent, but Chang-tsai said, "Why do you ask us, Father? It is for you to decide."

"Very well," said the father in reply to his youngest daughter, "you will be the one." Thus Chang-tsai became Heh's wife. According to legend, the couple went to a mountain and prayed for a son. When Confucius was born on September 28, 551 B.C., they named him Qiu (丘), in honor of their answered prayer. "Qiu" means "hill or mountain."

Little is known of the childhood and youth of Confucius. Heh died when Confucius was three, and Mother Chang-tsai also died at an early age. Because his family was poor, the boy had to work, and thereby learned many practical skills. When he was young, the game he liked best was to imitate the ceremony of sacrifices. This mystery of the sacrifice to God must have impressed and attracted him deeply. All his life he tried to research the lost ceremony of sacrifices to Shangdi. In later years he wrote:

> **He who understands the ceremonies of the sacrifices to Shangdi, would find the government of a kingdom as easy as to look into his palm!**[1]

He began teaching in his own home while in his twenties.

> **The Master [Confucius] said: "At fifteen, I had my mind bent on learning. At thirty, I stood firm. At forty, I had no doubts. At fifty, I knew the decrees of Heaven. At sixty, my ear was an obedient organ for the reception of truth. At seventy, I could follow what my heart desired, without transgressing what was right."**[2]

Confucius was thought to be a tall man—almost ten feet tall! According to his disciples, **"The Master was mild, and yet dignified; majestic, and yet not fierce; respectful, and yet easy."**[3]

Unlike a philosopher in the western world, Confucius was a man of many skills. He was a first class musician; actually music was an important course in the six skills he taught. He could cook good food. He was not only meticulous in mind and thought, but also in his appearance and behavior. His mastery of the martial arts was a wonderment to the professionals in this field, but the Master was a peace lover, as exemplified in his firm refusal to discuss military matters in the following quotation.

> **The Duke Ling of Wei (卫灵公) asked Confucius about tactics. Confucius replied: "I have heard all about sacrificial vessels, but I have not learned military matters." On this, he took his departure the next day.**[4]

Confucius died at the age of 73, in the year 479 B.C., about 500 years before the coming of Jesus Christ. He left a mountain of rich treasures. He compiled *The Book of Songs, The Book of Documents, Yi Jing,* and also *The Book of Rites.* There were other books, such as the *Book of Music,* destroyed during the Qin dynasty (p. 22). He was the sole author of *Spring and Autumn.* However with all these books written, Confucius claimed to be merely **"a transmitter and not an author."**[4a] This causes us to wonder what he meant by being merely a "transmitter." To whom was he referring as the "author?"

Confucius knew that his mission came from Heaven. One time when he was put in a dangerous situation, he assured his student of the protection of Heaven.

> **The Master was put in fear in Kuang (匡). He said: "After the death of King Wen, was not the cause of truth lodged here in me?**
>
> **"If Heaven [God] had wished to let this cause of truth [literature] perish, then I, a future mortal, should not have got such a relation to that cause. While Heaven does not let the cause of truth**

> [literature] perish, what can the people of Kuang do to me."5

Confucius told his disciples that he was doing his appointed work for Heaven and therefore was under Heaven's protection. His work was to "transmit" the messages from Heaven. It was Heaven who inspired him to write. Compare with the following verse from the Bible:

> *For prophecy never came by the will of man, but holy men of God spoke as they were moved by the Holy Spirit. (2 Peter 1: 21).*

It appears to be only logical that Confucius was also commissioned by the Holy Spirit! He even clearly told his disciples that there was no reason to be discouraged after he had been refused a position by the border-warden of Yi, for his Heavenly appointed work was the more important.

> **The border-warden at Yi requested to be introduced to the Master, saying: "When sons of the Prince (君子) have come here, I have never been denied the privilege of seeing them."**
> **The followers of the sage introduced him, and when he came out from the interview, he said: "My friends, why are you distressed by your master's loss of office? The kingdom has long been without the principles of truth and right; Heaven is going to use your master as a bell with its wooden tongue."6**

A metal bell with a wooden tongue was shaken to make important announcements, or to call people together. Heaven would employ Confucius in the same manner to proclaim truth and right. The Bible says: *"And God has appointed these in the church: first apostles, second prophets, third teachers." (1 Corinthians 12: 28).*

This bell with a wooden tongue can be compared with the tongue of a teacher. If Lao Zi was a prophet of the *Dao,* Confucius may well be called the teacher of the Dao. Both were chosen by Heaven!

Confucius did not fail his Heavenly appointment. How true a Chinese saying, "Ten thousand years could be in darkness without Confucius." The light that he carried to ancient China can also be today *"as a light that shines in a dark place," (2 Peter 1: 19)*, to lead many Chinese to the Great Light—even to the way of Truth and Righteousness!

As a great teacher, the Dao was always the center and focus of his interest.

> **When a son of the Prince is taught of the Dao,**
> **he loves man;**
> **When the son of a mean man is taught**
> **of the Dao, he is easily obedient.[7]**

Confucius knew how to lead his students step by step in pursuit of the Dao. Notice what his favorite student said of his teaching on this subject:

> **Yan Yuan(颜渊), in admiration of the Master's teaching, sighed and said: "I looked up to them [the Dao], and they seemed to become more high; I tried to penetrate them, and they seemed to become more firm; I looked at them before me, and suddenly they seemed to be behind.**
>
> **"The Master, by orderly method, skillfully leads men on. He enlarged my mind with learning, and taught me the restraints of ceremony and laws.**
>
> **"When I wish to give over the study of his teaching, I cannot do so, and having exerted all my ability, there seems something to stand right up before me; but though I wish to follow and lay hold of it [the Dao], I really find no way to do so."[8]**

The Dao and the knowledge of the Dao are certainly not easy to grasp fully. There is an ever deeper depth beyond what is already learned. We have studied the Dao of Lao Zi. Let us now see what definition Confucius gave to the Dao:

> Yin [阴 , the visible] and Yang [阳 , the invisible]
> are called the Dao.
> The loving one discovered it and calls it love;
> The wise man discovers it and calls it wisdom.⁹

Like the Dao of Lao Zi, the meaning of Dao in this statement of Confucius has also remained a riddle for thousands of years. None of the various explanations is widely accepted. In Chapter 6, we discovered that, in the light of the Bible, the Dao is the Godhead, and especially connotes Jesus Christ. We may use the same key to unlock this mystery here!

But before we do this, let us read one more sentence from Confucius which comes immediately after the above quotation:

> **That which cannot be fathomed in terms**
>   **of Yin [the visible]**
>   **and Yang [the invisible] is called**
>   **God [神 Shen].**¹⁰

So it is apparent that Confucius equated the Dao with God! The mystery of this Dao [God] is that He is both visible and invisible. In the Bible, we meet the same mystery in the incarnation of Jesus Christ, for in Christ, divinity (Yang, the invisible) was clothed with humanity (Yin, the visible). In Christ we behold the image of the invisible God. Man could not behold the unveiled glory of God in Christ and live. By faith we behold Christ standing between humanity and divinity, thereby connecting God and man, and earth with heaven.

Tradition says Confucius traveled to the state of Zhou where Lao Zi lived, and asked him the meaning of the Dao.¹⁰ᵃ The Dao of Lao Zi and the Dao of Confucius are one and the same. Now we can understand that their Dao was Jesus Christ, the Son of God (invisible), the Son of man (visible). Note the following verses from the Bible:

> *And without controversy great is the mystery*
> *of godliness:*
>   <u>*God was manifested in the flesh,*</u>

> *Justified in the Spirit, seen by angels,*
> <u>*Preached among the Gentiles,*</u>
> *Believed on in the world,*
> *Received up in glory. (1 Timothy 3: 16).*

The black and white symbol of Yin and Yang faintly shows a righteous God manifested in sinful flesh. Yet how far the original meaning has been perverted!

Both the Bible and Chinese Classics testify that this message has been preached to the Gentiles. *"That was the true light, which gives light to every man coming into the world." (John 1: 9).*

So important is the Dao that Confucius said:

> **The Dao may not be left for an instant. If it could be left, it would not be the Dao. On this account, a son of the Prince does not wait till he sees things, to be cautious, nor till he hears things, to be apprehensive [reverent and careful].[11]**

For in the Dao [Jesus Christ] was the way, the truth and the life. The disciple Peter said, *"Nor is there salvation in any other, for there is no other name under heaven given among men by which we must be saved." (Acts 4: 12).* Therefore, Confucius designed to set his students' minds on the Dao.

> **The Master said, "Let the will be set on the Dao. Let every action be based on morality and be firmly grasped. Let every work be motivated by love."[12]**

Likewise, the apostle Paul advised Christians to set their minds on Jesus Christ—the Dao. *"Let us lay aside every weight, and the sin which so easily ensnares us, and let us run with endurance the race that is set before us, looking unto Jesus, the author and finisher of our faith." (Hebrews 12: 1, 2).* The Dao should be the first priority in one's life.

> **The Master said, "The object of a son of the Prince is Dao. Food is not his object. There is ploughing:—**

even in that there is sometimes want. So with learning;—payment may be found in it. A son of the Prince is anxious lest he should not reach the Dao; he is not anxious lest poverty should come upon him."[13]

The reward of learning the Dao is in the Dao. *"He who comes to God must believe that he is, and that he is a rewarder of those who diligently seek him." (Hebrew 11: 6)*. This is also the teaching of Jesus Christ, the Dao:

> *"O you of little faith, . . . do not worry, saying, 'What shall we eat?' or 'What shall we drink?' or 'What shall we wear?' For after all these things the Gentiles seek. For your heavenly Father knows that you need all these things. But seek first the kingdom of God and His righteousness, and all these things shall be added to you." (Matthew 6: 30 - 33).*
>
> *For the kingdom of God is not eating and drinking; but righteousness, and peace, and joy in the Holy Spirit. (Romans 14: 17).*

Confucius himself did not set his mind on riches and honors as his priority.

> **The Master said: "With coarse rice to eat, with water to drink, and my bended arm for a pillow;—I still have joy in the midst of these things. Riches and honors acquired by unrighteousness are to me as a floating cloud."**[14]

Yan Hui was the favorite student of his Master. It was because of his joy in seeking the Dao.

> **The Master said: "Admirable indeed was the virtue of Hui (回)! With a single bamboo dish of rice, a single gourd dish of drink, and living in his mean narrow lane, while others could not have endured**

the distress, he did not allow his joy to be affected by it. Admirable indeed was the virtue of Hui."[15]

It was the same spirit that brought Paul and Silas joy even when they were in prison. *"But at midnight Paul and Silas were praying, and singing hymns to God; and the prisoners were listening to them." (Acts 16: 25).*

Confucius warned his disciples:

The Master said, "Those who follow a different Dao [Way] cannot lay plans with each other."[16]

Compare this statement with the following biblical counsel :

Do not love the world or the things in the world. If anyone loves the world, the love of the Father is not in him. For all that is in the world—the lust of the flesh, the lust of the eyes, and the pride of life—is not of the Father but is of the world. And the world is passing away, and the lust of it; but he who does the will of God abides forever. (1 John 2: 15 - 17).

Great teacher as he was, Confucius was humble. He knew that it was Heaven that gave him the virtue that was in him.

The Master said, "Heaven produced the virtue that is in me."[17]

And he knew that the same Heaven who gave and sustained life to everyone could also produce virtue in others. Therefore Confucius learned from everyone.

The Master said, "When I walk along with two others, they may serve me as my teachers. I will select their good qualities and follow them, their bad qualities and avoid them."[18]

He was aware of his imperfections, and in great humility he said:

The Master said, "The sage and the man of perfect virtue:—how dare I rank myself with them?

> **It may be simply said of me, that I strive to become such without satiety, and teach others without weariness."**[19]

Diligently teaching the Dao as he was, Confucius had a strong desire to see the Dao he taught, even as the Hebrew prophets desired to see the coming Messiah of whom they prophesied. The Chinese Master said:

> **"If a man in the morning hear the right Way, he may die in the evening without regret."**[20]

It seemed that Confucius often had dreams of former sages.

> **The Master said: "Extreme is my decay. For a long time, I have not dreamed, as I was wont to do, that I saw the Duke of Zhou."**[21]

We can see from this statement the old Master's desire to see the sages and hear from them the lessons of the Dao. This faithful teacher of the Dao seemed to have realized that the Dao he sought, the Dao he taught of, may have been one and the same as the "Holy Man." He not only wanted to hear the Dao, but dreamed of seeing the Holy Man in Person!

> **The Master said, "A Holy Man (聖 人) is not mine to see;**
> **Could I see a man of real talent and virtue, that would satisfy me."**
>
> **The Master said: "A good man it is not mine to see; could I see a man possessed of constancy, that would satisfy me."**[22]

This dream of the Master remained unrealized in his life. His teaching was also not very much appreciated and practiced. He himself was not popular, and had to move from one place to another, living in poverty. Yet he was not dissatisfied with Heaven. He knew there was One who knew him and his dream.

The Master said: "Alas! there is no one that knows me."

Zi Gong said: "What do you mean by thus saying that no one knows you?"

The Master replied: "I do not murmur against Heaven. I do not grumble against men. My studies lie low, my penetration rises high. But there is Heaven—that knows me!"[23]

Yet Confucius was not the only one whose dreams were not realized. Many Hebrew prophets had the same experience. They died without seeing the coming Messiah of whom they prophesied all their lives.

These (men and women through the ages who were looking for the Savior of mankind) all died in faith, not having received the promises, but having seen them afar off were assured of them, embraced them and confessed that they were strangers and pilgrims on the earth. (Hebrews 11: 13).

Who could this Holy Man be that the Chinese Master dreamed of and desired to see? When was He to come? If He were to come, would He meet all the expectations of the ancient Chinese and therefore be easily recognized by today's Chinese?

10

Behold the Holy Man!

> The Master said, "A Holy Man is not
> mine to see;
> Could I see a man of real talent and
> virtue, that would satisfy me."[1]

In the Chinese language, the words for "sage" and the "Holy Man" are the same. However, all the sages realized that they were not that perfect Holy Man. All of these wise men made mistakes and committed offenses in their lives. Confucius, commonly known as the greatest Chinese sage, knew well his personal failings. His disciples said of him:

> Though there might be a large quantity of meat, he would not allow what he took to exceed the due proportion for the rice. It was only in wine that he laid down no limit for himself, but he did not allow himself to be confused by it.[2]

In a list of things to which he failed to attain, one item was **"not to be overcome of wine."** [3] Confucius would never allow his disciples to call him the "Holy Man." Even Mencius said of him:

105

"Oh!" formerly Zi Gong asked Confucius, saying, "Master, are you the Holy Man?"

Confucius answered him, "The Holy Man is what I cannot rise to. I learn without satiety, and teach without being tired."

Zi Gong said, "You learn without satiety:—that shows your wisdom. You teach without being tired:—that shows your benevolence. Benevolent and wise:—Master, you are the Holy Man."

Confucius said, "Now you want to put the title of Holy Man on me? What are you talking about?"[4]

Mencius himself was later titled "the second sage," but he did not consider himself worthy of even this appellation, for he said,

I have not attained to do what they [the sages of antiquity] did. But what I wish to do is to learn to be like Confucius.[5]

Since both Confucius and Mencius denied the title of the Holy Man, who, then, could He be? Who was this Person that all of the Chinese sages through the years wrote of, and longed to see?

How great is the Way of the Holy Man! Like overflowing water, it sends forth and nourishes all things and rises up to the height of heaven. All-complete is its greatness! It embraces the three hundred rules of ceremony, and the three thousand rules of royal behavior. It waits for the Proper Man, and then it is fulfilled.[6]

According to this teaching of Confucius, this Holy Man is the One who "**nourishes all things and rises up to the height of Heaven.**" It is the Holy Man who "**embraces the three hundred rules of ceremony, and the three thousand rules of royal behavior.**" He is the One who comes to practice and fulfill the law of Heaven!

Surely the God of heaven has numberless **"rules of royal behavior."** In the book of *Hosea 8: 12*, God speaks, *"I have written for him the <u>great things of My law</u>, but they were counted as a strange thing."* The original meaning of "great things" here mentioned in the law is "ten thousand."[7] Even though God has a perfect law, man disregarded it. But *"<u>he will magnify the law, and make it honorable</u>." (Isaiah 42: 21, KJV).*

Who is this **"Proper Man"** who "will magnify the law, and make it honorable?"

> *Therefore, when He came into the world, He said:*
> *"Sacrifice and offering You did not desire,*
> *But <u>a body You have prepared for Me</u>.*
> *In burnt offerings and sacrifices for sin*
> *You had no pleasure.*
> *Then I said, '<u>Behold, I have come</u>—*
> *In the volume of the book it is written of Me—*
> *<u>To do Your will</u>, O God.'" (Hebrews 10: 5 - 7).*

Jesus Christ, who was equal with God, **"rises up to the height of heaven."** Was He not able to **"send forth and nourish all things,"** for He upheld *"all things by the word of His power?" (Hebrews 1: 3)*. When Jesus was on earth, he stated, *"Do not think that I came to destroy the Law or the Prophets. <u>I did not come to destroy but to fulfill</u>." (Matthew 5: 17)*. Was not Jesus Christ the **"Proper Man"** whose body was prepared by God to **"fulfill"** His law?

How much more in the "volume of the book" of Chinese classics do we find information written about the Holy Man? Even though China has long been considered a "pagan" nation, yet in her archives are descriptions of this **"Proper Man"** which rival the Bible in their anticipation of the coming Messiah.

Let us see what kind of a mosaic we can portray of the Holy Man as we put together a number of quotations. In some cases we will be describing the Dao, which we have identified as the Godhead, or Jesus. So the term "Dao" used here is interchangeable with the "Holy Man." In fact, in the

Dao De Jing there are about 30 references describing the Holy Man. Considering the fact that the whole book consists of only 5,000 words, the Holy Man is certainly an important theme. Perhaps these various references were cited according to His mission.

The Holy Man As Creator

> **Therefore the Holy Man goes about**
> **Doing no action and**
> **Teaches with no words,**
> **Creating, yet not possessing,**
> **Working, yet not taking credit.**
> **Work is done, but no boasting**
> **Therefore it lasts forever.**[8]

We have already seen that Jesus Christ is the Creator (Chapter 6): *"For by Him all things were <u>created</u> that are in heaven and that are on earth, visible and invisible, whether thrones or dominions or principalities or powers. All things were created through Him and for Him." (Colossians 1: 16).*

Yet Jesus was "**not taking credit**" to Himself and did His work with "**no boasting.**" As He said, *"<u>The Son can do nothing of Himself</u>, but what He sees the Father do; for whatever He does, the Son also does in like manner." (John 5: 19).* Jesus did not work on His own, but God the Father worked through Him. He was a Man of **"no action"** (无为).

The Holy Man's [Jesus Christ's] work **"lasts forever,"** for His salvation and kingdom are eternal. *"And having been perfected, He became the author of <u>eternal salvation</u> to all who obey Him." (Hebrew 5: 9).* His believers are promised an everlasting Kingdom. *"For so an entrance will be supplied to you abundantly into the <u>everlasting kingdom</u> of our Lord and Savior Jesus Christ." (2 Peter 1: 11).*

The Holy Man As the Life Provider

> The Holy Man provides nourishment for the wise and thus reaches the whole people. Truly great is the time of Providing Nourishment" (頤).[9]
>
> The Holy Man leads by emptying people's minds and filling their stomachs.[10]

These sayings from the Chinese Classics are hard to understand. Why was **"the Holy Man emptying people's minds and filling their stomachs?"** Why is **"the time of Providing Nourishment"** so important? The Holy Man knows that man's mind is full of self, and selfishness leads to death. Self has be to emptied so that the Spirit of life can come in. His "special food" will give them eternal life.

> *"I am the living bread which came down from heaven. If anyone eats of this bread, he will live forever; and the bread that I shall give is My flesh, which I shall give for the life of the world." (John 6: 51).*

> *"Whoever drinks of the water that I shall give him will never thirst. But the water that I shall give him will become in him a fountain of water springing up into everlasting life." (John 4: 14).*

The Holy Man As Teacher

> The Holy Man is the Teacher of hundreds of generations.[11]

Said a ruler of the Jews, Nicodemus, *"Rabbi, we know that <u>You are a teacher come from God</u>; for no one can do these signs that You do unless God is with him." (John 3: 2).*

> From the beginning until now, His name has not disappeared, so the Father of all things can be seen.

> From whom do I see the image of the Father of all
> things? It is from Him.[12]

Hiding in the garment of humanity, Jesus came to reveal the **"Father of all things"** to the world. Jesus told his disciples: *"He who has seen Me has seen the Father," (John 14: 9),* because *"He is the **image** of the invisible God." (Colossians 1: 15).*

How did the Holy Man teach?

> **The Holy Man teaches with the Dao [Word] of God,
> and the entire universe surrenders to Him.[13]**

The Holy Man's purpose was to direct all minds to **"the Dao [word] of God,"** that man might have this foundation of truth and doctrine. Jesus said, *"For I have not spoken on My own authority; but the Father who sent Me gave Me a command, what I should say and what I should speak." (John 12: 49).*

The Holy Man As Sin Pardoner

In Chapter 8 we discovered that a **"Son of the Prince pardons offenses and sins."** He was also called the Holy Man. Lao Zi referred to Dao extensively in his brief and profound book, *Dao De Jing*. The Dao was so highly esteemed by him and the other ancient sages that there was no rival.

> **Therefore to be established as the emperor,
> With three officers installed,
> And be presented with a gift of gems and
>   a team of horses,
> Is not as good as to sit in Dao.
> Why did the ancient Masters esteem
>   the Dao so much?[14]**

To become an emperor is certainly an honor in this world. Such a person is surrounded by high ranking officers and receives not only their respect,

but many valuable presents. But to be in the Dao is still better. Why?
> **Because, being one with the Dao,**
> **When you seek, you find;**
> **When you commit a sin, you can be forgiven.**
> **That is why everybody loves the Dao.**[14]

Man who has committed a sin longs to be free of guilt, and to walk without a burden. Only God can forgive sin and offenses, either to man or to Himself. No man has the authority to forgive the sin of others. But Jesus, the Son of God and the Son of Man, was given the full authority. By dying in man's stead, He made forgiveness possible. He said, *"But that you may know that the Son of Man has power on earth to forgive sins." (Mark 2: 10)*. However, sin is not forgiven unless confessed. *"If we confess our sins, He is faithful and just to forgive us our sins and to cleanse us from all unrighteousness." (1 John 1: 9)*.

The Holy Man As Mediator and Protector

> **Dao is the mystery of myriads of things,**
> **He is the treasure of the good and the**
> **Mediator [保, Protector] of the wicked.**[14]

From the Bible we understand that there are other intelligences in the universe. *"For we have been made a spectacle unto the world, and to angels and to men." (1 Corinthians 4: 9, KJV)*. The creation of man was an expansion of the heavenly family already in existence. Christ (*Dao*) was not only the Creator of man, but of all living intelligences in God's family. (Colossians 1: 16 - 17; Ephesians 1: 10). He is the *"mystery of God" (Colossians 2: 2)*, therefore Jesus **"is the mystery of myriads of things."**

In Chapter 7, we discovered that there was a war in heaven, when Satan with his angels rebelled against God and were cast out (Revelation 12: 7 - 9). But the unfallen angels are still faithful and loyal to God. They are **"of the** good," and holy. Christ is still their Head and Friend. **"He is the treasure of the good."**

God has not forsaken man, but man became **"wicked"** and his *"iniquities have separated"* him from God. *(Isaiah 59: 2)*. Therefore Christ came to be **"Mediator"** and to supplicate before God for our benefit.

> *For there is one God, and one mediator between God and men, the Man Christ Jesus.*
> *(1 Timothy 2: 5).*

> *And if anyone sins, we have an Advocate with the Father, Jesus Christ the righteous. And He Himself is the propitiation for our sins, and not for ours only but also for the whole world. (1 John 2: 1, 2).*

The Holy Man As Our Righteousness

> **[The Holy Man] knows the white,
> But keeps the black.** [15]

It may be universally true that black is often used to represent unrighteousness, and white righteousness. When Adam and Eve sinned against God, they lost their **"white"** robe of righteousness and innocence, and put on the **"black"** clothes of unrighteousness and guilt.

But the God of Heaven sent His Son to take on the blackness <u>of the sinner</u>, so that he might be clothed with the pure white righteousness of Christ.

> *For He made Him who knew no sin to be sin [black] for us, that we might become the righteousness [white] of God in Him. (2 Corinthians 5: 21).*

Perhaps one of the most beautiful of Chinese characters is that for *righteousness* 義.[16] It depicts a *lamb* 羊 over *me* 我, signifying that the blood of the Lamb covers my sin so that I then stand righteous and justified before God.

The Holy Man As Our Example

One commonly known Chinese proverb says: "Teaching by example is better than teaching by empty words." Advice, however wise, may be confusing, but an example is always clear. An example is like a shining star in the darkness. The Holy Man, in Chinese expectation, is not only a Teacher of words, but an example for all.

> **Therefore the Holy Man embraces the one**
> **And sets an example for all.**[17]

In His life on earth, Jesus set an example of being *"gentle and lowly in heart" (Matthew 11: 29)* for all to follow. He was the Creator and Master, yet when all the disciples were unwilling to wash one another's feet, Jesus performed the task as a servant. He said plainly:

> *So when He had washed their feet, taken His garments, and sat down again, He said to them,*
> *"Do you know what I have done to you?*
> *You call Me Teacher and Lord,*
> *and you say well, for so I am.*
> *If I then, your Lord and Teacher, have washed your feet, you also ought to wash one another's feet.*
> *<u>For I have given you an example</u>, that you should do as I have done to you."   (John 13: 12 - 15).*

Continuing the above quotation from *Dao De Jing* regarding the Holy Man, Lao Zi said:

> **Not putting on a display, He shines forth.**
> **Not justifying Himself, He is distinguished.**
> **Not boasting, He receives recognition.**
> **Not bragging, He never falters.**
> **He never contends, so no one can ever**
>   **defeat Him.**[17]

Again and again, Jesus was confronted by the Jewish leaders with difficult questions presented to trap Him, and thereby bring about His execution. However, when confronted, many times, His gentle, clever answers defeated them. True is Lao Zi's statement concerning the Holy Man: **"He never contends, so no one can ever defeat Him."** A perfect example of how Jesus outwitted His rivals in a calm, authoritative, wise manner is found in *Mark 11: 27 - 33:*

> *Then they came again to Jerusalem. And as He was walking in the temple, the chief priests, the scribes, and the elders came to Him. And they said to Him, "By what authority are You doing these things [driving money-changers from the temple]? And who gave You this authority to do these things?"*
> *But Jesus answered and said to them, "I will also ask you one question; then answer Me, and I will tell you by what authority I do these things: The baptism of John—was it from heaven or from men? Answer Me."*
> *And they reasoned among themselves, saying, "If we say, 'From heaven,' He will say, 'Why then did you not believe him?' But if we say, 'From men'— they feared the people, for all counted John to have been a prophet indeed. So they answered and said to Jesus, "We do not know."*
> *And Jesus answered and said to them, "Neither will I tell you by what authority I do these things."*

Has it not become obvious how closely Jesus, the humble, unpretentious, wise One fulfilled all the ancient Chinese sages' prophecies of the coming Holy Man? Is He also the One whom the Chinese expected to come and save the world?

The Holy Man As Our Savior

> **Therefore the Holy Man**
> **Is good at saving all men**
> **So that no one is forsaken.**
> **He takes care of all things**
> **And abandons nothing.**[18]

God cares for everyone. *"Are not two sparrows sold for a copper coin? And not one of them falls to the ground apart from your Father's will. But the very hairs of your head are all numbered. Do not fear therefore; you are of more value than many sparrows." (Matthew 10: 29 - 31).* The Lord God *"is longsuffering toward us, <u>not willing that any should perish</u> but that all should come to repentance" (2 Peter 3: 9)* and be saved.

The Bible tells of the amazing love of our heavenly Father. *"For scarcely for a righteous man will one die; yet perhaps for a good man someone would even dare to die. But God demonstrates His own love toward us, in that while we were still sinners, Christ died for us." (Romans 5: 7, 8).*

> **The one who closes the door well**
> **Closes it without a lock.**
> **Yet no one can open it.**
> **The one who makes good knots**
> **Needs no rope,**
> **Yet no one can loosen it.**[18]

In one of Jesus' final messages, He announced to His listeners regarding Himself: *"He who has the key of David, He who opens and no one shuts, and shuts and no one opens, I know your works. See, <u>I have set before you an open door, and no one can shut it.</u>" (Revelation 3: 7, 8).*

The door of salvation is open to all; the invitation is for everyone! Said Jesus, *"<u>Behold, I stand at the door and knock.</u> If anyone hears My voice and opens the door, I will come in to him and dine with him, and he with Me." Revelation 3: 20*

The key is to open the door of our hearts to Jesus, then He will open the door of heaven for us. He **"makes good knots**, but **needs no rope"** to bind our human hearts to Him, for the knots are made of love. Thus said the Lord:

> *"I drew them with gentle cords,*
> *With <u>bands of love</u>,*
> *And I was to them as those who*
> *<u>take the yoke from their neck</u>.*
> *I stooped and fed them." (Hosea 11: 4).*

Yes, the loving, gentle Jesus Christ was the long-awaited Holy Man!

11

Suffering of the Holy Man

> Therefore said the Holy Man:
> "He who is disgraced for the kingdom is the Lord
>   of the kingdom;
> He who suffers for the Kingdom is the King
>   of the universe."[1]

Human suffering began with the dawn of human history when Adam and Eve were banished from the Garden of Eden. Sin lies at the root of all human suffering; such distress is no respecter of persons and comes to everyone. Facing adversity, people either pray to God, trusting and hoping—or curse God without hope. How many, when undergoing an ordeal, consider that the God of heaven has suffered more keenly and for a longer time? True are the words of St. Augustine, "God had one Son on earth without sin, but never one without suffering."[2] God endured anguish for man even before man was created!

Is it possible that the ancient Chinese sages prophesied in their writings of One equal with God suffering, not because of His own sin and offenses, but for all under heaven? Lao Zi (c. 570 B.C.) recorded what he understood of the Holy Man:

> **He who is humiliated for the kingdom**
> **is the Lord of the kingdom;**
> **He who suffers for the Kingdom**
> **is the King of the universe.**
> **The truth often sounds paradoxical.**[3]

How could this Man's suffering and humiliation make him the **"Lord of the Kingdom"** and **"the King of the universe?"** It is necessary for us to discover the meaning of human life in order to understand why the Holy Man had to suffer. Confucius' opening words in *The Great Learning* state his concept of the whole purpose of man's existence.

> **What the Great Learning teaches is to**
> **illustrate illustrious virtue;**
> **to renovate the people; and to rest**
> **in the highest excellence.**[4]

What does Confucius mean by the term, **"illustrious virtue"**? Concerning one's virtue, Confucius himself answers this important question:

> **Heaven [God] produced the virtue**
> **that is in me.**[5]

Confucius was pointing out here that all virtues possessed by man come from God. It is up to man to allow this gift of virtue to shine out of the life—to "glorify" the God of heaven; to reflect God's character. It was the realization of an ancient Chinese sage that:

> **Heaven and earth are the parents**
> **of all creatures;**
> **Of all creatures man is the**
> **most highly endowed.**[6]

This teaching is repeatedly emphasized by all the sages. In *The Book of Filial Piety,* Confucius taught, **"Man is the most precious among all the creatures between heaven and earth."**[7] The idea of evolving life forms never crossed his mind. How far China has come from the thinking of her ancestors! Man was created in God's likeness, for God had said, *"Let us make man in Our image, according to Our likeness,"* *(Genesis 1: 26),* with a character reflecting that of a loving God.

After man sinned, God's likeness in Adam was replaced with that of the tempter Satan, the fallen angel. Man was no longer able to obey God as before. The sins which followed disobedience took many forms: hatred, suspicion, disloyalty, sorrow, pain, and every kind of suffering. *"For all have sinned and fall short of the glory of God." (Romans 3: 23).* The resultant *"wages of sin"* was death. *(Romans 6: 23).*

But *"God is love" (1 John 4: 16)*, and the fundamental element of love is freedom. So God gave to man the freedom of choice. He could say "yes" or "no" to his Maker, according to his own free will. Concerning man's free-will gift from God, Confucius said,

> **The commander of the forces of a large State may be carried off, but the will (志) of even a common man cannot be taken from him.**[8]

When God created man, He took a risk, for if only one person chose to say "no" to the loving Creator, the perfect harmony in all His heavenly family would be lost. There would be an immediate problem with just one disobedient choice. In that eventuality, God must find a solution so that His other created beings would still willingly and happily choose not to follow the disobedient course. In God's dealing with disobedience, He must demonstrate that He is love. He must convince all that the best choice is willing obedience. Only thus would the safety and peace of the entire universe be restored and forever assured.

God had just such a wonderful plan, though it entailed an infinite cost. Lao Zi described the work of Dao thus: **"Restoration is the motion of the Dao."**[9] When man sinned, he lost his likeness to God, and became filled with evil passions. Sinful man changed his concept of a loving God to a selfish Being with purposes much like his own. <u>To restore the image of God in humans</u>, God sent His only Son to the world to suffer and die for mankind everywhere. To glorify God—<u>to demonstrate what God's true character is</u>—was the purpose of Christ's mission.

> *Jesus lifted up His eyes to heaven, and said: "Father, the hour has come. <u>Glorify Your Son, that Your Son also may glorify You</u>, as You have given Him authority over all flesh, that He should give eternal life to as many as You have given Him. And this is eternal life, that they may know You, the only true God, and Jesus Christ whom You have sent. <u>I have glorified You on the earth</u>. I have finished <u>the work which You have given Me to do</u>." (John 17: 1 - 4).*

To glorify God—to demonstrate what God's real character is—this was Christ's mission on earth, and the purpose of His life was to reflect God's character in human flesh. By His suffering, Christ paid the price for restoring God's perfect character in fallen man. There could be no restoration of man without Jesus' suffering.

Jesus is called the *"Lamb slain from the foundation of the world." (Revelation 13: 8).* Jesus was committed to a life of suffering and final death even before man was created. Thus the anguish of God the Father and Son, in their plan for man's eventual salvation and restoration, became *"things which angels desire to look into." (1 Peter 1: 12).* Suffering and poverty accompanied Jesus from the time of his earthly birth when the angels sang, *"Glory to God in the highest, and on earth peace, good will toward men!" (Luke 2: 14).*

Jesus, the long-awaited Holy Man did not come as an angel or as a prince in a palace, but was born to a poor peasant mother in a stable. His first cradle was a feeding trough for cows. But wise men from the East, who were acquainted with the prophecies of a Holy Man to come, were attracted by a moving star that led them to Jerusalem. *"Where is He who has been born King of the Jews?"* they inquired. *"For we have seen His star in the East and have come to worship Him." (Matthew 2: 2).*

The jealous King Herod in Jerusalem commanded the priests to search the Scriptures. They found the prophecy which said, *"For out of you [Bethlehem] shall come a Ruler Who will shepherd My people Israel." (Matthew 2: 6).* Thus the wise men continued their quest and journeyed on to Bethlehem, where they paid homage to the newborn Child. Shortly after the visit of the wise men, Herod sent soldiers to kill all the male children under two years of age in the district of Bethlehem, hoping to eliminate the One he considered his rival. But God had already sent an angel to the parents of Jesus, warning them to flee immediately to Egypt and remain there until they were directed to return.

The exact time of Jesus' birth is not known from the Bible in order that the day not receive the honor that should be given to Christ as Redeemer. Unfortunately, a pagan day [Christmas] has been instituted and become commercialized. By promoting what is not in the Bible, the world has chosen to forget what is required of them by God, and the real meaning of Christ's coming to earth.

Such humiliation it was for Jesus Christ, man's Creator, to step down from His heavenly throne and be born *"in the likeness of sinful flesh," (Romans 8: 3)*—not even like Adam before his fall! In summary, we find Christ's earthly mission:

> *And without controversy great is*
> *the mystery of godliness:*
> *God was manifested in the flesh,*
> *Justified in the Spirit,*
> *Seen by angels,*

> *Preached among the Gentiles,*
> *Believed on in the world,*
> *Received up in glory.*
> *(1 Timothy 3: 16).*

The Bible is nearly silent regarding His first 30 years. How interesting is Confucius' statement: **"If truly a King were to arise, it would still require thirty years for His love to be manifested."**[10] As a youth, Jesus worked in His father's carpenter shop and was a devoted and obedient Son of His earthly parents.

> **The Master said, "While a man's father is alive,**
> **look at the bent of his will;**
> **When his father is dead, look at his conduct.**
> **If for three years he does not alter from the way of**
> **his father, he may be called filial(孝)."**[11]

The Bible does not tell when Jesus' earthly father died, but we know that two months after His baptism, Jesus performed His first miracle when His mother, without His father, was with Him. This began His public ministry. The fifth commandment of God's holy law requires one to *"honor your father and your mother, that your days may be long upon the land which the Lord your God is giving you." (Exodus 20: 12)*. Among the ancient peoples of the world, China is the only one stressing filial piety to the point of having a book, *Xiao Jing [The Book of Filial Piety]*, with contents devoted to these teachings. Is it any wonder that China's days have been long upon the land which the Lord has given her? God is faithful in keeping His promises. Although China did not enjoy the privilege of full revelation from God like the Jewish people, yet she was not wholly ignorant of saving truths.[12]

Even when Jesus was dying on the cross, He had caring thoughts for His mother who stood by, grief-stricken. *"He said to His mother, 'Woman, behold your son!' Then He said to the disciple [John], 'Behold your mother!' And from that hour that disciple took her to his own home."* (John 19: 26, 27). Jesus was a perfect example of filial love.

When the time came for Jesus to enter His public ministry, He had first to go through a heaven-appointed trial. Note this impressive prophecy of Mencius:

> **Thus, when Heaven is about to confer a great office on this Man, He first exercises his mind with suffering, and sinews and bones with toil. He exposes his body to hunger, and subjects him to extreme poverty. Heaven confounds his undertakings. By all these methods, Heaven stimulates his mind, strengthens his nature, and supplies his weakness.**[13]

In order to restore man to his original sinless character, Jesus had to meet each temptation where man had fallen, and successfully overcome. After His baptism, *"Jesus was led up by the Spirit into the wilderness to be tempted by the devil. And when He had fasted forty days and forty nights, afterward He was hungry."* (Matthew 4: 1, 2). The devil thought to take advantage of Him in His weakened state, for he remembered how easily the first couple fell to the temptation of appetite. Said Satan to Jesus, weak from hunger, *"If you are the Son of God, command that these stones become bread."* But Jesus answered, *"It is written, 'Man shall not live by bread alone, but by every word that proceeds from the mouth of God.'"* (Matthew 4: 3, 4). Jesus, as a human, was relying only on the word of God, where power is hidden.

"Then the devil took Him up into the holy city, set Him on the pinnacle of the temple, and said to Him, 'If you are the Son of God, throw Yourself down. For it is written: "He shall give His angels charge over you. In their hands they shall bear you up, Lest you dash your foot against a stone."' Jesus said to him, 'It is written again, "You shall not

tempt the LORD *your God.'" (Matthew 4: 5 - 7)*. A second time, Christ was tempted to answer the devil's "if You are the Son of God," but He did not accept any suggestion of this doubt. Jesus would not presume upon God's goodness, forcing God to protect Him, outside the path of obedience.

Although Satan can tempt, he can never force one to do evil. He cannot control one's mind unless one yields to his control. To glorify God, or self; to be obedient, or disobedient; to have faith, or presumption; the choice is one's own to make. Presumption leads one to transgress God's expressed command, assuming that His great love will still deliver from the consequence of willful sin. One must comply with the conditions on which mercy is to be granted—obedience.

"Again, the devil took Him up on an exceedingly high mountain, and showed Him all the kingdoms of the world and their glory. And he said to Him, 'All these things I will give You if You will fall down and worship me.' Then Jesus said to him, 'Away with you, Satan! For it is written, "You shall worship the LORD *your God, and Him only you shall serve."'* *(Matthew 4: 8 - 10)*. Satan, who had revolted in heaven, offered Christ the kingdoms of this world, to buy His homage. But Jesus would not be bought.

Mencius said, **"How is it possible that a son of the Prince should be bought with a bribe?"**[14] Jesus had come to establish a kingdom of righteousness, and He would not forsake this purpose. Again Mencius wrote,

> **To be above the power of riches and honors to make one dissipated; of poverty and mean condition to make one swerve from principle; and of power and force to make one bend: these characteristics constitute the Great Man (大丈夫).**[15]

Jesus surely was the Great Man who met these standards of which Mencius wrote. But to accomplish His goal, He must pass through a life of hardship, sorrow, conflict and an ignominious death. He must bear the sins of the whole world and endure separation from His heavenly Father. God intends that man be the conqueror of Satan and sin through His Son Jesus Christ. Only the suffering and victory won by Jesus makes this possible.

During His three-and-a-half years of public ministry, Jesus met with constant rejection by the religious leaders in Jerusalem. He healed all the sick who came to Him and raised three persons from death to life again. On one occasion when He raised a paralyzed man to walk again, Jesus said to him, *"Man, your sins are forgiven you."* When the religious leaders heard this, they said, *"Who is this who speaks blasphemies? Who can forgive sins but God alone?"* Jesus, reading their thoughts, asked, *"Which is easier, to say, 'Your sins are forgiven you,' or to say, 'Rise up and walk'?"* So He healed the man. *"And they were all amazed. . .saying, "We have seen strange things today!" (Luke 5: 20, 21, 23, 26)*.

From the time of Adam, God promised a Savior to defeat the devil. To the Serpent in Eden He had said, *"I will put enmity between you and the woman, and between your seed and her Seed; He shall bruise your head, and you shall bruise His heel." (Genesis 3: 15)*. The "Seed of the woman" [Jesus] was to bruise the head of the serpent [destroy Satan], but in so doing the Seed's heel would be bruised [He would suffer death]. At the gate of Eden, the first sacrifice of a lamb was made that looked forward to the sacrificial death of the Savior millennia later.

The prophet Isaiah foretold in great detail the suffering which would come to the holy Servant of God.

> *He is despised and rejected by men,*
> *<u>A man of sorrows and acquainted with grief</u>. . . .*
> *Surely He has borne our griefs*
> *And carried our sorrows;*
> *Yet we esteemed Him stricken,*
> *Smitten by God, and afflicted.*
> *But He was wounded for our transgressions,*

> *<u>He was bruised for our iniquities;</u>*
> *The chastisement for our peace was upon Him,*
> *And by His stripes we are healed. . . .*
> *And the* LORD *has laid on Him the iniquity of us all.*
> *He was oppressed and He was afflicted,*
> *Yet He opened not His mouth;*
> *He was led as a lamb to the slaughter,*
> *And as a sheep before its shearers is silent,*
> *So He opened not His mouth.*
> *He was taken from prison and from judgment,*
> *And who will declare His generation?*
> *For He was cut off from the land of the living;*
> *For the transgressions of My people He was stricken.*
> *And they made His grave with the wicked—*
> *But with the rich at His death,*
> *Because He had done no violence,*
> *Nor was any deceit in His mouth . . .*
> *And He was numbered with the transgressors,*
> *And He bore the sin of many,*
> *<u>And made intercession for the transgressors.</u>*
>   (Isaiah 53: 3 - 9, 12).

Through centuries and millennia the blood of innocent sheep and bullocks flowed—all as a promise for the ultimate sacrifice of the Son of God. Jesus' ministry was nearly over. Looking forward to His coming suffering and death, Jesus told His disciples, *"Most assuredly, I say to you, unless a grain of wheat falls into the ground and dies, it remains alone; but if it dies, it produces much grain." (John 12: 24)*. The Passover ceremony, first celebrated when the Israelites fled from the slavery of Egypt, was drawing nigh. Jesus knew His mission. He knew He had to die in order for men to be saved. Yet His humanity trembled at the coming separation from His Father. *"Now My soul is troubled, and what shall I say? 'Father, save Me from this hour'? But for this purpose I came to this hour. Father, glorify Your name." (John 12: 27)*.

Suffering of the Holy Man

After eating the Passover supper with His disciples and instituting a new service with the symbolic bread and wine, He with three of His disciples went to the Garden of Gethsemane, where He fell on His face and prayed, saying, *"O My Father, if it is possible, let this cup pass from Me; nevertheless, not as I will, but as You will." (Matthew 26: 39).* Then He came to His disciples, hoping to find some comfort and encouragement, but He found them sleeping. In great disappointment, He went away, making the same request to the Father the second and third time.

"And being in agony, He prayed more earnestly. Then <u>His sweat became like great drops of blood</u> falling down to the ground." (Luke 22: 44). The burden of sin was so heavy, the destruction of it was so painful that His human nature could hardly bear it. *"My soul is exceedingly sorrowful, even to death." (Matthew 26: 38).* His terrible death began in the Garden of Gethsemane. He saw that all the transgressors of God's holy law would have to perish if left to themselves. The death penalty had to be executed and the justice of God's law had to be satisfied. Through the death of the sinless suffering Holy Man of God, millions could gain everlasting life. He could not turn from His mission. The decision was made, *"If this cup cannot pass away from Me unless I drink it, Your will be done." (Matthew 26: 42).* He tasted *"death for everyone." (Hebrews 2: 9).*

Then came a mob to the garden, searching for Him, led by one of His own disciples, Judas the betrayer. Jesus could have escaped from them, but He knew the purpose of this hour. He voluntarily offered His life for sinful man.

> **The Holy Man puts all others before Him.**
> **He laid down His life, and His life exists.**
> **Through selfless action, He attains fulfillment.[16]**

Jesus was arrested and brought to court for a mock trial. Many hundreds of years of both Hebrew and Chinese prophecies concerning Him were fulfilled in one day. He was betrayed, beaten, spit upon, despised and mocked. Yet He remained silent, without complaint. Seven hundred years before, Isaiah had prophesied, *"I was not rebellious, Nor did I turn away. I gave my back to those who struck Me, And My cheeks to those who plucked out the beard; I did not hide My face from shame and spitting." (Isaiah 50: 5, 6).*

Lao Zi also foretold the same disgraceful abuse of the Holy Man:

He knows his glory, yet remains in disgrace.[17]

The sinless, righteous Servant of the Lord was despised, beaten, and nailed to a wooden cross. Our peace and healing come by His suffering. Our righteousness comes by His sinless offering. While the Roman soldiers were pounding the nails through His palms, He prayed for them, saying, *"Father, forgive them, for they do not know what they do." (Luke 23: 34).* The prayer of Christ for the soldiers embraced the world, for it included every sinner that ever lived or should live. Upon all rests the guilt of crucifying the Son of God. He offered Himself, bleeding and lacerated upon the cross as a sacrifice of love for each of us.

Jesus suffered silently. At about the ninth hour, He cried out, *"My God, My God, why have You forsaken Me?" (Matthew 27: 46).* His Father's face was hidden from Him. Jesus was left alone as a Substitute for the sinner, totally separated from the Father, under the wrath of God. His heart was broken. He died alone.

Some may think that Jesus died with hope, knowing that His Father would raise Him up after three days. But this thinking undermines the infinite sacrifice of the Savior. In after years many of His followers died martyr's deaths with the future hope of their Master's acceptance in heaven. But Jesus died as the sinner under the condemnation of God, without hope of a resurrection. His final cry, *"My God, why have You forsaken Me?"* emphasizes that He did not have this hope of a future glory.

How did the death of God's Son differ from that of martyrs who have been tortured and killed for God's truth? Bodily pain was only a small part of the agony Christ suffered. <u>He alone experienced the penalty of sin</u>. When the Father turned away from Him, He felt the separation that sinners will feel when perishing.

But all heaven suffered with Christ, and this did not begin with His humanity. From the first sin, disobedience of His creatures has been painful to God. Every wrong deed, every failure of man brings grief to Him. *"In all their affliction He was afflicted. . . .In His love and in His pity He redeemed them; And He bore them and carried them all the days of old."* *(Isaiah 63: 9).* The death of Jesus testified that God's perfect law is immutable and requires complete obedience. *"In this the love of God was manifested toward us, that God has sent His only begotten Son into the world, that we might live through Him." (1 John 4: 9).*

Jesus became sin in order to end sin, and died to destroy death forever. *"The sting of death is sin, and the strength of sin is the law. But thanks be to God, who gives us the victory through our Lord Jesus Christ." (1 Corinthians 15: 56).* We find the same thought in the *Shu Jing*: **"The end of punishment is to make an end of punishing."**[18]

Love and hate, good and evil, sin and righteousness, selfishness and sacrifice, justice and mercy—all met on the cross of Jesus. What amazing love God manifested toward man! How can we continue to bring sorrow and suffering to the Father, Son and Holy Spirit who together are longing to save us? Our consciences must surely be awakened to their wonderful free gift of salvation!

12

Poetry of the Creator

As might be expected, a Nobel Prize winner in physics stood amazed at the basic laws of nature. Dr. Zhengning Young (杨振宁), the first Chinese Nobel winner in this category, marveled at the beautiful simplicity and wonderful inclusiveness of primary laws discovered in nature. He quoted the following verses for comparison:

> To see a World in a Grain of Sand,
> And a Heaven in a Wild Flower;
> To hold Infinity in the palm of your hand,
> And Eternity in an hour.
> —*William Blake (1757-1827)*

> Nature and nature's law lay hid in night:
> God said, let Newton be! And all was light.
> —*A. Pope (1688-1744)*

Dr. Young wrote in the *21st Century,* a journal of the Chinese University of Hong Kong, "These two quotes are not enough to tell the complete feelings of a physicist on examining the beauty of basic laws. Something is missing—a feeling of solemnity, holiness and fear at the first encounter with the mystery of the universe. The beauty of the sublime, the beauty of the soul, the beauty of religion and the beauty of the ultimate for which the architect of a Gothic church offers his praise, is missing. This basic law of nature I call the 'Poetry of the Creator.'"

The predictable movements of the sun, moon and stars; the unchanging succession of the four seasons; and the vastness of the universe tell us that the Creator is a God of absolute order. These are all a reflection of wondrous laws which have mystified scientists for centuries. In fact, all major scientific "discoveries" are but the unlocking of God's hidden laws in the universe!

The Creator-God not only wrote His "poems" in the physical universe, but personally wrote with His own finger, on stone, the moral "poetry of the Creator" to govern and guide human life. This law is commonly called "The Ten Commandments."

It was the year 1445 B.C., and after ten terrible plagues had fallen on Egypt, the Pharaoh fearfully commanded the Israelite slaves, under the leadership of God through Moses, to leave his country. Over a million people with their belongings and livestock streamed out into the unfriendly wilderness of the Red Sea region. As they fled, God opened the waters of the Red Sea for the vast throng to walk over the seabed on dry land. But He closed the waters over the pursuing chariots of the Egyptians. (Exodus 14).

Generations of Israelites had lived and died in Egypt. Surrounded by the idol-worshiping Egyptians, they had nearly forgotten their original Creator-God and their former homeland in Canaan. The third month after leaving Egypt, the multitude of ex-slaves approached the magnificent Mount Sinai. Their God-appointed leader, Moses, went up into the mountain to commune with God, who promised,

> *"If you will indeed obey My voice and keep My covenant, then you shall be a special treasure to Me above all people; for all the earth is Mine."...Then all the people*

answered together and said, "All that the LORD has spoken we will do." (Exodus 19: 5, 8).

By this bold promise to God, the Israelites failed to understand their inability to keep the law in their own strength. The "old covenant" was thus made at Sinai. God further commanded that the people wash their clothes to prepare for the LORD's descent on the mountain top. A boundary was set around the base of the Holy mountain so that no one would cross over and die. On the third day, in the morning,

> *There were thunderings and lightnings, and a thick cloud on the mountain; and the sound of the trumpet was very loud, so that all the people…trembled.…Now Mount Sinai was completely in smoke, because the LORD descended upon it in fire…and the whole mountain quaked greatly. (Exodus 19: 16, 18).*

Then God proclaimed His sacred precepts—the ten-line "Poetry of the Creator:"

- *I am the LORD your God, who brought you out of the land of Egypt, out of the house of bondage. You shall have no other gods before Me.*
- *You shall not make for yourself any carved image, or any likeness of anything that is in heaven above, or that is in the earth beneath, or that is in the water under the earth; you shall not bow down to them nor serve them. For I, the LORD your God, am a jealous God, visiting the iniquity of the fathers on the children to the third and fourth generations of those who hate Me, but showing mercy to thousands, to those who love Me and keep My commandments.*
- *You shall not take the name of the LORD your God in vain, for the LORD will not hold him guiltless who takes His name in vain.*
- *Remember the Sabbath day, to keep it holy. Six days you shall labor and do all your work, but the seventh*

> day is the Sabbath of the LORD your God. In it you shall do no work: you, nor your son, nor your daughter, nor your male servant, nor your female servant, nor your cattle, nor your stranger who is within your gates. For in six days the LORD made the heavens and the earth, the sea, and all that is in them, and rested the seventh day. Therefore the LORD blessed the Sabbath day and hallowed it.
> - Honor your father and your mother, that your days may be long upon the land which the LORD your God is giving you.
> - You shall not murder.
> - You shall not commit adultery.
> - You shall not steal.
> - You shall not bear false witness against your neighbor.
> - You shall not covet your neighbor's house; you shall not covet your neighbor's wife, nor his male servant, nor this female servant; nor his ox, nor his donkey, nor anything that is your neighbor's. *(Exodus 20: 2 - 17).*

The Ten Commandments, like all the rest of God's words, are a reflection of His character. *"The law is holy, and the commandment holy and just and good." (Romans 7: 12).* Differing from the laws of nature, this *"law is spiritual," (Romans 7: 14).* It is so brief that even a child can quickly memorize it, yet it is profound, covering the duty of man to God and man to fellow man. God's law is so sacred that,

> He gave Moses two tablets of the testimony, tablets of stone, <u>written with the finger of God</u>. *(Exodus 31: 18).*

The importance of this law is shown in the fact that these <u>are the only words in the whole Bible written by God's own hand</u>. By this act, God emphasized what His will truly is, and there should be no excuse or misunderstanding.

Although we find no complete Ten Commandments in any of the Chinese Classics, the ancient sage kings knew that there was a law given by Heaven, and understood its principles. We may learn that the early Chinese kings believed their government also should be regulated by law, one given by God, Himself.

If we who are charged with government do not treat parties who proceed to such wickedness as offenders, the law given by Heaven to our people will be thrown into great disorder or destroyed.[1]

Such was the guiding principle of administration. **"The law given by Heaven"** was the assurance of peace and order in the kingdom. Let us now see which of the ten precepts of God's holy law have been practiced among the ancient Chinese:

- The first commandment forbids worship of other gods, It is widely understood that the early Chinese worshiped only one supreme God. Even today in the Temple of Heaven in Beijing, the name of the "Heavenly Sovereign Shangdi" is written in the Imperial Vault and in the Hall of Prayer for Good Harvests.

- The ancient Chinese were not idol worshipers. The first recorded history of making an image was that of King Wu Ting (武丁), who was "without Dao." He made an idol, calling it "the Spirit of Heaven," and then shot at it. Wu Ting reigned 4 years and died in 1191 B.C.[2]

- The third commandment forbids taking God's name in vain. Even in the time of Confucius, the name of Shangdi was sacred. His name was connected with the sacrifice which was not to be spoken of carelessly.

- The fourth commandment is in reference to keeping the seventh-day Sabbath as a memorial of creation. Did the ancient Chinese keep this day? Perhaps.

- The fifth commandment deals with filial piety. Only the Chinese have a *Book of Filial Piety* to teach this principle.

The rest of the five commandments, from the sixth to the tenth, can be found even in today's Chinese law, let alone in the teachings of the sages. But in the course of time, the law given by Heaven was lost. Gone with it was the most precious truth and true knowledge of God. Idol and spirit worship came in as early as the Shang dynasty. With regret and deep sorrow, Confucius declared, **"The Great Dao is lost."**[3]

Though the detailed precepts of the law were lost, its essence and principles were handed down. The standard of righteousness was still the center of all the teachings of the ancient sages.

> *For when Gentiles, who do not have the law, by nature do the things contained in the law, these, although not having the law, are a law to themselves, who <u>show the work of the law written in their hearts</u>, their conscience also bearing witness, and between themselves their thoughts accusing or else excusing them.*
> *(Romans 2: 14, 15).*

Mo Zi, (Chapter 3, p. 28), whose teachings are the foundation of the Mohist school of thought, had extensive teaching on righteousness and the will of Heaven.

> **The will of Heaven is truly the standard of righteousness.** [4]
>
> **To obey the will of Heaven is to accept righteousness as the law.**
> **To oppose the will of Heaven is to accept force as the law.**[5]

What, then, is the **"will of Heaven?"** What does Heaven desire? Mo Zi explains:

> **Now what does Heaven desire and what does He abominate? Heaven desires righteousness and abominates unrighteousness.**[6]

By Mo Zi's statement we may understand his great interest in the law of Heaven. **"The desire and will of Heaven is righteousness."** He continues to reason:

> And Heaven likes to have the world live and dislikes to have it die; likes to have it rich and dislikes to have it poor; and likes to have it orderly and dislikes to have it disorderly. Therefore we know Heaven desires righteousness and abominates unrighteousness.[6]

Truly, God has no pleasure in the death of people. Rather, He sent His Son to die in their place and give them life. *"'For I have no pleasure in the death of one who dies,' says the LORD God. 'Therefore turn and live!'"* (Ezekiel 18: 32). *"I have come that they may have life, and that they may have it more abundantly." (John 10: 10).*

Although a book of Mo Zi's writings has survived, little is known of the author. The messenger, however, is not important, but rather his message:

> When I do what Heaven desires, Heaven will also do what I desire. I desire blessings and advantages, and abominate calamities and misfortunes. When I do not do what Heaven desires, neither will Heaven do what I desire.[7]

When we do things pleasing to God, we have the assurance that our prayers will be answered. The Bible in both the Old and New Testaments says, *"One who turns away his ear from hearing the law, even his prayer is an abomination." (Proverbs 28: 9).* Also, *"And whatever we ask we receive from Him, because we keep His commandments and do those things that are pleasing in His sight." (1 John 3: 22).*

The nature of the lawgiver determines the nature of the law. Concerning the lawgiver, Mo Zi said,

> Heaven is honorable, Heaven is wise,
> So, then, righteousness must originate with Heaven.[8]

The Bible confirms that *"There is one Lawgiver, who is able to save and destroy." (James 4: 12).* The prophet Isaiah said, *"For the LORD is our*

Judge, the LORD *is our Lawgiver, the* LORD *is our King; He will save us." (Isaiah 33: 22).* By this we learn that the Savior is also the Lawgiver. This Person is Jesus Christ. It was He who spoke the words of the law from Mount Sinai and wrote the law with His own finger on tables of stone.

Not only Mo Zi spoke of the importance of the law in governing a nation, but so also did Confucius.

> **Confucius said: "To govern a nation without the law is like a blind person walking without a guide. Where should he go? It is also like seeking in a dark room. How can one see without a candle?"**[9]

Similarly the Bible says,

> *For the commandment is a lamp,*
> *And the law a light;*
> *Reproofs of instruction are the way of life.*
>   *(Proverbs 6: 23).*

Without the law, man is likely to be deceived and cheated. Confucius made a vivid comparison. He said:

> **The law is to govern a nation like the scale for the weighing of matter, or a carpenter's marking thread for making a straight line, and the compass and square to make right squares and circles... Therefore, a son of the Prince who knows the law, cannot be cheated.**[10]

The Bible says that people die for lack of knowledge of the law. God's law is a safeguard to prevent being deceived by human philosophers.

> *Beware lest anyone cheat you through philosophy and empty deceit, according to the tradition of men, according to the basic principles of the world, and not according to Christ. For in Him dwells all the fullness of the Godhead bodily; and you are complete in Him, who is the head of all principality and power. (Colossians 2: 8 - 10).*

Confucius also had another reference to "a son of the Prince:"

> **The Master said: "A son of the Prince thinks of virtue; a mean man thinks of comfort. A son of the Prince thinks of the sanctions of law; a mean man thinks of favors which he may receive."**[11]

We have observed from the above that the ancient Chinese sages and kings understood that Heaven was an honorable and wise Lawgiver, that His law was essential to guide the people in the way of truth and insure that the kingdom was in order. The law given by Heaven clearly delineates right from wrong. As Mo Zi pointed out,

> **Taking the will of Heaven as the law of standard, one tells things as clearly as black and white.**[12]

As a standard, the law helps man know what is righteousness and what is unrighteousness. In the Bible, all unrighteousness is called sin. *"Sin is the transgression of the law." (1 John 3: 4, KJV)*. Like a mirror, the law shows whether one has sinned or not. Without the law, none knows what sin is. *"By the law is the knowledge of sin." (Romans 3: 20)*. Adam and Eve, at their creation, had a knowledge of the law of God. It was printed on their hearts and they understood its requirements. Otherwise they could not have known that they had sinned.

Although the ancient Chinese teachers did not have a full knowledge of the "poetic" precepts of the Creator, they realized that the high standard of the law could not be lowered. Listen to a conversation between Mencius and his student:

> **Gong Sun Chu (公孙丑) said, "Lofty are your principles and admirable, but to learn them may well be likened to ascending the heavens, something which cannot be reached. Why not adapt your teaching so as to cause learners to consider them attainable, so daily exert themselves."**
> **Mencius said, "A great artificer does not, for**

> the sake of a stupid workman, alter or do away with the marking line.
>
> "Yi [the famous archer of ancient China] did not, for the sake of a stupid archer, change his rule for drawing the bow."[13]

Because the law of the Lord is perfect, and therefore changeless, it is impossible for sinful men, of themselves, to meet the standard of its requirement. Therefore, God sent Jesus to *"save His people from their sins." (Matthew 1: 21)*. This was why Jesus came as our Redeemer. By faith in Christ we may reach the standard set by law. The Apostle Paul asks, *"Do we then make void the law through faith? Certainly not! On the contrary, we establish the law." (Romans 3: 31)*.

On the same subject of the "old law," Confucius said,

> **The law is to clear up the causes for disorder, just as the bank is built for resisting a flood. To think that the old bank is of no use and destroy it will surely bring a flood. To think of the old law as of no use and abandon it will bring calamity and disorder upon oneself.**[14]

Even though the Ten Commandments were given at Sinai thousands of years ago, it is still God's will and standard for humans. Neglect or ignorance of it accounts for the crimes and problems in our modern society. How interesting that we find words in the *Li Ji* voicing the same idea.

> **Where the law is emphasized,**
> **social order will be well kept;**
> **Where the law is abandoned,**
> **social disorder will abound.**[15]

Furthermore we read from the same source:

> **Therefore only the Holy Man knows the law is not to be destroyed. If a nation is in disorder, a family**

broken, and people being killed, these are the result of destroying the law first.[16]

Like the natural law in the universe, the moral and spiritual law cannot be destroyed without drastic results. In the world today, where the law is well honored, society is usually also well ordered. Where the law is poorly kept, crime and corruption abound. Furthermore, the "Poetry of the Creator" is perfect, even as He is perfect. His laws are not subject to amendment and change, as human laws made by finite man. *"God is love." (1 John 4: 16).* God's nature, His law, is love. It will ever be a reflection of God's love. God does not change. With Him *"is no variation or shadow of turning." (James 1: 17).*

Jesus, in His famous sermon on the Mount of Blessing, declared,

"Do not think that I came to destroy the Law or the Prophets. I did not come to destroy but to fulfill. For assuredly, I say to you, till heaven and earth pass away, one jot or one tittle will by no means pass from the law till all is fulfilled. . . .For I say to you, that unless your righteousness exceeds the righteousness of the scribes and Pharisees, you will by no means enter the kingdom of heaven." (Matthew 5: 17, 18, 20).

Jesus Christ, the Creator of all, the Giver of the law, declared that it was not His purpose to disregard its precepts. Everything in nature is under law and depends upon these principles for harmony. It was Jesus' purpose to bring man back to obedience to the everlasting law. <u>By His own obedience to the law, Christ testified to its changelessness</u> and proved that through His grace it could be perfectly obeyed by all mankind.

We have read (pp. 132, 133) that the "Old Covenant" was the promise of the people, at the giving of the law from Mount Sinai, who said, *"All that the LORD has spoken we will do." (Exodus 19: 8).* They attempted to keep the law in their own strength, and failed. The "New Covenant" promise of God is, *"I will put My laws into their hearts, and in their minds I will write them." (Hebrews 10: 16).*

Jesus Himself, summarized the Ten Commandments when He said,

> "'You shall love the LORD your God with all your heart, with all your soul, and with all your mind.' This is the first and great commandment [first four commandments]. And the second is like it: 'You shall love your neighbor as yourself' [last six commandments]. On these two commandments hang all the Law and the Prophets." (Matthew 22: 37 - 40).

These two principles are also expressed in the words of Mo Zi.

> **All those whom I love, these love also,**
> **And all those whom I benefit these benefit also.**
> **Their love to men is all-embracing *and their benefit to men is most substantial*.**[17]

The law of God and the gospel of Christ go hand in hand. *"I and My Father are One."* (John 10: 30). They are in perfect balance.

> *A false balance is abomination to the LORD:*
> *But a just weight is His delight. (Proverbs 11: 1, KJV).*

Without the law, one does not know what sin is, and will feel no need for a Savior. The law, without faith in the salvation that Christ offers, cannot save the sinner. The law and Christ's salvation are a perfect whole. At the cross, *"Mercy and truth have met together; Righteousness and peace have kissed." (Psalm 85: 10).* The law points to Christ. Christ points to the law. The gospel calls men from their transgression back to obedience to the law of God.

Christ died that the honor of God's law might be preserved. As the Son of Man, He left us an example of obedience; as the Son of God, He gave the power to be obedient to the law. The law is the standard by which all shall be judged. Through the grace of Jesus, not one need miss heaven. To live a life in Jesus is the foundation of the New Covenant of the gospel.

The Lord has promised to bring man back to perfect obedience to Him:

"I will bring you back from your captivity; I will gather you from all the nations...." *(Jeremiah 29: 14).*

In today's world of hundreds of religions, how can one choose the right one? Mo Zi suggests three valid tests:

> **Now that the truth and error [of a doctrine] in the world is hard to tell, there must be three tests. What are the three tests? They are the test of its basis, the test of its verifiability, and the test of its applicability.**[18]

He explains further:

> **To test the basis of a doctrine we shall examine the <u>will of Heaven</u> and the deeds...of the sage-kings. To test its verifiability, we shall go to the books of the early kings. As to its applicability, it is to be tested by its use in the administration of justice and government. These then are the three tests of a doctrine.**[19]

We will see if the principles Mo Zi put forth are still applicable today. First: We are to test a doctrine by **"the will of God"** [His Commandments, p. 136], and the <u>deeds of Jesus Christ and His faithful apostles.</u> The Bible says:

> *To the law and to the testimony! If they do not speak according to this word, it is because there is no light in them. (Isaiah 8: 20).*

Of Jesus it is written: *"That was the true Light which gives light to every man coming into the world." (John 1: 9).*

Second: Mo Zi's test of verifiability of doctrine was the standard of the **"books of the early kings."** These sage kings were Yao, Shun, Yu, Tang, Wen, and Wu. Some of their books have been lost, but we now have the complete Word of God in the Bible, which fully relates truthful doctrine.

Said Martin Luther (1483 - 1546 A.D.) during the Protestant Reformation, "The Bible, and the Bible only is where I stand."

Third: In the use of doctrine in the **"administration of justice and government,"** are the results good? Jesus advised His disciples:

> *You will know them by their fruits. . . . A good tree cannot bear bad fruit, nor can a bad tree bear good fruit. Every tree that does not bear good fruit is cut down and thrown into the fire. Therefore by their fruits you will know them. (Matthew 7: 16, 18, 19).*

Finally, this is the advice that Mo Zi gave his fellow men in his day:

> **If the gentlemen of the world really desire to practice love and righteousness, and be a son of the Prince, seeking to attain the way of the sage-kings on the one hand and to procure blessings to the people on the other, they must not neglect to understand the will of Heaven. The will of Heaven is truly the standard of righteousness.**[20]

<u>Deeds, not words, count in the sight of God.</u>

> *"Not everyone who says to Me, 'Lord, Lord,' shall enter the kingdom of heaven, but he who does the will of My Father in heaven. Many will say to Me in that day, 'Lord, Lord, have we not prophesied in Your name, cast out demons in Your name, and done many wonders in Your name?' And then I will declare to them, 'I never knew you; depart from Me, you who practice lawlessness!'"*
> *(Matthew 7: 21 - 23).*

13

The Most Excellent Way

Fan Chi (樊迟) asked about love. The Master said, "It is to love men."[1]

Now, love is the most honorable dignity conferred by Heaven, and the safest home in which man should dwell.[2]

The human heart is made for the sole purpose of accepting and transmitting love. The apostle Paul calls it *"the most excellent way."*

> *Love suffers long and is kind; love does not envy; love does not parade itself, is not puffed up; does not behave rudely, does not seek its own, is not provoked, thinks no evil; does not rejoice in iniquity, but rejoices in the truth; bears all things, believes all things, hopes all things, endures all things. Love never fails.*
> *(1 Corinthians 13: 4 - 8).*

Jesus, the Holy Man, who came and died on the cross to teach the lesson of love, said:

> *"If you love me, keep my commandments." (John 14: 15).*

Jesus' commandments and those of God are one and the same, for He did not speak on His own authority, *"but the Father who sent Me gave Me a command, what I should say and what I should speak." (John 12: 49)*.

The love of God and the law of God are inseparable, for *"love is the fulfillment of the law." (Romans 13: 10)*. Did the Chinese sages teach love toward God and man? Were they actually teaching the keeping of God's commandments? The God of Heaven inspired most of the sages to teach this same lesson: reverence to God and love to man!

"Love," in English is used to express every kind of admiration for God, man, and even inanimate objects. The Chinese, on the other hand, have many different characters for "love" in their language; each has a specific meaning for different relationships. For example, there are several words to describe man's love to God: to revere Heaven (敬天); to be obedient to Heaven (順天); to fear Heaven (畏天); to serve Heaven (事天); and to follow Heaven (法天).

The respectful, grateful, and fearful attitude of the ancient Chinese toward God can be described by the following statement of the great sage, the Duke of Zhou:

> **We should be apprehensive and careful,**
> **As if we were on the brink of a deep gulf,**
> **As if we were treading on thin ice.**[3]

Simultaneously, the great king of Israel, Solomon (970 - 930 B.C.), wrote:

> <u>*Walk prudently*</u> *when you go to the house of God and draw near to hear rather than to give the sacrifice of fools, for they do not know that they do evil.*
> *Do not be rash with your mouth,*
> *And let not your heart utter anything hastily before God.*
> *For God is in heaven, and you on earth;*
> *Therefore let your words be few.*
> *(Ecclesiastes 5: 1, 2)*.

Solomon, in his old age, wrote his autobiography in the book of Ecclesiastes. He described the emptiness of all the pleasures of earth; he showed that the vanities of the world failed to meet the heart's real desires. He had pursued intellectual goals, carried out schemes of commercial enterprise, and had lived to the full the splendor of court life. But he summed up his experiences in this sad record:

> *I have seen all the works that are
> done under the sun; and indeed,
> <u>all is vanity and grasping</u> for the wind.
> What is crooked cannot be made straight,
> And what is lacking cannot be numbered. . . .
> Let us hear the conclusion of the whole matter:
> <u>Fear God and keep His commandments,</u>
> <u>For this is man's all (the whole duty of man, KJV)</u>.
> For God will bring every work into judgment,
> Including every secret thing, whether good or evil.*
>   (Ecclesiastes 1: 14, 15; 12: 13, 14).

Almost simultaneously as Solomon made this declaration, the great Chinese sage, the Duke of Zhou, advised the king whom he assisted that he should learn from the example of those ministering in the first dynasty of China—that they were the ones to lead people to "fear God." They had right principles for both the kingdom and its people.

Confucius' disciples likewise recorded their Master's teaching concerning man's duty:

> **The Master said: "Without recognizing the
> ordinances of Heaven,
> it is impossible to be a son of the Prince."**[4]

"**A son of the Prince**" is the ideal person according to Confucius. The ideal person in God's eyes is a *"son [child] of God."* The apostle John could hardly find words to express his feelings of gratitude for the love of

God, and exclaimed, *"Behold what manner of love the Father has bestowed on us, that we should be called <u>children of God</u>! Therefore the world does not know us, because it did not know Him." (1 John 3: 1).*

While the Chinese never knew who "the Prince" was, the Bible makes it clear. Jesus was not only the Holy Man, but the *"Prince of peace," (Isaiah 9: 6)* and *"the Prince of life." (Acts 3: 15)*. He was God. Therefore, **"sons of the Prince"** in Chinese could mean the same as *"sons of God."* How accurate was the Chinese designation for the ideal person! It is the love of God that makes man "a child [son] of the Prince [Jesus Christ]."

A **"son of the Prince"** should **"fear the decree of Heaven,"** but not in the sense of being frightened, as in the heathen tradition of fearing their gods. Rather the ancient Chinese viewed God as their heavenly Father. Note how Confucius put these thoughts together:

> **Confucius said: "Therefore, the loving man serves his parents as if he serves Heaven, and he serves Heaven as if he serves his parents."**[5]

Modern scholars tend to place Confucius as an early forerunner of humanism. However, Confucius' own testimony does not bear this out. It is true that he did not talk too much about the God of Heaven, but all his teachings are based on his deep reverence for God. He said that by the age of fifty, he knew the decree of Heaven (Chapter 9, p. 94). He taught heavenly principles in order to reflect the way of Heaven in human life. How sad that his teachings have been used to disprove the very belief of his spiritual Fountain, the God of Heaven!

For Confucius, love was the keynote of all his teachings. In the short *Confucian Analects,* there are more than 180 references to love! The following conversation between him and a student, from another source, illustrates his opinion on this subject.

Zi Lu (子路) said: "If a man treats me well, I will also treat him well; and if a man does not treat me well, I will not treat him well."

Zi Gong (子贡) said: "If a man treats me well, I will also treat him well; and if a man does not treat me well, I will [try to] lead him [to do so], simply conducting him forward, or letting him fall backward."

Yan Hui (颜回) said: "If a man treats me well, I will also treat him well, and if a man does not treat me well, I will still treat him well."[6]

These three attitudes are inclusive of all man's feelings toward his fellow man. Note Confucius' comments:

> As each of the three had his own view on the subject, they asked the Master about it, who said: "Yu's (由, Zi Lu) words are those of a barbarian; Ci's (赐, Zi Gong) those of a friend; and Hui's (回, Yan Hui) those of a relative.
>
> The ode says:
> 'This man is all vicious,
> and I regard him as my brother.
> This woman is all vicious, and I regard her
> as a marchioness! [wife of a marquis]'"[7]

The first attitude was greatly condemned by the Master who identified the speaker as a "barbarian." Put in biblical terms, the attitude of a sinner. The apostle Luke recorded Jesus' words: *"But if you love those who love you, what credit is that to you? For even sinners love those who love them."* (Luke 6: 32). Even sinners, who are not entirely closed to God's Spirit, will respond to kindness. They may give hate for hate, but they may also give love for love. However, it is only the Spirit of God that gives love in return for hatred. Solomon had this to say: *"A friend loves at all times, and a brother is born for adversity."* (Proverbs 17: 17).

The attitude of friends and relatives are what Confucius approves. Hui was his favorite student, and he frequently used him as an example to encourage others in pursuing *Dao*. When Hui died, Confucius wept bitterly, fearing that no one could carry on his mission given by Heaven. It was finally given to Zi Gong, who retired from public office for six years after Confucius' death, in order to spread his master's teaching across the land of China.

The ancient Chinese sages taught that the world is but one family. A Confucian student thus comforted one who had no brothers:

> **Let a son of the Prince never fail reverently to order his own conduct, and let him be respectful to others and observant of the law. . .then all within the four seas will be his brothers. What has a son of the Prince to do with being distressed because he has no brothers?**[8]

The genuine "children of the Prince" should treat one another as family, for they have God's nature of love that is not dependent upon royal birth, nationality or special rank in order to be a member of this family. Their love embraces all humanity, doing good to the evil and unthankful, without hope of returned favor. This is the characteristic of the royal children of Heaven. This is similar to Confucius' "golden rule":

> **Do not do to others what you would not wish done to yourself.**[10]

This is what Jesus taught to His disciples: *"Therefore, whatever you want men to do to you, do also to them, for this is the Law and the Prophets." (Matthew 7: 12).*

Efforts have been made to decide which of these two principles given by Confucius and Jesus was the greater, in order to conclude which of the two teachers was the greater. Confucius' followers have argued that Confucius taught 500 years before Jesus, and therefore his statement is the original. On the other hand, some professed Christian scholars have argued that Jesus taught a positive lesson while Confucius approached it negatively, therefore they have held that Jesus was the greater. Both Christians and Confucianists have failed to see that their teachings have come from the same source: *"for love is of God; and everyone who loves is born of God and knows God." (1 John 4: 7).*

The golden rule is a principle covering all human relationships. One enters into another's feelings, joys, sorrows, difficulties and identifies with that one as if exchanging places. This is a wonderful rule of courtesy and honesty—actually the standard of true Confucianism and Christianity.

Yet there is a deeper significance to the golden rule. Everyone who has received the grace of God is called upon to impart to those in darkness and ignorance, as if in their place, what one would desire them to impart to him. The apostle Paul said, *"I am a debtor both to Greeks and to barbarians, both to wise and to unwise." (Romans 1: 14).* Each of us has a debt to impart this gift to others. The free gift from God is heaven and eternal life through Jesus Christ, the Holy Man.

> **This is what is called love: to establish oneself in Dao and desire to establish others in Dao as well: to practice Dao in the world and seek to help others to practice Dao in the world as well.**[9]

The highest establishment of oneself is in Dao [Jesus]. Therefore those who have followed Jesus should **"desire to establish others in Dao as well, and seek to help others to practice Dao [faith in Christ] in the world as well."**

THIS IS REAL LOVE. This is Jesus' great command at His departure from this earth:

> *"Go ye therefore, and teach all the nations, baptizing them in the name of the Father, and of the Son, and of*

> *the Holy Ghost: Teaching them to observe all things whatsoever I have commanded you: and lo, I am with you alway, even unto the end of the world."*
> *(Matthew 28: 19, 20, KJV).*

The Chinese have had a "family concept" which, according to Confucius, may extend to the world, seeing all men as "relatives in God." With this stand, there can be no real enemies, for all have the same heavenly Father. This is why Yan Hui still wanted to deal well with those who mistreated him. Mencius adds a further practical step:

> **Mencius said: "The loving one transfers his love for whom he cares to those he does not love, while the unloving one transfers his hate for whom he loves not to those he loves."**[11]

Let us pause and compare these thoughts with a lesson that Jesus taught:

> *"You have heard that it was said, 'You shall love your neighbor and hate your enemy.' But I say to you, love your enemies, bless those who curse you, do good to those who hate you, and pray for those who spitefully use you and persecute you, <u>that you may be sons of your Father in heaven.</u>" (Matthew 5: 43 - 45).*

In Jesus' teaching, the source of this matchless love is revealed: "your Father in heaven." Love is not a man-made product, but a gift from Heaven! Said Mencius:

> **Now, love is the most honorable dignity conferred by Heaven, and the safest home in which man should dwell.**[1]

Again and again Mencius emphasized the fact that to love is the easiest way to live, for it is the only harmonious way with Heaven. He appealed to the people of his time:

> Love is the most tranquil habitation of man, and righteousness his straight path. Alas for them who leave the tranquil dwelling empty and do not reside in it, and who abandon the right path and do not pursue it.[13]

Even though both Confucius and Mencius taught reverence to Heaven, the true knowledge of God had been lost by their time. It might have been for this reason that Confucius did not talk too much about the worship of Heaven, whom he greatly revered. However, he had much to say about love, as expressed in the remaining six of the ten commandments.

The fifth commandment requires that children honor their parents, as exemplified by the story of the Ruler Shun. Mencius wrote rather extensively of Shun, the last of the so-called "legendary rulers." He used Shun as a worthy example of filial love of children toward their parents. Even though Shun's goodness and industry had been recognized by the then ruling sovereign, Yao—to the extent that Yao designated Shun to superintend the kingdom as a co-regent, and gave him his two daughters as wives—yet Shun was filled with sorrow. The reason for Shun's distress was that his parents were not in accord with him.

Shun's father was blind and his mother had died. His father remarried, and the new wife had a son whom the father loved more dearly than Shun. In fact, his father came to hate Shun and plotted with his new wife on several occasions to kill him. Reported Mencius:

> His parents set Shun to repair a granary, and after removing the ladder, Ku Sou [Shun's father] set it on fire. They also made him dig a well. He got out, but they, not knowing this, covered it up. Xiang (象) [Shun's younger brother by his stepmother] said, "Of the schemes to cover up the city-forming prince, the merit is all mine. Let my parents have his oxen and sheep. Let them have

his storehouses and granaries. His shield and spear shall be mine. His flute shall be mine. His bow shall be mine. His two wives I shall make attend for me to my bed."

Xiang (象) then went into Shun's palace, and there found Shun on his couch playing on his flute. Xiang said, "I am come simply because I was thinking anxiously about you." At the same time, he blushed deeply. Shun said to him, "Here are all my officers, do you want to undertake the government of them for me?"[14]

Shun was too wise not to be aware of Xiang's intention to kill him, but he cherished no resentment against his half-brother, only regarding him with affection and love in an effort to win his heart. This is an example to us of how Christ deals with us—He knows our thoughts and the intentions of our hearts, that we have no righteousness to offer. But to win our love and trust, He treats us with the kindness and mercy that we do not deserve.

Shun's great sorrow was that his parents did not love him. In spite of the fact that Ruler Yao put everything he had—nine sons and two daughters, his various officers, oxen and sheep, storehouses and granaries—all under the stewardship of Shun; although multitudes of scholars in the kingdom flocked to Shun; because his parents were not in accord with him, he felt like a poor man who had nowhere to turn. The possession of riches, beauty, and honors were not sufficient to remove his sorrow. This is a story of true filial piety and love! Shun's story became the model of loyalty to family for ages to come.

Love must begin in the home. This is a starting point for the development of love for all of mankind. Society is composed of families, and is actually what the heads of the families make it. The family household is the heart of the community, the church, and the nation. Ultimately, the success and well-being of society and the nation depend upon home influences. The ancient Chinese put so much emphasis on the family that their name for the nation was the "national family" (国家). All the principles practiced at home were transferred to the government. Consequently, family values had a very high place in society.

Parents were to teach their children the importance of implicit obedience. Correct home training was a means of avoiding misery and crimes in society. Children, trained to fear Heaven and honor their parents at home, were prepared to practice these principles of truth in society and the world.

The Book of Filial Piety says:

> **He who loves not his parents, yet loves others is against virtue;**
> **He who respects not his parents, yet respects others is against courtesy.**[15]

Confucius said:

> **Love towards parents should be first taught so that people will be peaceful with one another; respect towards the elderly should be first taught so that people learn to be obedient. In teaching people to be friendly to one another, parents will be honored; by respect shown to the elderly, the law of government will be honored. By serving one's own parents with filial piety, and treating government's law with due respect, everything will be successful.**[16]

Confucius was asked by his disciples on various occasions to define filial piety:

> **Meng Yi (孟懿子) asked what filial piety was. The Master said, "It is not being disobedient."**[17]

> **Zi You (子游) asked what filial piety was. The Master said: "The filial piety of nowadays means the support of one's parents. But dogs and horses likewise are able to do something in the way of support. Without reverence, what is there to distinguish one support given from the other?"**[18]

155

Confucius was saying that the best way to honor one's parents and show reverence to them was by obedience. And ultimately it is obedience or disobedience which decides everyone's destiny. It was because of disobedience to God's command by our first parents in the Garden of Eden that sin and suffering came into the world, and man was lost! The lesson is that children must love, trust and obey God as they love, trust and obey their parents.

When Jesus came to earth, He set a perfect example of obedience for the world, and this is the same obedience that God requires from humans today. Jesus served His heavenly Father willingly and with love. *"I delight to do Your will, O My God,"* he declared. *"Your law is within my heart." (Psalm 40: 8).* Thus we should also serve God, with obedience from the heart. However, sin has weakened our powers of obedience, and in our own strength, we can never obey God. This is why God sent Jesus to our world—to live His law perfectly and to empower us to do likewise. *"I can do all things through Christ who strengthens me." (Philippians 4: 13).*

Children will learn to respect their parents when they observe the father giving kindly attention to the mother's needs, and the mother rendering respect for the father. The sacredness of marriage was greatly esteemed by the ancient Chinese sages. Confucius said: **"Marriage is the beginning of all generations."**[19] Marriage was ordained by God in the Garden of Eden. Eve was created from a rib taken from Adam's side. She was to stand by his side as a "helpmeet" and loving companion. Jesus performed His first miracle at a wedding feast, thus showing His interest in this institution.

Marriage is a blessing, for it protects the purity of, and gives happiness to, mankind. Paul counsels both husbands and wives:

> *Husbands, love your wives, just as Christ also loved the church and gave Himself for her, . . . So husbands ought to love their own wives as their own bodies; he who loves his wife loves himself. (Ephesians 5: 25, 28).*

*Wives, submit to your own husbands, as to the Lord.
For the husband is head of the wife, as also Christ is
head of the church; and He is the Savior of the body.
Therefore, just as the church is subject to Christ, so let
the wives be to their own husbands in everything.*
(Ephesians 5: 22, 23).

Love has its enemy—self. True love can never grow unless self and selfishness is subdued. Regarding this, the writings of Confucius record:

Yan Yuan (颜渊) asked about love. The Master said: "To subdue one's self and return to propriety [law], is love. If a man can for one day subdue himself and return to propriety [law], all under heaven will ascribe love to him."[20]

To love means to die to self. Self-denial is the most difficult attribute to learn and practice. Man cannot subdue self through his own efforts. Divine help is necessary for one to die to self. Jesus said,

"If anyone desires to come after Me, let him deny himself, and take up his cross, and follow Me."
(Matthew 16: 24).

When one surrenders self to Jesus, the Holy Spirit brings love into one's heart, and this is reflected in one's words and deeds. Again, the ancient Chinese writings speak:

Yan Yuan said: "I beg to ask the steps of that process."

The Master replied, "Look not at what is contrary to propriety; listen not to what is contrary to propriety; speak not what is contrary to propriety; make no movement which is contrary to propriety."

Yan Yuan then said, "Though I am deficient in intelligence and vigor, I will make it my business to practice this lesson."[21]

Of all Confucius' teachings on love, this is the most famous quote. Although Confucius himself did not fully understand the source of subduing oneself, yet he made clear the steps in the process—that the battle between good and evil is in the heart. Man can either choose to yield to Heaven's influence or to the evil one. One must avoid seeing or hearing all that even suggest impure thoughts. Solomon, the great, wise king advised, *"Keep your heart with all diligence, For out of it spring the issues of life." (Proverbs 4: 23)*. Those who carefully guard their thoughts and actions receive a promise:

> *He who walks righteously and speaks uprightly,*
> *He who despises the gain of oppressions,*
> *Who gestures with his hands, refusing bribes,*
> *Who stops his ears from hearing of bloodshed,*
> *And shuts his eyes from seeing evil:*
> *He will dwell on high;*
> *His place of defense will be the fortress of rocks;*
> *Bread will be given him. His water will be sure.*
> *(Isaiah 33: 15, 16).*

The mind can be strengthened and trained to run on subjects of purity until it will naturally take that turn. Genuine love comes from a pure heart and sound mind.

> *Finally, brethren, whatever things are true, whatever things are noble, whatever things are just, whatever things are pure, whatever things are lovely, whatever things are of good report, if there is any virtue and if there is anything praiseworthy—meditate on these things. (Philippians 4: 8).*

There is yet a most crucial element of love taught by the Chinese sages—forgiveness. Without it, love is but an empty word, for when man errs, forgiveness is demanded.

> **The Master said, "Shen (參), my doctrine is that of an all pervading unity."**

> The other disciples asked, saying, "What do these words mean?" Zeng Zi (曾子) said, "The doctrine of our Master is to be faithful [to the decree of Heaven] and forgiving to others—this, and nothing more."[22]

The Lord of Heaven is a forgiving God. Jesus, the Holy Man, died to make it possible for God to forgive our sins. This forgiveness is a great part of His love.

> *For if you forgive men their trespasses, your heavenly Father will also forgive you. But if you do not forgive men their trespasses, neither will your Father forgive your trespasses. (Matthew 6: 14, 15).*

How important it is to forgive! He who is unforgiving loses his opportunity for mercy from the God of Heaven. God's complete forgiveness is beyond our understanding.

> *As far as the east is from the west, so far has He removed our transgressions from us. (Psalm 103: 12).*

> *We love Him because He first loved us.*
> *(1 John 4: 19).*

> **Mencius said, "That whereby a son of the Prince is distinguished from other men is what he preserves in his heart:—namely, love and propriety [law]."**[23]

As already explained, the "sons of God" are those in a loving covenant relationship with God. Within their hearts is the law of God and a love for it.

> *"This is the covenant that I will make with them after those days," says the Lord: "I will put My laws into their hearts, and in their minds I will write them." Then He adds, "Their sins and their lawless deeds I will remember no more."*
> *(Hebrews 10: 16, 17).*

14

The Way of Man

> The Faithful is the Way of Heaven.
> Attainment of The Faithful is the way of man.[1]

The ancient Chinese writings have much to say about Heaven [God] and the Holy Man. The suffering of the Holy Man made us marvel at His unsearchable love for humanity and for His priceless sacrifice on behalf of lost sinners of the world. The God of Heaven did His part in sending Jesus Christ to the world and accomplishing salvation for man through the Savior's blood. He provided more than enough grace for all sinners to be saved. Now, what should man do? What is the "way of man?"

According to the above quotation, one must understand **"The Faithful"**(诚者) before it is possible to know the way of man, for **"The attainment of The Faithful (诚之者) is the way of man."** What, then, is "The Faithful," which is the way to Heaven?

Even though Jesus was the world's greatest instructor, His teachings were not understood by His disciples before His death. Although Confucius was a great teacher of Dao, his doctrine was also not fully grasped by his disciples in his time. Zi Gong, who was 31 years younger than Confucius, became the Master's most brilliant and favorite student (p. 150). Concerning him, Confucius said, **"From the time I got Zi Gong, scholars came daily, resorting to me from a distance."**[2]

Zi Gong was the most famous diplomat of his time, and a great statesman. When the Master died, Zi Gong led the funeral service and withdrew from public life for six years to mourn Confucius' death. It was during this time that he spread the teachings of Confucius throughout the land of China. He was to Confucius as the apostle Paul was to Jesus. Yet even Zi Gong came to this conclusion, saying, **"The Master's discourses about man's nature, the Way of Heaven, cannot be heard."**[3]

But Confucius' grandson, Zi Si, understood the great light in the Master's teaching on the Way of Heaven, and let this shine out brightly in the book, *The Doctrine of the Mean*. This book is an expository on "The Faithful" found in Confucius' teaching. We may be surprised to find that here the Way of Heaven is extensively discussed in great detail. Thus, new light and a better understanding has been given for the Chinese on the nature and attributes of Heaven [God].

> **The Faithful is the Way of Heaven.**
> **The attainment of The Faithful is the way of man.**
> **He who is The Faithful, is He who, without effort, hits what is right, and apprehends, without the exercise of thought ;—**
> **He is none other than the Holy Man who naturally and easily embodies the right way.**
> **He who attains to The Faithful, is he who chooses what is good, and firmly holds it fast.**[4]

What is this **"The Faithful" (Cheng, 诚者)**? Some say "The Faithful" means "free from all deception." Some say it means "truth and reality;" still others say it is "freedom from all moral error and ceaselessness."[5] This passage, according to common Chinese understanding, simply means being honest and sincere. The Chinese have held the view for thousands of years that as long as one is "honest and sincere," one is in good standing, and is assured of achieving heaven. And yet, a person may be entirely sincere, and still be entirely wrong! As a result of this view, the standard of right and wrong is lost sight of. This misunderstanding of "The Faithful" has led to the concept that it does not matter what one believes as long as one is sincere! This has been a common Chinese belief based upon the misinterpretation of the character for "The Faithful" in *The Doctrine of the Mean*. The question has been, therefore, since "The Faithful" is not an absolute, why is it important? This is a question which has puzzled the Chinese for ages!

According to the earliest Chinese Dictionary, *The Interpretation of Words [Shuo Wen 《说文》]*, the Chinese character (诚, Cheng) used here means "faithful" (信, Xin).[6] Our study thus far has shown that the Holy Bible is the key to unlocking the mysteries in the Chinese Classics. The Word of God has helped greatly in understanding the most mysterious passages in the *Yi Jing* and Lao Zi's writings. Is it possible that the Bible can also throw light on this particular teaching of Confucius?

> *It is the glory of God to conceal a matter,*
> *But the glory of kings is to search out a matter.*
> *(Proverbs 25: 2).*

Christ is the mystery of God, *"without controversy great is the mystery of godliness: God was manifested in the flesh," (1 Timothy 3: 16)*, for all the mysteries of God are hidden in Him. Lao Zi said, **[The Dao] "is the gate to all mysteries."**[5] Through **"the Gate,"** Christ, we can enter this mystery of Confucius.

Of Christ, John wrote,

> *These things says the Amen, the Faithful and*
> *True Witness, the Beginning of the creation of God.*
> *(Revelation 3: 14).*

> *Now I saw heaven opened, and behold, a white horse. And He who sat on him was called <u>Faithful and True</u>, and in righteousness He judges and makes war.*
> *(Revelation 19: 11).*

Surprisingly, **"The Faithful"** is one of Jesus' names! If we simply substitute "The Faithful" with "Christ" in the above quotation, we will see how easily it may be understood—that which has been a mystery and has puzzled Chinese for thousands of years!

> **[Christ] is the way of Heaven. The attainment of [Christ] is the way of man. He who is [Christ], is He who, without an effort, hits what is right, and apprehends, without the exercise of thought;—He is none other than the Holy Man who naturally and easily embodies the right way. He who is in [Christ], is he who chooses what is good, and firmly holds it fast.**

Is this substitution legitimate?

The Doctrine of the Mean has an extensive discussion on "The Faithful." We should compare all of its attributes with Jesus Christ to see whether our identification is correct. We have chosen the following five attributes of "The Faithful" for comparative purposes.

1. "The Faithful" Means Wisdom

> **Possessed of The Faithful, one shall be intelligent.**[7]

The Bible confirms that Jesus was the embodiment of wisdom:

> *In whom are hidden all the treasures of wisdom and knowledge. (Colossians 2: 3)*

Therefore the Bible says, *"but you are wise in Christ."*
> *(1 Corinthians 4: 10).*

2. "The Faithful" Is the Creator

The Faithful is the end and beginning of things. Without The Faithful there would be nothing.[8]

Jesus said, *"I am the Alpha and Omega, the First and the Last." (Revelation 1: 11).*
John wrote, *"In the beginning was the Word, and the Word was with God, and the Word was God....All things were made through Him, and without Him nothing was made that was made." (John 1: 1, 3).*

On this account, a son of the Prince regards the attainment of The Faithful as the most excellent thing.[8]

Yet indeed I also count all things loss <u>for the excellence of the knowledge of Christ Jesus my Lord</u>, for whom I have suffered the loss of all things, and count them as rubbish, that I may gain Christ. (Philippians 3: 8).

3. "The Faithful" Is Love and Wisdom

The Faithful does not merely stop at the perfection of Himself, but helps to perfect other men and things also. The perfection of Himself shows <u>His perfect love</u>. The perfection of other men and things shows <u>His wisdom</u>.[9]

When Jesus knew that His hour had come that He should depart from this world to the Father, having loved His own who were in the world, <u>He loved them to the end</u>."
(John 13: 1).

...but to those who are called, both Jews and Greeks, Christ the power of God and <u>the wisdom of God</u>.
(1 Corinthians 1: 24).

4. "The Faithful" Is Endless

Hence the most Faithful is without ending.[10]

Since Christ is He who gives eternal life to man, it is only logical that He Himself has life **without ending**. *"Jesus Christ is the same yesterday, today, and forever." (Hebrews 13: 8).*

5. "The Faithful" Alone Can Govern Human Relations

> **It is only the most Faithful under Heaven who can govern the great principles of invariable human relations; establish the great fundamental virtues of humanity and know the transforming and nurturing operations of Heaven and earth. Shall He have anything (other than being faithful to Heaven) on whom He depends? His love is earnest and sincere! His wisdom is as deep as an abyss, His vastness is that of Heaven!**[11]

Jesus Christ, as the Creator of everything, established the institution of marriage in the Garden of Eden. From marriage comes all human relationships. Jesus, *"upholding all things by the word of His power" (Hebrew 1: 3)*, is the One **"transforming and nurturing operations of Heaven and Earth."** Heaven [the Father] is the One **"on whom He [Jesus] depends."** He said, *"I do nothing of Myself," "but the Father who dwells in Me does the works." (John 8: 28; 14: 10).*

> **Who can know Him, but he who is holy and wise and has all embracing knowledge, possessing all heavenly virtues?**[11]

Who is this Person? The one described here is a very interesting Person, **"who is holy and wise and has all embracing knowledge, possessing all heavenly virtues."** The Bible confirms *"all have sinned and fall* *short of the glory of God." (Romans 3: 23)*. No one in the human family fits the description of this Person, and no man knows the Most Faithful [Christ Jesus] of himself. But there is One who knows even the deep things of God [the Father and the Son].

> *But God has revealed them to us through His Spirit. For the Spirit searches all things, yes, the deep things of God. For what man knows the things of a man which is in him? Even so <u>no one knows the things of God except the Spirit of God</u>. (1 Corinthians 2: 10, 11).*

This Person who knows the Most Faithful must be the Holy Spirit!

With these five parallel attributes showing that "The Faithful" in *The Doctrine of the Mean* refers to Jesus Christ, we can surely say that Jesus is the Way of Heaven.

Let us now listen to two beautiful ancient Chinese hymns. In fact, the ancient Chinese were famous for their singing. Confucius was a great musician. The Classics were not read, they were sung. Even those who received the traditional Chinese education in their youth, still today know how to sing the following two "hymns" from *The Doctrine of the Mean*. This hymn describes why "The Faithful" [Jesus Christ] could accomplish His mission on earth.

> **Hence the most Faithful is without ending.**
>   **Without ending,**
> **He continues long. Continuing long,**
>   **He evidences Himself.**
> **Evidencing Himself, He reaches far.**
> **Reaching far, He becomes large and substantial.**
> **Large and substantial, He becomes**
>   **high and brilliant.**
> **Large and substantial;—this is how He**
>   **perfects all things.**
> **High and brilliant;—this is how He**
>   **overspreads all things.**

> Reaching far and continuing long; this is how He perfects all things.
> So large and substantial, The Faithful is the co-equal of Earth. So high and brilliant, that makes Him the co-equal of Heaven.
> So far-reaching and long-continuing, that makes Him infinite.
> Such being His nature, without any display, He becomes manifested; without any movement, He produces changes; and without any effort, He accomplishes His end.
> The way of Heaven and Earth may be completely declared in a sentence.
> —They are without any doubleness, and so they produce things in a manner that is unfathomable.
> The way of Heaven and Earth is large and substantial, high and brilliant, far-reaching and long-enduring.[12]

The following song tells how men's hearts are drawn to "The Faithful" Holy Man.

> Therefore His fame overspreads the Middle Kingdom [China],
>   and extends to all barbarous tribes.
> Wherever ships and carriages reach;
>   wherever the strength of man penetrates;
>   wherever the heavens overshadow and the earth sustains,
>   wherever the sun and moon shines;
>   wherever frosts and dews fall;—
> All who have blood and breath unfeignedly honor and love Him.
> Hence it is said,—He is the equal of Heaven.[13]

The Way of Man

How wonderful is the adoration of the Faithful [Jesus Christ]! How beautiful are these "hymns" by which the ancient Chinese prophets praised Him.

****

Now we will come to a discussion of **"the Way of man."** It is sad that Confucius has been regarded by many as the "father of modern humanism." It is because he taught the "way of man," which has been wrongly translated as "humanism" in English. But how different was the "way of man" which he taught in *The Doctrine of the Mean*, whence the term was derived: **"The Faithful is the Way of Heaven. The attainment of The Faithful is the Way of man."**[14]

Knowing that "The Faithful" is Christ, and that He was surely the "Way of Heaven," we find that the essence of "the Way of man" is far from the modern humanistic teaching! To the contrary, the "way of man" is to have Christ dwelling in the heart.

The Chinese words for **"the attainment of The Faithful"** can also be interpreted as "to take or accept The Faithful as truth." Simply put, the way of man is to believe that the Faithful is Jesus Christ, for He is the Truth. Jesus said, *"I am the way, the truth, and the life." (John 14: 6)*.

To possess the truth intellectually is one thing, but to be possessed by the truth is quite another. It is not enough to just agree and accept theoretically that Jesus is the Truth. He is the Savior. One has to put one's belief into practice. Words are of no value unless they are accompanied by appropriate deeds. The test of The Faithful is not words, but deeds. How can one accomplish these "deeds?" Eight steps are given in the book, *The Great Learning*. These are:

> **To investigate things, to complete knowledge, have the Faithful thoughts, have the heart rectified, be self-cultivated, have a well-regulated family, a state well-governed, and the whole kingdom tranquil and happy.**[15]

These steps have been known by the Chinese for thousands of years, but not many know the source of the power to attain the desired achievement.

> **From the son of Heaven [king] down to the mass of the people, all must consider the cultivation of a person the root of everything.**[16]

> **When the mind is not present,
> we look and do not see;
> we hear and do not understand;
> we eat and do not know
> the taste of what we eat.**[17]

One's mind is **"the root of the cultivation of a person."** But the knowing and the doing are two different things.

> **It is not the knowing that is difficult,
> but the doing.**[18]

How then should one overcome the difficulty of the doing? Both Lao Zi and Mencius pointed the way.

> **Be true and unswerving,
> Become as a babe once more.**[19]

> **Mencius said, "The great man is he
> who does not lose the heart of a babe."**[20]

This advice from both Mencius and Lao Zi, to become as babes, is of great significance. Small children trust their parents for everything and accept their teaching as truth. The parents' words are authoritative in their lives. Babes generally do not insist on having their own ideas, but act according to their parents' instruction. Small children make mistakes, but readily accept correction. They are friendly and forgiving. They do not hold grudges. Babes are good learners—and good teachers for adults! In a word, they have faith and trust in their parents.

The moral is to trust in Heaven as babes do in their parents. The God of

Heaven knows best and His plan is the best. All heaven and earth are in His perfect control. If man submits to Heaven as a babe does to his parents, things will then be better. The Way of man is the Way of faith.

In the Bible, we read that man must become as a babe to understand the truth. *"Therefore, laying aside all malice, all deceit, hypocrisy, envy, and all evil speaking, <u>as newborn babes</u>, desire the pure milk of the word, that you may grow thereby." (1 Peter 2: 1, 2).* God loves to reveal His truth to man in every possible way. In nature, heavenly wisdom and the eternal *Dao* is imprinted, but fallen man cannot understand it. Sin has obscured the vision, and one cannot by oneself interpret nature without placing it above God. The teaching of nature has been so perverted that it turns the mind away from its Creator. For example, the title for God the Father, "Heaven," is now viewed as no more than the physical expanse of the skies.

God does not conceal truth from men. It is one's own selfish interest that closes the door to truth. Jesus spoke to God in front of His listeners, *"I thank You, Father, Lord of heaven and earth, that <u>You have hidden these things from the wise and prudent and have revealed them to babes.</u>" (Matthew 11: 25).*

The way of Heaven is hidden only to those who are wise in their own estimation, who are puffed up by the teaching of man's philosophy. *"The message of the cross is foolishness"* to them. *(1 Corinthians 1: 18).* They cannot see the beauty, power and mystery of God's plan of redemption. Many have eyes, but **"do not see;"** have ears, but **"do not understand;"** have intellect, but they discern not the hidden treasure.

Truth is revealed only to those little children who do not trust themselves, and truth is the only gate to heaven. Therefore, only "little children" can enter heaven. Jesus said, *"Assuredly, I say to you, unless you are converted and <u>become as little children</u>, you will by no means enter the kingdom of heaven. Therefore <u>whoever humbles himself as this little</u>*

<u>child</u> *is the greatest in the kingdom of heaven." (Matthew 18: 3, 4).*

The apostle Paul made it even more clear why the wise of the world cannot see. *"But even if our gospel is veiled, it is veiled to those who are perishing, <u>whose minds the god of this age has blinded</u>, who do not believe, lest the light of the gospel of the glory of Christ, who is the image of God, should shine on them." (2 Corinthians 4: 3, 4).*

We have found that God has given abundant evidence in the Chinese Classics to identify the Holy Man as Jesus Christ. In the light of the Bible, the Chinese can recognize Him as the One, long-awaited by the ancient sages. But for the discovery of Jesus to become meaningful, a decided change must take place in one's life. In accepting Christ, one must give up cherished maxims and traditions, as well as selfish, ungodly practices. The old mind has to be put to death upon hearing the Dao! As Confucius said,

> **If a man in the morning hears the Dao,
> he may die in the evening without regret.**[21]

It requires a sacrifice to receive the changeless, eternal *Dao*. To be converted and become as a little child requires one to give up one's own preconceived opinions. But how can one become a babe again when an adult? The same question was asked of Jesus two thousand years ago.

There was a man of the Pharisees named Nicodemus, a ruler of the Jews. This man came secretly to Jesus by night and said to Him,

> *"Rabbi, we know that You are a teacher come from God; for no one can do these signs that You do unless God is with him."*
>
> *Jesus answered and said to him, "Most assuredly I say to you, unless one is born again, he cannot see the kingdom of God."*
>
> *Nicodemus said to Him, "How can a man be born when he is old? Can he enter a second time into his mother's womb and be born?"*

> *Jesus answered, "Most assuredly, I say to you, unless one is born of water and the Spirit, he cannot enter the kingdom of God. That which is born of the flesh is flesh, and that which is born of the Spirit is spirit. Do not marvel that I said to you, 'You must be born again.' The wind blows were it wishes, and you hear the sound of it, but cannot tell where it comes from and where it goes. So is everyone who is born of the Spirit." (John 3: 2 - 8).*

To be born again in the Spirit, one's imperfect nature and character must be remade in Christ, who is perfect. To be "born again," one becomes entitled to receive the righteousness of the Holy Man and be justified before God as a sinless new person.

> **It is only He who is the most completely Faithful [Jesus Christ] under heaven, who can fully develop His nature [His perfect righteousness]. He can do the same to the nature of other men [imputing His righteousness to others who believe in Him].[22]**

The word of God is the transforming power in creating a new life. *"Therefore, if anyone is in Christ, he is a new creation; old things have passed away; behold, all things have become new." (2 Corinthians 5: 17).* It is God's will that *"we all come to the unity of the faith and the knowledge of the Son of God, to a perfect man, to the measure of the stature of the fullness of Christ." (Ephesians 4: 13).*

Born of the spirit, one will have a new heart—the heart of a new babe in Christ, "The Faithful." One will begin to see the glory of God, the beauty of the truth, and feel keenly the need for one's personal transformation.

This is the way of man.

15

The New Book of Changes

> The Master said: "If some years were added to my life, I would give fifty to the study of the Yi, and then I might come to be without great faults."[1]

"**O**neness of Heaven [God] and man (天人合一)" is the sole foundation of all Chinese philosophy and has been the goal of the Chinese for ages. How can one come to God and become one with Him? This is the question many have asked in the past, and is still the question being asked today. Many are seeking for the right answer to this fundamental question. The answer lies in the *Yi Jing, The Book of Changes.*

The theme of *The Book of Changes,* as the title suggests, is the importance of "changes" in one's life. "Changes," according to the book, may avoid misfortune and disaster; "changes" bring peace and prosperity; "changes" lead to success and auspiciousness! In a word, "changes" bring down blessings from Heaven.

Confucius himself thus explained the effect of "changes."

> When one runs to the end of one's course, one "changes." Through changes one achieves success;

through success one achieves eternity. Therefore, "They were blessed by Heaven with good fortune. There is nothing that does not further one." ²

In commenting on Confucius' words concerning his study of the *Yi Jing*, Liang Reng-kong (梁启超, 1873 - 1929 A.D.), the most prominent scholar in the last imperial dynasty, the Qing (清, 1616 - 1911 A.D.), said, "To *Yi Jing* students, the most important lesson to learn consists of only one word: Repent (悔)!" Repentance gives rise to change, and change can bring one into harmony with Heaven.

In the Bible, we find the same question, how to be one with God, asked by thousands of the people of Israel on the Day of Pentecost after Christ's crucifixion. Peter preached, for the first time after his denial of his Master, saying:

> *"Therefore let all the house of Israel know assuredly that God has made this Jesus, whom you crucified, both Lord and Christ."*
>
> *Now when they heard this, they were cut to the heart, and said to Peter and the rest of the apostles, "Men and brethren, what shall we do?"*
>
> *Then Peter said to them, "<u>Repent</u>, and let every one of you be baptized in the name of Jesus Christ for the remission of sins; and you shall receive the gift of the Holy Spirit. For the promise is to you and to your children, and <u>to all who are afar off</u>, as many as the Lord our God will call." (Acts 2: 36 - 39).*

When Peter called for repentance, he was speaking not only to the Israelites, but also to *"those who are afar off."* This could include the people *"in the land of Sinim."* Three thousand people responded to Peter's invitation to repentance that day.

This same principle of repentance has been taught both in the *Yi Jing* and in the Holy Bible. *"Baptism in the name of Jesus Christ"* was a new light that came into the world after Jesus started His ministry. Also included in Peter's promise was *"the gift of the Holy Spirit."* Did the ancient Chinese ever realize that there was such a precious gift from God to help them make right choices and guide them in every step of their lives? Did they ever receive any assistance from the Holy Spirit at all? Did the ancient Chinese understand repentance?

These are fair questions to ask, and deserve good answers. Let us refer to the ancient writings of the Chinese Classics for answers.

In *The Book of Poetry, Tian* [*Heaven*, God] is repeatedly mentioned. The ancient Chinese not only knew that there was a God, but that this Supreme Being had laws for everything He created.

> **Heaven [God] in giving birth to the multitude of men,**
> **To every endowment appointed its appropriate law.**
> **The people, holding fast this constant nature,**
> **Love the virtue which is admirable.**[3]

How could sinful man **"love the virtue which is admirable?"** The natural man is a transgressor, and his nature is in harmony with the first transgressor (Satan). It is only natural for man with a sinful nature to love evil and sin. Love for good, as well as enmity against evil in the human heart, has no natural existence. After Adam sinned, God put enmity [hatred] for sin in the human because of His love and pity for man, announcing:

> *"And I will put enmity between you and the woman,*
> *And between your seed and her Seed."*
> *(Genesis 3: 15).*

This "enmity" was created through the agency of the Holy Spirit. It is the Holy Spirit that *"convicts the world of sin, of righteousness, and of judgment." (John 16: 8).* In Chapter 7 we discovered that the Holy Spirit was mentioned in *The Book of Poetry* and by Mencius (p. 74). God's

Spirit is given to every individual in order to lead each on the right path. It is God's Spirit that strives to awaken one's conscience. However, the Holy Spirit does not strive forever if there is no response, as before the great worldwide flood, when He declared, *"My Spirit shall not strive with man forever. . . ." (Genesis 6: 3).*

This gift was well understood by the ancient Chinese. One of the most authoritative commentaries was printed in 654 A.D. where Kong Ying-da (孔颖达, 574 - 648 A.D.) said:

> **The people have been produced by supreme Heaven, and both body and soul are Heaven's gift. Men have thus a material body and a knowing mind, and Heaven further assists them, helping them to harmonize their lives.**[4]

How striking is this statement! It fully and clearly tells of the work of God's Spirit on the human heart. God does not just give man a body and intelligent mind, but **"Heaven further assists them."** It is this gift that leads men to harmonize with Heaven in all their words, thoughts and actions.

> **The right and wrong of their language, the correctness and errors of their conduct, their enjoyment of clothing and food, the rightness of their various movements; all these things are to be harmonized by what they are endowed with by Heaven. Accordance with the right way gives life, while error leads to death. Thus Heaven has not only given life to men, and conferred upon them a body and mind, but <u>it further assists them in harmonizing their conditions of life</u>, thereby making provision for its continuance.**[4]

The effect of God's Spirit on the human heart has been recognized, but the effect of the divine Worker has often been mistaken. Thus started the long dispute in Chinese philosophy about whether human nature was good or evil. On one side was Mencius who mistook the work of the Holy Spirit as something innate in man, and therefore concluded that human nature was good. On the other side was Xun Zi (荀子, 313-230 B.C.), a contemporary of Mencius, who concluded that human nature was evil. Xun Zi mistook the work of God's Spirit on human souls as mere human effort. The argument has gone on and on. Here is another example of how human reasoning and imagination alone fails without divine help. (The Chinese edition of this book has more details). But instead of going deeper into this dispute, we would like to present a Bible view on the subject. Note these several references to man's innate nature:

After the universal flood which wiped out all of mankind except for a family of eight survivors, the Lord said, *"I will never again curse the ground for man's sake, although <u>the imagination of man's heart is evil from his youth</u>." (Genesis 8: 21).*

> *Behold, I was brought forth in iniquity,*
> *And in sin my mother conceived me.*
>   *(Psalm 51: 5).*

> *The heart is deceitful above all things,*
> *And desperately wicked;*
> *Who can know it? (Jeremiah 17: 9).*

As puzzling as this issue may appear, we believe that God can clarify and settle the question. The word of God is authoritative. Even though the human heart may be evil, it can bear good fruit through the work of the Holy Spirit, showing *"love, joy, peace, longsuffering, kindness, goodness, faithfulness, gentleness, self-control." (Galatians 5: 22).* Through the Holy Spirit, sinful ones can also become the sons and daughters of God ["**sons of the Prince**"].

> *But as many as received Him, to them He gave the right to become children of God, to those who believe in His name: who were born, not of blood, nor of the will of*

> the flesh, nor of the will of man,
> but of God. (John 1: 12, 13).

This is God's promise for the whole world. It is interesting to see what Confucius' view was on this matter. He did not say directly whether man's nature was good or evil, He simply said:

> **By nature, men are nearly alike;
> by practice, they get to be wide apart.**[5]

A closer look at Confucius' teachings proves that he held a view similar to that of the Bible.

> **The Master said, "I have not seen one who loves virtue as he loves apparent beauty."** [6]

> **The Master said, "It is all over! I have not yet seen one who could perceive his faults, and inwardly accuse himself."**[7]

Without the assistance of the harmonizing power from Heaven, man cannot have love for good and hatred for evil within himself. Left alone, as the Master said, man will not **"inwardly accuse himself."** If there is nothing good in man, where does the virtue in him or in the sages come from?

> **The Master said, "Heaven produced the virtue that is in me."**[8]

Every desire for truth (Jesus said, *"I am the truth," John 14: 6*) and purity, every conviction of one's sinfulness, shows that the Holy Spirit is working upon the heart. One who listens to the voice of conscience from heaven will inwardly accuse himself.

The ancient philosopher, a beloved student of Confucius, Zeng Zi (曾子, 505 - 436 B.C.) said:

> **I daily examine myself on three points: whether, in intercourse with friends, I may have been unfaithful;**

whether, in intercourse with friends, I may have been insincere; where I may not have mastered and practiced the instructions of my teacher.[9]

These three points are far from the standards for perfection, but show the conviction of one's need for improvement by the Spirit.

> The Master said, "When we see men of worth, we should think of equaling them; when we see men of a contrary character, we should turn inward and examine ourselves."[10]

Through perceived and unperceived influences of the Holy Spirit, the minds of men are being attracted closer to God. A sincere desire for improvement makes more certain one's determination to abandon faults.

> *For when Gentiles, who do not have the law, by nature do the things in the law, these, although not having the law, are a law to themselves, who show the <u>work of the law written in their hearts</u>, their conscience also bearing witness, and between themselves their thoughts accusing or else excusing them.*
> *(Romans 2: 14, 15).*

God's law is written on every individual's heart, so that the conscience bears witness of right and wrong.

> The Master said, "When I walk along with two others, they may serve me as my teachers. I will select their good qualities and follow them, their bad qualities and avoid them."[11]

> The Master said, "The leaving of virtue without proper cultivation; not thoroughly discussing what is learned; not being able to move towards righteousness of which knowledge is gained; and not being able to change what is not good; these are the things which occasion me meditation."[12]

It is the Holy Spirit that appeals to the heart to change for the good, and gives a desire for righteousness. This heavenly influence keeps one humble and gentle. Whenever one becomes ashamed of one's own sinful ways and gives up some evil habits, it is a response to Heaven's [Christ's] drawing. The conscience is awakened, and endeavor is made to change the life.

To abandon faults is a good virtue highly regarded by all Chinese sages. It was reported of one of Confucius' students:

> **Zi Kong said, "The faults of a son of the Prince are like the eclipses of the sun and moon. He has faults, and all men see them; he changes, and all men look up to him."**[13]

It is not a shameful thing to repent and change. Everyone errs, even the admirable sages, such as King Yu and King Yao made their mistakes. When men desire to abandon evil, Heaven is happy to forgive and supplies power to overcome.

> **The Master said, "Hold faithfulness and sincerity as first principles. Have no friends not equal to yourself. When you have faults, do not fear to abandon them."**[14]

However, if one knows of a sin, and holds to it, there is no forgiveness from Heaven.

> **The Master said, "To have faults and not to reform them—this indeed, should be pronounced as having faults."**[15]

The following story told by Mencius illustrates how one should abandon his offenses and sins.

> **Mencius said, "Here I saw a man who every day stole some of his neighbor's chickens. Someone instructed him, 'Such is not the way of a good man.'**
> **"He replied, 'With your leave I will diminish my**

appropriations, and will take only one chicken a month. Next year, I will make an end of the practice.'
"If you know that the thing is unrighteous, then use all despatch in putting an end to it—why wait till next year?"[16]

This is a frequently made mistake. Many think they cannot completely stop doing something evil, and therefore attempt to stop it gradually. But if a thing is evil, is it not still evil, even though one does it less frequently? Is it not better to stop doing it entirely, and be rid of it from one's life? As noted above, the reforming, harmonizing Agency of Heaven is willing to help and give the power for a complete change.

The first chapter of *The Book of Changes* tells of Heaven as the Creator of everything. In the whole book, the will of Heaven is the highest standard for all man's action. In fact, the purpose of practicing "divination" was to find out the will of Heaven. One was advised not to do anything until finding the will of Heaven.

From the *Yi Jing* we read the following:

**If someone is not as he should be,
he has misfortune.
And it does not further him to
undertake anything.
If the will of Heaven does not protect one,
can one do anything?**[17]

This principle was included in the instruction of all the ancient Chinese sages. What a shame that many of those who study the *Yi Jing* today have lost sight of the true knowledge of **"the will of Heaven."** The standard is lost; the need for change is not felt; study of *The Book of Changes* does not bring real changes in one's life.

While the **"will of Heaven"** and sin have never been clearly defined in the Chinese Classics, these are precisely defined in the Bible. God's will concerning man is revealed in His holy law: *"Whosoever committeth sin transgresseth also the law: for sin is the transgression of the law." (1 John 3: 4, KJV).* We are called to change from *"the transgression of the law."*

Any transgression of God's holy law is sin. It was man's breaking of God's unchanging law that caused the death of Jesus on the cross in order to atone for our committed sins. One is not called to repent of a sinful nature, but of sin itself—the breaking of God's law. The concept of "original sin" was brought into the church by Saint Augustine (354 - 430 A.D.), and is a human theory, not a Bible term. It is true that everyone has inherited a sinful nature from Adam, namely, the tendency and propensity to disobey God, and has suffered the consequences of rebellion. But we are not responsible for Adam's sin and therefore not required to repent for his original sin in the Garden of Eden!

> *The soul who sins shall die. The son shall not bear the guilt of the father, nor the father bear the guilt of the son. The righteousness of the righteous shall be upon himself, and the wickedness of the wicked shall be upon himself. (Ezekiel 18: 20).*

This consequence of sin even affected Jesus Christ, for He *"was born of a woman, born under the law" "in the likeness of sinful flesh"* and *"inasmuch then as the children have partaken of flesh and blood, He Himself likewise shared in the same." (Galatians 4: 4; Romans 8: 3; Hebrews 2: 14).* Jesus had the same sinful nature as other descendants of Adam. Although He was made *"in the likeness of sinful flesh,"* He did not have a sinful mind as we do. Jesus, therefore, did not sin, but lived a perfect, obedient life to the law of God.

We are often blind to our own sins and fail to see that there is no power in human nature alone that can overcome temptation and sin. But when we behold the cross of the Holy Man, the love of God floods our hearts and we then recognize the sinfulness present in our own lives. Our eyes are opened to see how awful sin is, and how much we need God's forgiveness. Within the law itself there is no forgiveness. It is merely a schoolmaster to lead us to Jesus for forgiveness, and for strength to overcome sin.

> *This is a faithful saying and worthy of all acceptance, that Christ Jesus came into the world to save sinners.*
> *(1 Timothy 1: 15).*

> *Now the Lord is the Spirit; and where the Spirit of the Lord is, there is liberty. But we all, with unveiled face, beholding as in a mirror the glory of the Lord, are being transformed into the same image from glory to glory, just as by the Spirit of the Lord.*
> *(2 Corinthians 3: 17 - 18).*

The Holy Bible is the *New Book of Changes.* All the secrets of how to change are given in this sacred Book, as well as the power needed to make the change. Mere improvement is not enough. God desires a complete replacement of our sinful natures with His holy character. By beholding Jesus Christ, the Holy Man, we will be changed *"into the same image of Christ, just as by the Spirit of the Lord."*

Faith in Jesus is the real key to change!

16

Communication with Heaven

> Gems unwrought, can form nothing useful;
> So men untaught, can never know Dao.[1]
>
> The Master said, "My prayer has been for a long time."[2]

Learning was not only highly emphasized, but also had profound meaning in ancient China. Noting how Mencius' mother regarded the importance of her son's learning (pp. 29, 30), we can get a faint idea. "Live to learn, and learn to live" might well be the Chinese motto. For the Chinese, life itself is a process of learning of the Dao. If one stops learning, one's life has lost its meaning.

The Way of Learning

From the first quotation above in the *Li Ji*, one can see that if man does not learn, he can never know Dao. To know Dao, the Truth of life, is the sole purpose the Chinese have put on learning. The way of greater learning is to illustrate the illustrious virtue—that is to glorify God. It is to think, feel and act like God would if He were a human. Mencius, the great learner thus defines the goal of learning:

> **The end of learning is nothing else but to seek for the lost mind.**[3]

We have seen how the original human mind (that of Adam, the first man) reflected God's nature and character, but was lost because of disobedience (sin). To **"learn"** is **"to seek for the lost mind"** which was given by God at man's creation. The "lost mind" can be restored by the "second birth" through the Holy Spirit, as discussed in the previous chapter.

Being a great teacher and learner himself, Confucius was a man with deep thought—but listen to his advice:

> **The Master said, "I have been the whole day without eating, and the whole night without sleeping—occupied with thinking. It was of no use. The better plan is to learn."**[4]

What, then, should be the subject of his study? Perhaps you have noticed already that all the sages taught the same thing: one needs to learn the way of Heaven and man; to try to understand the decree of Heaven for man; and **"to stand in awe of the words of the Holy Man."**[5] It is in the words of sages that the most important ideas of the Dao are taught.

Of all of earth's books, the Holy Bible is the only word of God written by His sages, the prophets. On the other hand, in the ancient Chinese Classics we have found hidden, scattered heavenly light for "the land of Sinim." But the Word of God is a complete revelation and greater light for modern China and all the world. It is in the Bible that the most excellent treasures are hidden and await to be found by millions of sincere seekers after truth.

> **Even if it is the best food, one will not know its delicious taste if one doesn't eat it; nor of the most excellent Dao, one will not know its goodness if one does not learn it.**[6]

Experience is the best teacher. The Bible also encourages men to *"taste and see"*—

> *Oh taste and see that the LORD is good;*
> *Blessed is the man who trusts in Him!*
> *(Psalm 34: 8).*

However, as with food, if someone is sick, one cannot enjoy the good taste of the food. So it is, the goodness of God cannot be appreciated when our "sick natural self" is present. The sickness must be healed first if one would have good taste for the best food. In other words, "self" must die if one wants to see the goodness of the Lord. The apostle says:

> *Therefore, if anyone is in Christ, he is a new creation; old things have passed away; behold all things have become new. (2 Corinthians 5: 17).*

When a man is converted to God, a new spiritual taste is created. He loves the things that God loves, and hates the things that God hates. His life is bound up in the life of Jesus who shed His life blood for him. As he beholds Christ's righteousness and is pardoned for his sins through the merits of Jesus, he declares with the psalmist,

> *The law of the LORD is perfect, converting the soul;*
> *The testimony of the LORD is sure,*
>   *making wise the simple; . . .*
> *The commandment of the LORD is pure,*
>   *enlightening the eyes;*
> *The fear of the LORD is clean, enduring forever; . . .*
> *More to be desired are they than gold,*
>   *Yea, than much fine gold;*
> <u>*Sweeter also than honey and the honeycomb*</u>.
>   *(Psalm 19: 7-10).*

Even today, the ancient sages' teachings are still of benefit in searching for Bible truth.

> The Master said, "A son of the Prince, extensively studying all learning, and keeping himself under the restraint of the rules of the law, may thus likewise not overstep what is right."[7]

"**Extensively studying all learning**"—for those who make the Bible their textbook, this could mean that one should study the whole Bible without preference to either the Old or the New Testament. These are inseparable. The history of the birth, life, death and resurrection of Jesus as the Son of God in the New Testament cannot be fully understood without the multiple prophetic evidences of Him contained in the Old Testament. In order to appreciate it, the plan of redemption from the foundation of the world must be thoroughly understood. The miracles of Jesus are a proof of His divinity, but the strongest evidences that He is the world's Redeemer are found in the prophecies of the Old Testament compared with their fulfillment in the New.

Jesus said to the Jews, *"Search the Scriptures; for in them you think you have eternal life; and these are they which testify of Me."* (John 5: 39).

In Jesus' day, there was no other Scripture in existence, save that of the Old Testament, so the injunction of the Savior is plain.

In order to **"not overstep what is right,"** one must **"keep himself under the restraint of the rules of the law."** When our sin is pardoned, we will want to keep His law, not because we want to be saved by our own works, but because we are saved by the grace of Jesus. We will not want to **"overstep what is right,"** committing sin again. When the standard of righteousness is kept in view, we will see how far we have fallen short of God's requirement, and how great is His grace to forgive our sin. We may be always grateful for Jesus' abundant grace.

> The Master said, "If a man keeps refreshing his old knowledge, he will gain new insights and may be a teacher of others."[8]

The Master said, "Learn as if you could not reach your object, and were always fearing also lest you should lose it."[9]

In every age there is new development of truth: messages of God to the people of that generation. Old truths are essential. New truth is not independent of the old, but an expansion of it. Only by understanding the old truths can we comprehend the new. To be an ardent searcher of truth, one must not be satisfied, but diligently seek new light. Just before he was put to death for his faith, the apostle Paul told of his own experience in following the teachings of Jesus:

> <u>Not that I have already attained</u>, or am already perfected; but <u>I press on</u>, that I may lay hold of that for which Christ Jesus has also laid hold of me. Brethren, I do not count myself to have apprehended; but one thing I do, <u>forgetting those things which are behind and reaching forward</u> to those things which are ahead, I press toward the goal for the prize of the upward call of God in Christ Jesus. (Philippians 3: 12 - 14).

In giving the warning to those who think that once they are saved, they are always saved, Paul urged them to be watchful lest they should fall and be cast away: *"Therefore let him who thinks he stands take heed lest he fall."* (1 Corinthians 10: 12).

> *Therefore I run thus: not with uncertainty. Thus I fight: not as one who beats the air. But I discipline my body and bring it into subjection, lest, when I have preached to others, I myself should become disqualified.*
> *(1 Corinthians 9: 26, 27).*

The Master said, "Is it not pleasant to learn with a constant perseverance and application?"[9]

To hear and learn without practicing what one has learned is useless.

Practice deepens what we have learned and changes our thoughts and characters.

> *For not the hearers of the law are just in the sight of God, but the doer of the law will be justified.*
> *(Romans 2: 13).*

> *For if anyone is a hearer of the word and not a doer, he is like a man observing his natural face in a mirror; for he observes himself, goes away, and immediately forgets what kind of man he was. But he who looks into the perfect law of liberty and continues in it, and is not a forgetful hearer but a doer of the work, this one will be blessed in what he does.*
> *(James 1: 23 - 25).*

We need to practice what we believe, for our faith in the truth needs to be shown in our deeds. This counsel given by James, the brother of Jesus, is still applicable today:

> *But someone will say, "You have faith, and I have works." Show me your faith without your works, and I will show you my faith by my works. You believe that there is one God. You do well. Even the demons believe—and tremble! But do you want to know, <u>O foolish man, that faith without works is dead</u>?*
> *(James 2: 18 - 20).*

The Master said, "Learning without thought is labor lost; thought without learning is perilous."[11]

Human thought alone is powerless, for it is imperfect. Human thought alone will never find a solution to the problem of sin. It is through learning from our Creator-God that we may have power. If we meditate upon what we learn from the Bible, we will be filled with God's fullness.

> *That he would grant you, according to the riches of His glory, to be strengthened with might through His Spirit in the inner man, that Christ may dwell in your hearts through faith; that you, <u>being rooted and grounded in love, may be able to comprehend with all the saints what is the width and length and depth and height</u>—to know the love of Christ which passes knowledge; that you may be filled with all the fullness of God.*
> *(Ephesians 3: 16 - 19).*

Meditation upon holy things will elevate and refine the mind, and develop us into **"sons of the Prince."** There is a practice of meditation in the school of Confucianism: namely sitting silently. That is totally different from mystical eastern meditation. What Confucius taught was for one to meditate upon what one has learned about the *Dao*. Eastern, mystical meditation is a counterfeit of genuine meditation. The Bible speaks of meditation. King David wrote:

> *Oh, how I love <u>Your law! It is my meditation all the day</u>.*
> *You, through Your commandments,*
>   *make me wiser than my enemies;*
> *For they are ever with me.*
> *I have more understanding than all my teachers.*
> <u>*For Your testimonies are my meditation.*</u>
> *I understand more than the ancients,*
>   *because I keep Your precepts.*
> *I have restrained my feet from every evil way,*
> *That I may keep Your word. (Psalm 119: 97 - 101).*

- Biblical meditation is to contemplate on a personal, powerful, loving Creator-God of the universe; false meditation is to see the "god" within oneself, or meditate on the image or idols created by human hands.

- Biblical meditation is to meditate upon the word of God and His wonderful creation of nature, His Providence in one's life and the character of God as manifested through all these; the false is to meditate through sound vibration, secret mantras, codes, or so-called "inner light."

- In genuine meditation, the mind is filled and surrendered to the will of God; in false meditation the mind is emptied, and thus the devil can capture it.
- Genuine meditation is to seek for a new mind and heart (second birth) without any imperfection; false meditation is to clear "dust" from the old mind.
- Genuine meditation is aimed at an intimate relationship with God; the false is to awaken the "dormant inner consciousness."
- Genuine meditation is to find peace with God through Christ; the false aims at reaching peace with oneself, or having peace with God by self-effort.

By disciplining the mind to dwell upon heavenly things, we can increase in *"the knowledge of the Son of God, to a perfect man, to the measure of the stature of the fullness of Christ." (Ephesians 4: 13)*.

There are other good lessons that we can learn from the Chinese sages. For example:

> **The Master said, "To tell, as we go along, what we have heard on the way, is the enemy of attaining virtues."**[12]

If we want to know what is truth, we must search carefully for ourselves that we may gain this knowledge personally. We cannot put our trust in what we hear alone; we must search the Scriptures for ourselves and compare what we hear with the Scripture, so that we are not led astray. <u>There are all kinds of doctrines in our world, but there is only one truth</u>. There is no earthly treasure attainable without painstaking effort. Why should we expect to understand the treasures of the Word of God without diligently searching the Scripture? Jesus said,

> *"Search the Scriptures; for in them you think*
> *you have eternal life;*
> *and these are they which testify of Me." (John 5: 39)*.

This instruction we need to take to heart today.

> The Master said, "The study of strange doctrines is injurious indeed!"[13]

It seems that never a month goes by but that we hear of some strange, new cult. These may be easily tried for truthful content simply by applying this test: *"To the law and to the testimony! If they do not speak according to this word, it is because there is no light in them."* (Isaiah 8: 20). What does the Bible say? Does the doctrine agree with Bible teachings? We must not regard the interpretation of men, but look to the Bible for the real truth! The Bible must be its own interpreter.

> *For precept must be upon precept,*
> *precept upon precept,*
> *Line upon line, line upon line,*
> *Here a little, there a little.*
> *(Isaiah 28: 10).*

> Mencius said, "Confucius ascended the eastern hill, and Lu (鲁) appeared to him small. He ascended to the Tai (泰) mountain, and all beneath the skies appeared to him small. So he who has contemplated the sea, finds it difficult to think anything of other waters, and he who has walked into the gate of the sage, finds it difficult to be interested in the words of others."[14]

When we really learn of Jesus, the Holy Man, we will lose interest in speculative human theories and fables. Through the study of the Bible, we will have a close communication with God. Every truth discovered in the Word tells new aspects of God's character. The will of God will be clearly seen, and human theories will be set aside.

The Way of Prayer

Human life is dependent on God's love and mercy for its existence and development. By means of prayer, man can call upon Heaven for help, especially in one's distress. Note what the greatest Chinese historian, Xi Ma Qian had to say about this:

> **From Heaven man derives his beginning; from his parents he grows as from roots. When a man is brought to extremity, he turns back to his roots, and thus it is that when men are embittered and worn out, afflicted, and grieved, we hear them always calling on their parents.**[15]

The ancient Chinese often prayed to Heaven in the form of praise or thanksgiving, asking for blessings for a good harvest, confessing sins, or for other needs. All are recorded in the ancient writings, as shown from the following examples:

- Prayer of praise:
  > **Great is God,**
  > **Beholding this lower world in majesty,**
  > **He surveyed the four quarters of the kingdom,**
  > **Seeking for someone to give**
  > **settlement to the people.**[16]

- Prayer of worship:
  > **I have brought my offerings,**
  > **A ram and a bull.**
  > **May Heaven accept them!**[17]

- Prayer of confession by a ruler [King Tang]:
  > **Throughout all the states that enter on a new life under me, do not, ye princes, follow lawless ways; make no approach to insolent dissoluteness; let every one observe to keep His statutes: so that we may receive the favor of Heaven. The good in you, I will not dare to conceal; and for the evil in me, I will not dare to forgive myself; I will examine these things in harmony with the mind of God [Shangdi]. When guilt is found anywhere in you who occupy the myriad regions, it must rest on me. When guilt**

is found in me, the one man, it will not attach to you who occupy the myriad regions. Oh! let us attain to be sincere in these things, and so we shall likewise have a happy consummation.[18]

- Prayer for the blessing of Heaven:
  Dwelling in the new city, let the king now sedulously cultivate the virtue of reverence. When he is all devoted to this virtue, he may pray to Heaven for a long abiding decree in his favor.[19]

- Appeal to Heaven for justice:
  The mass of the people were gradually affected by this state of things, and became dark and disorderly. Their hearts were no more set on good faith, but they violated their oaths and covenants. The multitudes who suffered from the oppressive terrors, and were in danger of being murdered, declared their innocence to Heaven. God surveyed the people, and there was no fragrance of virtue arising from them, but the rank odor of their cruel punishments.[20]

It is most interesting to note that Confucius was a man of prayer!

> **The Master being very sick, Zi Lu asked leave to pray for him.**
> **He said, "May such a thing be done?"**
> **Zi Lu replied, "It may. In the Eulogies it is said, 'Prayer has been made for thee to the God of Heaven and earth.'"**
> **The Master said, "My prayer has been for a long time."**[21]

We have previously mentioned many times that Confucius was a worshiper of Heaven. He knew his mission, that of a "transmitter," was given by Heaven, and that it was protected by Heaven. From his own mouth here, we read that Confucius was a man of prayer.

There are two kinds of prayers: the prayer of form, and the prayer of faith. The former is repetition of set, customary phrases—formal prayer. Nowhere do we find Confucius' disciples recording his formal prayers. His prayers must have been of the second type—prayers of faith, shown by sincere thoughts, and faithful deeds in following the will of Heaven. The prayer of faith reaches the throne of God. Confucius also taught that if one knew he was acting against the will of Heaven, his prayer was useless. He said:

> **He who offends against Heaven has none to whom he can pray.** [22]

God provides pardon for sins of ignorance, but not for deliberate stubbornness. Even sin against Christ can be forgiven if committed in ignorance and there is true repentance. But if one continues to be deaf to warnings against sins, and the working of the Holy Spirit in the heart, he faces committing the unpardonable sin against Heaven.

While prayers to Heaven from the kings, as well as from common people, have been found in the writings of ancient China, no direct teaching on the subject of praying to God is found. The Bible is different. In it is much instruction concerning prayer. Jesus Christ was a Man of prayer and therefore a Teacher and Example for us.

The highest form of prayer is communion as friend to Friend. We are not informing God of anything concerning ourselves, since He knows all. Prayer is a way of lifting us up to God's throne, rather than bringing Him down to our level. It is not necessary for us to move God by our tears, as if God has a cold heart. Rather His love and influence, through prayer, molds our hearts and changes our attitudes. Prayer brings us close to God so that we may enter into His will and plan.

Jesus' disciples noticed that their Master spent much time in prayer to His Heavenly Father. They requested that He teach them how to pray.

Jesus said to them:

> *"And when you pray, you shall not be like the hypocrites. For they love to pray standing in the synagogues and on the corners of the streets, that they may be seen by men. Assuredly, I say to you, they have their reward. But you, when you pray, go into your room, and when you have shut your door, pray to your Father who is in the secret place; and your Father who sees in secret will reward you openly. And when you pray, do not use vain repetitions as the heathen do. For they think that they will be heard for their many words. Therefore do not be like them. For your Father knows the things you have need of before you ask Him." (Matthew 6: 5 - 8).*

The Jesus gave an ideal prayer for them, and for us:

> *" In this manner, therefore, pray:*
>   *'Our Father in heaven, Hallowed be Your name.*
>   *Your kingdom come. Your will be done*
>   *On earth as it is in heaven.*
>   *Give us this day our daily bread.*
>   *And forgive us our debts,*
>   *As we forgive our debtors.*
>   *And do not lead us into temptation,*
>   *But deliver us from the evil one.*
> *For Yours is the kingdom and the power*
> *and the glory forever. Amen.'*
> *For if you forgive men their trespasses, your heavenly Father will also forgive you. But if you do not forgive men their trespasses, neither will your Father forgive your trespasses." (Matthew 6: 9 - 15).*

The Lord's prayer was so simple, a child can recite it; yet so profound that the greatest mind can never discover all its meanings. Prayer is an experience that can only be gained through practice.

Heaven is compassionate to the people. What the people desire, Heaven will fulfill.[23]

The ancient Chinese prayed to Heaven because they believed that Heaven heard and answered their prayers. Jesus assured His followers:

Most assuredly I say to you, whatever you ask the Father in My name He will give you. (John 16: 23).

What a wonderful promise this is! As with all of God's promises, this one also is conditional. The Bible reveals how our prayers may be answered, and how we may receive things that we ask for. First we must feel our need of help from God. The heart must be open to the Spirit's influence, or else God's blessing cannot be received. The prayer of the sincere, penitent soul is always accepted.

Secondly, we must pray in faith. Jesus said, *"Whatever things you ask when you pray, believe that you receive them, and you will have them." (Mark 11: 24).* But to claim that prayers will always be answered in the way that we desire is presumption. God does not err, He answers according to what is best for us.

Thirdly, we must persevere in prayer. This will cause our faith to grow.

Be anxious for nothing, but in everything by prayer and supplication, with thanksgiving, let your requests be made known to God, and the peace of God, which surpasses all understanding, will guard your hearts and minds through Christ Jesus. (Philippians 4: 6, 7).

17

The Temple of Heaven

> Someone asked the meaning of the Great Sacrifice. The Master said, "I do not know. He who knows its meaning would find it as easy to govern the kingdom as to look on this."—pointing to his palm.[1]

In the last chapter, we found that the ancient Chinese were a people of prayer. The prayers to Heaven were usually offered on a mountain, at an altar, or in a temple.

Today's visitors to China have probably walked through the famous Temple of Heaven park in Beijing(北京天坛公园), which is twice as large as the Imperial Palace. There are three edifices in the complex: the Temple for Good Harvests, the Imperial Vault, and the Altar of Heaven—the first built in 1420 A.D. Through the years, Chinese emperors came here to worship and offer a bull sacrifice to Shangdi, the God of Heaven. In 1911, Dr. Sun Yat Sen (孙逸仙, 1866 - 1925) founded the Republic of China, and the last emperor was deposed. This forever ended the great 4,000-year-old Border Sacrifice.

The tradition of worshiping and offering sacrifices to Shangdi dates back to the very beginnings of China's history. Even before the first dynasty, during the "Legendary Period of Five Rulers," the last of these rulers, Shun, **"sacrificed to Shangdi."**[2]

Confucius, himself, climbed Mount Tai's hundreds of steps and observed the ceremony at the ancient altar there. He made many references to the "Great Sacrifice," or the "Border Sacrifice" (郊祭). Since childhood, he had been fascinated with the ceremonies, the vessels, and the animal sacrifice. But he did not understand its significance and it became a mystery that he tried to solve his entire life. In fact, Confucius traveled through the various states collecting descriptions of the ceremony, but was unable to solve the enigma which, indeed, has remained a mystery also for the Chinese ever since. What was the meaning of the ancient "Border Sacrifice?" Where and how did it originate? Why was this rite conducted for over 4,000 years in China?

In the book, *Li Ji*, there are several chapters that specifically deal with sacrifices. The one offered to God is called the "Border Sacrifice," and its purpose, as described, is as follows:

> **Heaven gave the pattern and the Holy Man followed it. <u>The Border Sacrifice is to manifest the Dao of Heaven</u>.**[3]

> **By the ceremonies of sacrifices to Heaven and earth, they serve God.**[4]

According to *Li Ji*, the ceremonies of sacrifices to Heaven were offered at the winter solstice in the southern suburb of the imperial city. Its original purpose was to demonstrate the Dao of Heaven, and was a way to serve God and God only. Sadly, its real meaning was lost in the course of time. Sun and moon worship was later mixed into the Border Sacrifice. Why was the sacrifice to be conducted outside the imperial city? The answer is not recorded in the Chinese Classics. However, by examining the ancient, pictographic

Chinese character-writing, as well as the Bible, we can solve this riddle.

The first animal sacrifice in earth's history was performed *outside* of the Garden of Eden when God introduced the rite to Adam and Eve. They had been expelled from the garden for their disobedience in eating from the forbidden tree, as previously mentioned (pp. 15, 16, 82, 83).

> *So He [God] drove out the man; and He placed cherubim at the east of the garden of Eden, and a flaming sword which turned every way to guard the way to the tree of life. (Genesis 3: 24).*

The Serpent (Satan) had tempted Eve by promising that the forbidden fruit would make them like God, but instead they lost their original glorious God-likeness and became naked. Hastily they had sewed fig leaves together to cover themselves. After the LORD expelled them from Eden, *"the LORD God made tunics of skin, and clothed them." (Genesis 3: 21).* The use of skins, of course, indicated the death of animals—the first death on the lovely newly-created earth. This first sacrifice of animals represented Jesus Christ, the *"Lamb slain from the foundation of the world," (Revelation 13: 8),* whose eventual death would symbolically provide a "garment of salvation" for sinners.

According to the ancient pictographic Chinese characters, there was a *gate* 門 at Eden's border, a *barrier* 閑 which prevented the couple from taking and eating fruit from the *tree* 木 of life. With no access to this tree, God thereby prevented them from living forever and becoming immortal sinners. How interesting that the ancient Chinese drew a tree inside the gate to represent a *barrier* 閑 ! Furthermore, it was at this gate where God's presence was manifest in *fiery* 閃 glory, for again we find a *fire* 火 at the *gate* 門.[5] Repeatedly God said, in after years, to His ancient people:

> *"I will speak with you... from between the two cherubim." (Exodus 25: 22).*

203

We have just learned that there were cherubim [angels] at the "east of the garden of Eden." God's presence must have been there to commune with Adam and Eve.

> *Give ear...You [God] who dwell between the cherubim, shine forth! (Psalm 80: 1).*

God's glorious presence shone forth from between the two angel-cherubim. Here man could communicate with God, for again, according to the Chinese writing, Adam and his descendants must have come to the gate *to ask* 問 of God, as a *mouth* 口 for speaking is pictured. Also they came *to listen* 聞 with the *ear* 耳 at the *gate* 門.[6]

We have previously quoted Confucius' words:

If a man in the morning hear the Dao, he may die in the evening without regret.[7]

The Chinese words for "hear the Dao" are 聞道, in which the above character for "listen" is used.

It was to this *border* 囿, the gate of Eden, that Adam's son, Abel, later made his offering:

> *Abel also brought of the firstborn of his flock and of their fat. And the LORD respected Abel and his offering.*
> *(Genesis 4: 4).*

The older brother, Cain, brought an offering of fruit, but this was not acceptable, since only the death of an animal was symbolic of the future death of Jesus for the sins of the world. Consumed by jealousy and rebellion, Cain became angry and killed his brother, Abel. After being rebuked for the evil deed by the LORD, it is said that, without remorse,

> *Then Cain <u>went out from the presence of the LORD</u>....*
> *(Genesis 4: 16).*

He left the place where Abel's sacrifice had taken place before God's presence at the gate, the *border* 囲 of the garden. (For a complete, meaningful analysis of the most ancient forms of this character, see the chapter note).[8] That the "border of Eden" is the original reference for the "Border Sacrifice" becomes even more clear after examining *Hebrews 13: 12:*

> *Therefore Jesus also, that He might sanctify the people with His own blood, <u>suffered outside the gate</u>.*

When Jesus was crucified, He was taken outside the gate of the holy city, Jerusalem, to the hill of Golgotha where He suffered and died. This was actually a fulfillment ["antitype"] of the ancient prophetic promise ["type"], symbolized by the "border sacrifices" through the ages. Jerusalem was in turn the "antitypical fulfillment" of the Garden of Eden "type." So, we find that the crucifixion of Jesus outside the gate of Jerusalem was the BORDER SACRIFICE to which all previous and later sacrifices pointed!

The earliest Chinese sacrifice to God is found in the *Book of Huai Nan Zi* (《淮南子》), written in the 2nd century B.C., where Nu-Wa was said to **"patch together azure skies."** In Chapter 2 (p. 16, 17) we mentioned briefly how Noah [Nu-wa] **"fused together stones"** to build an altar on which to offer his sacrifices. In turn, God set a rainbow **"of five colors,"** promising there would never be another world-wide flood.[9] <u>This is the first Chinese legend suggesting a sacrifice to God.</u>

The tradition of animal sacrifice, however, came down through the centuries. We read in the *Book of Documents* that King Shun (before 2205 B.C.) sacrificed to God.

> **Thereafter, he sacrificed specially, but with the ordinary forms, to God.**[10]

We have noted, in some detail, the hidden Chinese explanation of the "Great Sacrifice," as well as the Biblical record. Now, let us see how God prepared the Hebrew people for the coming of the Holy Man, Jesus Christ, who would actually give His life in sacrifice as an atonement for sin.

After God's people, the Israelites—over one million in number, had been rescued from years of Egyptian slavery by a series of miracles, God led them, through Moses (c. 1525 - 1405 B.C.), to the Sinai wilderness where they encamped. It was there, as already noted (pp. 132), that God announced, from Mount Sinai, His holy law and afterward inscribed it with His own finger on tables of stone. After their prolonged sojourn in Egypt, the Hebrews had nearly forgotten their God. Therefore, He wanted to restore this knowledge among them, telling Moses:

> *"And let them make Me a sanctuary, that I may dwell among them."* *(Exodus 25: 8).*

A "sanctuary" is a sacred edifice for the worship of God. Recall a quote from the Chinese writings that we discussed a little earlier. Confucius said:

> **<u>Heaven gave the pattern and the sage followed it.</u>**
> **The Border Sacrifice is to manifest the Dao of Heaven.**[3]

The ancient Chinese recorded that a pattern for the Border Sacrifice service had been given to them by Heaven, yet this had been lost. Moses also received a "pattern" from God for a sanctuary, the details of which are recorded in the Bible. God said to Moses,

> *"And see to it that you make them <u>according to the pattern</u> which was shown you on the mountain."*
> *(Exodus 25: 40).*

The plan that Moses received was for a small, portable, tent-like tabernacle. It consisted of two beautiful apartments, set in an enclosed courtyard in the very center of their encampment. God was the architect who directed each meaningful detail. The ceremonies conducted there by the appointed priests, were to demonstrate the whole Plan of Salvation.

Each of the furnishings in the first apartment: the bread of Presence, the golden candles, the altar of incense, were all symbolic of the coming Messiah. The second, square, Most Holy place apartment, housed the golden chest that contained God's law written on tables of stone. The top of the golden chest ["ark of the covenant"] was the "mercy seat" representing God's throne. At either end of the mercy seat stood golden cherubim with outstretched wings, and from between them the glory of God's very presence shone out.

A sinner must bring an unblemished lamb (representing the Savior to come) into the outer courtyard. There, outside of the sanctuary, he confessed his sins over the lamb, and then with his own hand, slew the animal. The officiating priest then collected into a vessel the flowing blood from the sacrifice. Carrying the blood into the sanctuary, the priest sprinkled it on the altar of incense and the heavy veil that separated the two apartments, being drawn before the ark of the covenant. The sin was thereby transferred into the sanctuary by the "sin-laden" blood of the sacrifice that was sprinkled before the broken law of God in the golden ark. This heavy, embroidered veil on which the blood of the sacrifice was sprinkled also represented Jesus Christ who stood between the sinner and God's broken law, as we shall shortly learn.

Hundreds of years passed since the tabernacle was built during Moses' day. When King David came to reign about 1011 B.C., the original sanctuary must have been quite dilapidated with its more than 400 years of exposure to the elements. Therefore, David announced to his people:

> *"I had it in my heart to build a house of rest for the ark of the covenant of the LORD, and for the footstool of our God, and had made preparations to build it. But God said to me, 'You shall not build a house for My name, because you have been a man of war and have shed blood.'"* (1 Chronicles 28: 2, 3).

Instead, God chose Solomon, David's son, to build Him a temple. The construction of the large, permanent, beautiful temple, patterned after the wilderness tabernacle, took seven years to complete (1 Kings 6: 37 - 38). The golden ark containing the ten commandments written on two tables of stone by God's own finger, was the central focus. Two golden cherubim with touching outstretched wings stood at either end of the mercy seat.

It has been Satan's designed scheme to mislead men and women by separating God's mercy from His justice. It was Satan's accusation that God could not be a God of mercy and of justice simultaneously. Prior to the cross, the devil, through the legalism of the Jewish nation, portrayed God as a judge without mercy. After Jesus died on the cross, through misinterpretation of God's saving grace as understood in much of Christendom, another deception arose—that God's mercy had done away with His law. <u>But mercy and justice, the gospel and the law, are forever linked together, as shown in the sanctuary.</u>

> *Righteousness and justice are*
> *the foundation of Your throne.*
> *Mercy and truth go before Your face.*
> *(Psalm 89: 14).*

Although the original meaning of the Border Sacrifice was lost, and not many details of the services were recorded, yet one thing remained certain: <u>blood had to be shed</u>.[11] The blood, in the Chinese ceremony, came from animals, never from a human sacrifice, as found in some satanic religions.

The bull is used as the sacrificial animal in the Border Sacrifice.[12]

In the *Confucian Analects* an interesting conversation was recorded concerning the sacrifice of an animal:

> Zi Gong wished to do away with the offering of a sheep connected with the inauguration of the first day of each month. The Master said: "Chi [Zi Gong], you love the sheep; I love the ceremony."[13]

The Temple of Heaven

Zi Gong wanted to perform the service without a sheep, but Confucius sensed that there could be no ceremony without the sacrifice of an animal. He did not know, however, that the lamb represented the suffering Holy Man, nor the real import of the sacrifice.

The sanctuary service in Israel consisted of daily sacrifices and sacrifices made on the Day of Atonement. Outside the sanctuary in the court yard, stood the altar of burnt offering. Each morning a lamb was offered for the nation. This was slowly consumed by the fire on the altar. In the evening, another lamb was offered that was to burn until the morning offering was ready. Thus there was always a sacrifice on the altar, day and night—symbolizing the perpetual atonement provided in Christ for the whole world. On the seventh day Sabbath this offering was doubled.

The temple and the temple service constituted a wonderful object lesson for Israel. It was intended to demonstrate man's sinfulness, God's holiness, and the way to God. A chief lesson of the sacrificial system was to teach both the priests and the people to abhor and shun sin—which is the transgression of God's law (1 John 3:4). Through the killing of the animals, they must learn that sin means death. God also wanted to impress upon Israel that forgiveness of sin can be obtained only through confession and the ministration of blood. It costs something to forgive, and the cost is life, even the life of the Son of God.

The Jews were proud of their later, second temple for its splendor. It was still being used in the time of Christ, and was then being refurbished by Herod the Great. It was Jesus Christ whose presence in the second temple made it glorious, even superior to the former temple erected by Solomon and destroyed by the Babylonians. One of Christ's disciples marveled at its beauty, remarking to Him,

> *"Teacher, see what manner of stones and what buildings are here!"*

> *And Jesus answered and said to him,*
> *"Do you see these great buildings?*
> *Not one stone shall be left upon another,*
> *that shall not be thrown down." (Mark 13: 1, 2).*

Jesus here prophesied of the burning of the temple and the destruction of Jerusalem in 70 A.D., about 40 years after His crucifixion and death. When the Jewish nation rejected Jesus as their Messiah, the temple had no more meaning, *"for the glory has departed from Israel." (1 Samuel 4: 21)*. At the very moment of Jesus' death, something *important* happened in the temple.

> *Jesus cried out again with a loud voice, and yielded up*
> *His spirit. Then, behold, the <u>veil of the temple was torn</u>*
> *<u>in two from top to bottom</u>.*
> *(Matthew 27: 50, 51).*

Christ, the Veil (p. 212), the real Lamb of God, had been offered for the sin of the world; type had met the antitype; the shadow had met the body. The Border Sacrifice as well as Israel's temple, *"which are a shadow of things to come; but the body is of Christ," (Colossians 2: 17),* had forever become history. The Mosaic ceremonial law of sacrifices pointing to the coming Messiah had accomplished its mission and was abolished at the cross. Never again were animal offerings needed.

How can one approach God today? What offering should one bring to God? Is it necessary to build another temple? Where should God meet His people today? Even Confucius asked these questions 2,500 years ago:

> **Someone asked the meaning of the great sacrifice.**
> **The Master said, "I do not know. He who knows its**
> **meaning would find it as easy to govern the king-**
> **dom as to look on this."—pointing to his palm.**[1]

No man has all the answers concerning the temple of Heaven, or the worship of God. But with the word of God and the help of the Holy Spirit, one can understand more and more.

Paul talked about the type of offering for today when he said:

> *I beseech you therefore, brethren, by the mercies of God, that you present your bodies a living sacrifice, holy, acceptable to God, which is your reasonable service."*
> *(Romans 12 :1).*

Through the blood of Christ, we, who were sinners before, are now a royal priesthood, a holy nation. Said the apostle Peter:

> *But you are a chosen generation, a royal priesthood, a holy nation, His own special people, that you may proclaim the praises of Him who called you out of darkness into His marvelous light; who once were not a people but are now the people of God, who had not obtained mercy but now have obtained mercy.*
> *(1 Peter 2: 9, 10).*

Never more is there need to build another temple for God, because

> *You are the temple of the living God.*
> *As God has said:*
> *"I will dwell in them and walk among them.*
> *I will be their God,*
> *And they shall be My people." (2 Corinthians 6: 16).*

The church of Christ, which consists of His people, is the earthly sanctuary today, and Jesus Himself is the cornerstone. *(1 Peter 2: 4).*

> *But the hour is coming, and now is, when the true worshipers will worship the Father in spirit and truth; for the Father is seeking such to worship Him. God is Spirit, and those who worship Him must <u>worship in Spirit and truth</u>. (John 4: 23 - 24).*

Yet there is benefit by studying the deep meanings of the ancient sanctuary service. In it is found not only the way of Christ, but the way of being a Christian as well. The confession and washing before entering the first apartment of God's temple represented the experience of baptism. The service in the first apartment (the holy place) symbolized justification by faith, the forgiveness of sin. The second apartment (the Most Holy) represented sanctification by faith. The study of the sanctuary will prove to be a rich blessing to enhance the understanding of the Gospel of Christ.

Christ has entered the real sanctuary in Heaven, after which the earthly sanctuary was modeled, and become the High Priest. In Christ, there is no more veil separating the people from God.

> *Therefore, brethren, having boldness to enter the Holiest by the blood of Jesus, <u>by a new and living way</u> which He consecrated for us, through the veil, that is, His flesh, and having a High Priest over the house of God, let us draw near with a true heart in full assurance of faith, having our hearts sprinkled from an evil conscience and our bodies washed with pure water. Let us hold fast the confession of our hope without wavering, for He who promised is faithful. (Hebrews 10: 19 - 23).*

Through the blood of Christ, the widely opened door of sin will be closed forever; through the grace of Christ, the closed gate of Eden, where the Border Sacrifice was offered for ages, will be opened again forever.

> *Blessed are those who do His commandments, that they may have the right to the tree of life, and may enter through the gates into the city. (Revelation 22: 14).*

18

The First Truth and the First Deception

> Zi Lu asked about serving the spirits of the dead. The Master said, "While you are not able to serve men, how can you serve their spirits?"
> Zi Lu added, "I venture to ask about death." He was answered, "While you do not understand life, how can you know about death?"[1]

To be or not to be: that is the question."[2] The subject of life and death has been an intriguing topic through all time, and remains such for each of us today, since all inescapably face it. Where does life come from? Where does it go? Why does man die, and what happens to the dead? Is there life after death? Do the dead know anything? Who am I? Do I consist of just a body, or of both body and soul? Is the soul immortal? What are the chances of having eternal life, and if so, how does one obtain it?

For many, life seems unfair. One is not born according to one's own will. Most want to live, but have to die because that seems to be the fate of natural man. Some are born with disease or handicap; others die young when they desperately want to live. Where is freedom of choice in one's birth? If God is love and just, where is His justice if one cannot choose whether or not to be born into a life of suffering? Where is God's love when we are doomed to die? Many reject the idea of God because of the apparent injustice and sorrow in life. How can an intelligent and loving God allow this? To their logical reasoning, the reality of death does not match with a good and fair God. The question of life and death is therefore set aside as unanswerable.

These are important questions and deserve studied answers.

Through the ages, innumerable theories concerning life and death have been devised, yet the answer remains a mystery. Confucius, the great thinker, was a sincere worshiper of Heaven, but was also puzzled by this mystery. Without having the right answers, Confucius, however, pointed to a proper approach. For him, the answers to life and death could not be separated. To understand one, was to understand the other. In order to understand death, one must first understand life. In his commentary to the *Yi Jing*, Confucius said:

> **Going back to the beginning of things
> and pursuing them to the end,
> we come to know the lessons of
> life and of death.**[3]

Unfortunately, the records concerning "the beginning of things" were lost—possibly even during Confucius' time. Once again, we must come to the Bible for light. In fact, the "first truth" and the "first deception" coming to man were both on the subject of "to be or not to be." All human theories on this subject find their roots here. So, as Confucius advised, we must go back to "the beginning" and first learn of what man himself consists.

> *And the* LORD *God formed man of the dust
> of the ground, and breathed
> into his nostrils the breath of life; and man
> became a living being [soul, KJV]. (Genesis 2: 7).*

According to the Bible, man did not evolve from any earlier form of life, but was "formed" directly by God. <u>Man is simply "dust" plus "breath of life."</u> The dust man became a being [soul] when the "breath of life" was breathed into his nostrils [see Chapter 7]. The Bible tells us that a man is a *"living soul."* It is the breath of God that gives life to the dustman. God did not breathe into the dustman an "immortal soul," and the soul did not exist before the dustman was formed, therefore he is simply a combination of the dust and the life-spirit given by God. It is the Spirit of God that makes the dustman to will and to think. Without the Spirit of God, dust is dust.

God's first lesson for man was a command, *"Of every tree of the garden you may freely eat; but of the tree of the knowledge of good and evil you shall not eat, for in the day that you eat of it you shall surely die." (Genesis 2: 16, 17).*

It should be understood that God desires all to live, but He gave a warning of the severe consequences of disobedience. When God said, *"You shall surely die,"* He meant the whole man [soul] shall surely die. Disobedience of God's commandment is sin, and *"the wages of sin is death." (Romans 6: 23).* Likewise, *"the soul [man] who sins shall die." (Ezekiel 18: 20).*

Jesus, Himself, made it clear, there is no immortal "soul."

> *"And do not fear those who kill the body but cannot kill the soul. But rather fear Him who is able to destroy both soul and body in hell." (Matthew 10: 28).*

Even before Eve was created, God had warned Adam not to eat of the forbidden tree. If man obeyed God's first command, he would live; if he disobeyed, he would lose his life. This was the first truth man received from God.

The Chinese character for "life" is, interestingly, the same word as "commandment" 命 [4] This word often carries the meaning of the "commandment of Heaven," as used in the earliest Chinese Classics. Why should the Chinese view the commandment of Heaven as life? Notice also what Jesus said;

"And I know that His [the Father-God's] command is everlasting life." (John 12: 50).

All power and life are in the command of God. When the world was created, God simply spoke it into being.

> *By the word of the LORD*
> *the heavens were made,*
> *And all the host of them*
> *by the breath of His mouth.* . . .
>
> *For He spoke, and it was done;*
> *He commanded, and it stood fast.*
> *(Psalm 33: 6, 9).*

When Adam and Eve chose to disobey God's command, they sinned and cut themselves off from the source of life. Death was the unavoidable result. Following Adam's disobedience, God announced:

> *In the sweat of your face you shall eat bread*
> *Till you return to the ground,*
> *For out of it you were taken;*
> <u>*For dust you are, and to dust you shall return.*</u>
> *(Genesis 3: 19).*

To return to dust is to die. From "to be" to "not to be," from man to dust—that is death. What happened to the "breath of life?" **"Then the dust will return to the earth as it was, and the spirit will return to God who gave it." (Ecclesiastes 12: 7).** The "spirit" mentioned in this verse is the same as the "breath of life." The ancient righteous man, Job, understood that, *"The Spirit of God has made me, and the breath of the Almighty gives me life." (Job 33: 4).* When the "breath of life" is gone, only the dust of man remains. There is no life, no consciousness, no immortality!

How do the Chinese Classics compare with Biblical truth? A famous Chinese philosophy professor, Dr. Wei Zhengtong (韦政通), wrote in his book, *The Wisdom of China* (《中国的智慧》), which quoted from Confucius' contemporary, *Lu's Spring and Autumn* (《吕氏春秋》):

> That which is called death is this:
> he knows nothing and returns to the
> original state before he was created.[5]

Confucius also said in the *Book of Rites,* or the *Li Ji:*

> Every creature will die, and when he dies,
> he returns to dust.[6]
>
> The spirit returns to heaven;
> the body returns to the earth.[7]

The Bible and the ancient Chinese writings are identical! It is of special interest for us to read Dr. Wei's comment on the subject of the "immortal soul," which expresses a typical Chinese belief. "The Chinese philosophers seldom discuss the issue of the 'immortal soul,' and few believe in 'the soul of immortality.' This is mainly due to the influence of Confucius who taught, **'While you are not able to serve men, how can you serve their spirits? While you do not understand life, how can you know about death?'** What he [Confucius] emphasized was that man should try his best in his lifetime and should not pay too much attention to what will happen after death, for it will depend on what he had done before death. This thought has blocked the way for spreading the belief of the 'immortality of the soul.'"[8]

Once again, this Chinese understanding of death gives another proof that they had received the true light from the Source of truth. So, the question is—where did the belief in the "immortality of the soul" arise? This dogma is even widely accepted among many professed Christians. If the teaching is not from God, from whom did it come? We find the answer in the Bible as we listen to the first dialog between the serpent and the woman:

> *Now the serpent was more cunning than any beast of the field which the* LORD *God had made. And he said*

> to the woman, "Has God indeed said, 'You shall not eat of every tree of the garden?'"
> And the woman said to the serpent, "We may eat the fruit of the trees of the garden; but of the fruit of the tree which is in the midst of the garden, God has said, 'You shall not eat it, nor shall you touch it, lest you die.'"
> And the serpent said to the woman, "<u>You will not surely die</u>. For God knows that in the day you eat of it your eyes will be opened, and you will be like God, knowing good and evil." (Genesis 3: 1 - 5).

The first truth [*"in the day that you eat of it you shall surely die,"*] and the first deception [*"You will not surely die"*] were regarding the question of life and death. Satan, God's enemy, was saying that Adam and Eve had natural immortality, and would not die. Their bodies may go back to dust, but their souls are eternal and immortal. If they could not live in their bodies, they would continue to live in the form of the "immortal soul." They would not lose anything. Instead, they would gain knowledge and be like God.

Here lies the origin of all false theories concerning "the soul." One such popular false belief is that of reincarnation—a spiritual form of evolution, as found in Hinduism and Buddhism. These teachings came into China after the first century and corrupted the authentic belief and teachings of the Chinese sages. The origin of this dogma can be traced in the book, *Bhagavad-gita,* which states: "As the embodied soul continuously passes in one's body from childhood to youth to old age, the soul similarly passes into another body at death."[9]

The Hindu belief includes a personal god and reincarnation. On the other hand, in Buddhism, its founder, Gautama Siddhartha (c. 563 - 483 B.C., "Buddha," "Sakyamuni"), could not accept why the personal god of Hinduism did not stop the birth and death cycle. Therefore, he renounced the concept of a god, but kept the dogma of reincarnation, for he believed there was a "soul" in every living entity. The law of karma, reason and effect, was used to explain the unfairness and injustices in life. According to this theory, one's previous life determines how one suffers in this life. He established his primitive Buddhism upon his observation of the sufferings of those around him. Buddha did not understand that suffering is caused by sin. Neither did he know the true God or that the Son of God would become the greatest victim of suffering, and that His death would bring an end to all suffering.

Many take Buddhism as truth, and believe in reincarnation. Yet a closer look at its central assumptions and teachings presents a different picture. According to Buddhism, every living entity originally existed in a state of full and blissful enlightenment, which means that everyone had every truth and light. All Buddhist practices try to bring men and women back to that perfect state. This theoretically would bring an end to all suffering in this "bitter sea of birth and death." However, both Buddha and his disciples failed to tell the exact reason which caused men and women to fall into the suffering cycle of birth and death [reincarnation] in the first place. Buddhism has no answer to what caused the fall originally. The question, therefore, which needs to be answered by all who believe in reincarnation is, how can one be sure that by following the teachings of Buddhism, one can be "liberated" and return to his "original blissful world," never to be reincarnated again? If we fell from perfection once, what guarantees that it will not happen again? Similarly, we might ask, can a doctor really restore a patient's health without knowing the cause of his sickness?

Whether Buddha himself knew the answer or not, we do not know. He did not teach the truth—that man fell because of the deception of Satan and his disobedience to God. Reincarnation is not truth, but rather a theory based on the first deception from Satan.

The Greeks also introduced false beliefs invented first by Socrates (470 - 399 B.C.) and taught by his student, Plato (429 - 347 B.C.). This dogma of an "immortal soul" existing prior to the body, came into the Christian church soon after the death of the apostles. It was believed that the soul could never perish.[10] Socrates was famous for his statement that his knowledge was to know the fact that he knew nothing. What contradicts his own announcement is that he insisted and taught that his reasoning concerning the immortal soul was truth!

To this concept of an "immortal soul" was added an additional man-made idea: those worthy of heaven go directly to heaven after death, while those unworthy go either to a torturing hell, or to an intermediate place called "purgatory"—another non-biblical doctrine. According to *The Convert's Catechism of Catholic Doctrine,* "Purgatory is the state in which those suffer for a time who die guilty of venial sins, or who die without having fully satisfied for the punishment due to their forgiven sins."[11] All of these theories of "immortality of the soul" have originated from the first deception of Satan concerning life and death. It is profitable to recall Mencius' words here:

> **He who has walked into the gate of the sage, finds it difficult to be interested in the words of others.**[12]

Jesus said: *"I am the Truth." (John 14: 6). "For this cause I was born, and for this cause I have come into the world, that I should bear witness to the truth. Everyone who is of the truth hears My voice." (John 18: 37).* Human theory or church organizations have no say as to what is truth, the word of God alone is the authority. Those who follow the *"Truth"* need to put mere man's speculative ideas aside.

The apostle James gave this warning:

> *Brethren, if anyone among you wanders from the truth, and someone turns him back, let him know that he who turns a sinner from the error of his way will save a soul from death and cover a multitude of sins.*
> *(James 5: 19, 20).*

The First Truth and the First Deception

The Bible teaches that immortality is an attribute of God alone: *"[the Lord of lords]* <u>who alone has immortality,</u> *dwelling in unapproachable light, whom no man has seen or can see, to whom be honor and everlasting power." (1 Timothy 6: 16).*

While disobedience brought death, obedience is the only way for receiving the gift of immortality from God. God is willing to give this gift to all men. It is for this reason that Jesus came into the world.

> *God so loved the world that He gave His only begotten Son, that whoever believes in Him <u>should not perish but have everlasting life</u>. (John 3: 16).*

Now, what do the ancient Chinese sages teach about immortality? Or do they teach about the "immortality of the soul" at all? In the book of *Zhuo Zhuang,* the meaning of immortality is discussed.

> **When Mu Shu (穆叔) went to the State of Jing (晋国), Fan Xuanzi (范宣子) met him, and asked the meaning of the saying of the ancients, "They died but were immortal."**
>
> **This may be what the saying intended. I have heard that the highest meaning of it is when there is established [an example of] virtue; the second, when there is established [an example of] successful course; and the third, when there is established [an example of] words. When these examples are not forgotten with length of time, this is what is meant by the saying, "They died but were immortal."**[13]

This is the only famous doctrine on human immortality in ancient China, yet <u>it has nothing to do with "immortality of the soul!"</u> Sadly, after Buddhism came in with its disbelief in the God of Heaven and false concepts of reincarnation, spiritualism became ever more popular in China. Even famous advocates of Confucianism in later generations failed to understand the first lesson of life and death, and began to incorporate this false belief into their philosophy. The "immortal soul" theory became the basis for what is now called "Chinese Culture," which is simply a combination of two God-believing religions [Confucianism and Daoism] with one God-disbelieving religion [Buddhism].

It is true that the ancient Chinese did not understand the gift of eternal life. But God did put a desire in their hearts which only He could fill. Solomon stated:

> *He has made everything beautiful in its time. Also He has put eternity in their hearts, except that no one can find out the work that God does from beginning to end. (Ecclesiastes 3: 11).*

With the clear teaching of the Bible and the fulfillment of Jesus as the Holy Man, according to the predictions in the Chinese Classics, the Chinese can look back at the truth given their ancestors and distinguish truth from error in the false promises of an "immortal soul" offered by Satan in the first deception.

> *And this is the testimony: that God has given us eternal life, and this life is in His Son. He who has the Son has life; he who does not have the Son of God does not have life. (1 John 5: 11, 12).*

This is the GOOD NEWS. This is the GOSPEL: *"whoever believes in Him should not perish but have everlasting life." (John 3: 16).*

But there remain some questions. Is God fair in dooming all men to death because of Adam's fall? The Bible says that the *"wages of sin is death." (Romans 6: 23).* Are there two death penalties for sin, first when man's life ends, and the second a resurrection to be condemned again and suffer the *"second death"* in the *"lake of fire?" (Revelation 21: 8).* If everyone must die, why does the Bible say that Jesus died for everyone?

God has never forced men to serve Him—He gave men free will. But

Adam and Eve misused their freedom, doubted God's love, in spite of the evidences in Eden all about them, and chose to sin against their Maker and best Friend for selfish purposes. Thus death came into the world. But God has never intended that man should die twice for his sin.

The life we are living is, strictly speaking, just a "probationary life"—a chance to choose between God and Satan, good and evil, eternal life and eternal death. We normally call the end of this "probational life" death, but strictly speaking, it may be better called the "end of probation." This is NOT the penalty for sin. What is it then? Let us understand better what "death" is by reading the famous story of Jesus and His friend, Lazarus, who became so sick that his sisters, Martha and Mary, sent word to Jesus, saying:

> *"Lord, behold, he whom You love is sick."*
> *When Jesus heard that, He said, "This sickness is not unto death, but for the glory of God, that the Son of God may be glorified through it."*
> *Now Jesus loved Martha and her sister and Lazarus. So, when He heard that he was sick, He stayed two more days in the place where He was. Then after this He said to the disciples, "Let us go to Judea again. . . ." and after that He said to them, "Our friend Lazarus sleeps, but I go that I may wake him up."*
> *Then His disciples said, "Lord, if he sleeps he will get well."*
> *However, Jesus spoke of his death, but they thought that He was speaking about taking rest in sleep. Then Jesus said to them plainly, "Lazarus is dead. And I am glad for your sakes that I was not there, that you may believe. Nevertheless let us go to him."*
> (John 11: 3 - 7; 11 - 15).

Notice that Jesus called Lazarus' death a "sleep." When He first heard of Lazarus' illness, He commented, *"This sickness is not unto death."* By this he simply meant that Lazarus' sickness was not because of sin, for the "*wages of sin is death.*" Jesus had another purpose in mind. He was going to "wake Lazarus from sleep"—but not an ordinary sleep for the purpose of resting. Jesus plainly told His disciples that Lazarus' death ("end of probation") was not "death" but "sleep."

Upon Jesus' arrival, He found that Lazarus had been dead for four days. Then Jesus said:

> *"I am the resurrection and the life. He who believes in Me, though he may die, he shall live. And whoever lives and believes in Me shall never die. Do you believe this?"*
> *(John 11: 25, 26).*

Unfortunately, many do not believe these words of Jesus because they do not believe that the natural "end of probation" is not death in God's sight, but sleep. Now, let us read another story in the Bible about the natural "end of probation," and see how Jesus dealt with it.

> *And behold, there came a man named Jairus, and he was a ruler of the synagogue. And he fell down at Jesus' feet and begged Him to come to his house, for he had an only daughter about twelve years of age, and she was dying. . . . While He was still speaking, someone came from the ruler of the synagogue's house, saying to him, "Your daughter is dead. Do not trouble the Teacher. . . ."*
>
> *Now all wept and mourned for her, but He said, "Do not weep; she is not dead, but sleeping." And they ridiculed Him, knowing that she was dead. But He put them all outside, took her by the hand and called, saying, "Little girl, arise." Then her spirit returned, and she arose immediately. (Luke 8: 41 - 42; 49, 52 - 55).*

On the way to the ruler's house, the report came that the child had died. They must have checked carefully and found no life in her. But Jesus said, *"She is not dead, but sleeping."* The mourners ridiculed Jesus, knowing that the child had truly died. Here again, Jesus called this "end of probation" a sleep.

The apostles also taught that the death that comes to all men was "a sleep." Paul wrote,

> *After that He [Jesus] was seen by over five hundred brethren at once, of whom the greater part remain to the present, but <u>some have fallen asleep</u>.*
> *(1 Corinthians 15: 6).*

> *But I do not want you to be ignorant, brethren, concerning <u>those who have fallen asleep</u>, lest you sorrow as others who have no hope. For if we believe that Jesus died and rose again, even so God will bring with Him those who sleep in Jesus.*
> *(1 Thessalonians 4: 13, 14).*

Peter said the same concerning the dead:

> *For since <u>the fathers fell asleep</u>, all things continue as they were from the beginning of creation.*
> *(2 Peter 3: 4).*

This term, *"slept with his fathers"* is repeatedly used in the Old Testament to describe someone's death, e.g. 1 Kings 2: 10; 11: 43; 14: 20; 14: 31; 15: 8; 22: 50; 2 Kings 8: 24; 9: 28; 10: 35; 13: 9, etc. The Bible is clear that none of the human family has yet died for *"the wages of sin."* Jesus, alone, has died the death caused by sin. *"But God demonstrates His own love toward us, in that while we were still sinners, Christ died for us. (Romans 5: 8).* Jesus paid the *"wages of sin"* for every believing person, so that, as Jesus told Lazarus' sister, Martha, *"<u>Whoever lives and believes in Me shall never die.</u>" (John 11: 26).*

The Bible speaks of the "real death," or the *"second death" (Revelation 20: 14, 15),* which is complete annihilation of body, mind and soul. Although all die the natural "end of probation" (sleep), the natural birth does not necessarily lead to this real, second death. It may be averted by belief in, and obedience to Jesus Christ, the Savior of mankind.

Yes, the God of Heaven is fair and just. He gives to each the freedom to choose the "second birth" (see Chapter 14, p. 172, 173) through His Spirit, and be entirely free from death (extermination) forever. Each individual must make the decision "to be or not to be." God the Father sent His only Son, Jesus, to die in our place. The love manifested on the cross is the strongest argument that God is fair and just—and He is love!

Because of Jesus' sacrifice, man is bought back from death and gains another chance to live eternally. Everyone who beholds God's love and chooses to be born again in Christ, chooses life. Even though this "probationary life" ends with a sleep in the grave, this is not the end. There follows a resurrection to a new, eternal life with God the Father, the Son, and the Holy Spirit. *"God is not the God of the dead, but of the living." (Matthew 22: 32)*. He is not interested in seeing how many He can condemn and put to death, but in how many He can save and give eternal life! For He *"is longsuffering toward us, not willing that any should perish but that all should come to repentance." (2 Peter 3: 9)*.

Jesus is the source of life. To know Him is to know life; to have Him is to have life. To ignore Him is to know death. There is no death in life, and no life in death.

> *"And <u>this is eternal life</u>,*
> *that they may know You,*
> *the only true God,*
> *and Jesus Christ*
> *whom You have sent."*
> *(John 17: 3)*.

19

The Time Has Come

Heaven's net casts wide. Though its meshes are coarse, nothing slips through.[1]

Wan Zi (文子) asked, "If the dead shall come alive, with whom do you think I will come back?"[2]

From the very beginning, the Chinese knew that the God of Heaven was not only merciful, but righteous and just, for this is a teaching seen in all of the ancient Chinese Classics. Other important moral teachings contained in venerable folk literature, sayings and proverbs—which even the illiterate know by heart—carry the same ideal. However, during the "cultural revolution" (1966 - 1976), the Chinese Classics and religious books (including the Bible) were burned and declared "forbidden reading." But the heavenly teaching contained in the common people's hearts and in the folk literature [such as *Three Character Classics* 《三字经》 / *A collection of Moral Essays* 《增广贤文》] helped to keep the flame of truth burning in Chinese hearts.

It was a common sight to see old, poorly-dressed, rustic men selling handwritten folk literature on the streets after China began to reform in 1978. The older generation has been afraid that the great, ancient teachings would be lost, for these are no longer taught anywhere in China's schools. But God always has His way of preserving truth.

God will some day judge the world; virtues will be rewarded and vice punished—these have always been widely believed heavenly principles, handed down from antiquity. In the *Shu Jing, The Book of Documents,* we read:

> **The way of heaven is to bless the good and to punish the bad.**[3]

The ancient Chinese believed this was how the God of Heaven dealt with His people below. The early kings were considered the representatives of Heaven on earth. Therefore they should be just and fair in their judgment of the people.

> **The King said, "Oh! Let there be a feeling of reverence. Ye judges and chiefs, and all ye who are my relatives of the royal House, know all that I speak in much fear. I think with reverence of the subject of punishment, for the end of it is to promote virtue. Now Heaven, wishing to help the people, has made us its representatives here below. Be intelligent and pure in hearing one side of a case."**[4]

Kings as Heaven's representatives? This seems a questionable statement, for today's leaders are not always moral, even according to human standards. But the Bible teaches the same. Note what Paul said in general of the governing authority:

> *Let every soul be subject to the governing authorities. For there is no authority except from God, and the authorities that exist are appointed by God. Therefore whoever resists the authority resists the ordinance of God, and those who resist will bring judgment on themselves. For rulers are not a terror to good works, but to evil. Do you want to be unafraid of the authority? Do what is good, and you will have praise from the same.* <u>*For he is God's minister to you for good.*</u> *But if you do evil, be afraid; for he does not bear the sword in*

> vain; for he is God's minister, and avenger to execute wrath on him who practices evil. (Romans 13: 1 - 4).

The ancient King continued to urge his officers that while they are to judge the people, they themselves must be in awe of the Judgment of Heaven. For Heaven is just and impartial.

> **The correct ordering of the people depends on the impartial hearing of the pleas on both sides; do not seek for private advantage for yourselves by means of those pleas. Gain gotten by the decision of cases is no precious acquisition; it is an accumulation of guilt, and will be recompensed with many evils. You should ever stand in awe of the punishment of Heaven. <u>It is not Heaven that does not deal impartially with men, but men ruin themselves</u>. If the punishment of Heaven were not so extreme, the people would have no good government at all under heaven.**[5]

The early Chinese knew that government was of Heaven, built on love and justice; that Heaven had laws for the government. Human authority was Heaven's governing agency; breaking the law incurred punishment.

> **Heaven sends down misery or happiness according to one's conduct.**[6]

The God of Heaven does not judge blindly, but judges each individually according to his own conduct.

> *You are treasuring up for yourself wrath in the day of wrath and revelation of the righteous judgment of <u>God, who will render to each one according to his deeds</u>; eternal life to those who by patient continuance in doing good seek for glory, honor, and immortality; but to those who are self-seeking and do not obey the truth, but obey unrighteousness—indignation and wrath, tribulation and anguish, on every soul of man who does evil, of the Jew first and also of the Greek; but glory,*

honor, and peace to everyone who works what is good, to the Jew first and also to the Greek. <u>For there is no partiality with God.</u> (Romans 2: 5 - 11).

The apostle John recorded the words of Jesus in the book of Revelation: *"And behold, I am coming quickly, and My reward is with Me, <u>to give to every one according to his work.</u>" (Revelation 22: 12).* According to the *Shu Jing,* everyone is subject to the judgment.

There is no mistake about the decree of Heaven.[7]

With the judgment of God in view, Confucius wrote with confidence:

A virtuous family is sure to have an abundance of happiness; but a family without virtue an abundance of misery.[8]

However, living in the real world, the evildoer does not necessarily receive severe punishment, neither the virtuous person a good reward. There were questions!

Among his seventy excellent students, Confucius recommended only Yan Yuan as the most diligent. But Yan Yuan was so poor he had only husks and chaff for food and sometimes nothing at all. Also, he died young [age 18]. <u>Is this the way that Heaven rewards the virtuous?</u> On the other hand, the evil Zhi (跖) killed innocent people every day, even ironing their flesh with a burning iron. He was cruel and heinous, had several thousand followers. Zhi ran wild for a time and died a natural death. What was his virtue to have a peaceful ending.[9]

King Solomon noticed the same seeming inconsistency, writing:

There is a vanity which occurs on earth, that there are just men to whom it happens according to the work of the wicked; again there are wicked men to whom it happens according to the work of the righteous. I said that this also is vanity. (Ecclesiastes 8: 14).

Jesus Himself called the world a *"faithless and perverse generation."* *(Luke 9: 41)*. Then how can one see in a perverse generation the uprightness of God? How can one still believe that God is just and makes no mistakes in His judgment? How can one still believe that God is love when bad things happen to good people?

The ancient Chinese believed that a time of judgment would come. This is found in common Chinese sayings, such as:

Virtue and vice are sure to be rewarded in the end; only at times sooner, or at times later.

It is a common Chinese belief that there will be a right time for Heaven to judge the world and give either reward or punishment. From past history, there is sufficient evidence to trust His justice. Questions regarding God's justice have come only because of misunderstandings regarding death.

In the previous chapter, we found that when a man dies, it is for him, "the end of probation." He simply sleeps. He knows nothing of what goes on around him.

*For the living know that they will die,
but <u>the dead know nothing</u>,
And they have no more reward,
for the memory of them is forgotten.
Also their love, their hatred, and their
envy have now perished;
Nevermore will they have a share in
anything done under the sun.*
(Ecclesiastes 9: 5).

<u>*The dead do not praise the Lord*</u>*, nor any
who go down into silence.*
(Psalm 115: 17).

It is profitable here for us to point out a misunderstanding of the Chinese. Modern Chinese are labeled as atheists, though few, including the finest Chinese Christian scholars, know that the Chinese teaching of *Wu Shen Lun* (無神論) is totally different from western atheism.

As we discussed in Part II of this book, the Chinese language has several words to describe God. *Heaven* 天, who seldom speaks, is a name for God the Father; and we discovered that *Shangdi* (上帝) is the Only Begotten Son, Christ Jesus (see p. 78). In Chapter 7, we discussed about the *Qi* (氣) and *Spirit* (靈), which is the breath of God, or Holy Spirit. There are also two general terms for the Godhead: *Dao* (道) (see Chapter 6) and *Shen* (示申) (see pp. 78, 79). In the course of time, the meanings of all these names for God, except for the name *Shangdi*, have gone through some changes. *Heaven* is used, in some cases, to indicate only nature. *Qi* and *Spirit* are mostly misused (the modern movement of *Qi Gong* sprang from a misconception of the Holy Spirit, but will not be dealt with here). *Dao* has become more or less mystical, while the word *Shen* (示申) is used in many ways—one of which is for man's consciousness. Chinese philosophers have held that when a man dies, his consciousness (示申) is dead, as well. That is the true meaning of the Chinese phrase for "nonconsciousness" (無神論), which has mistakenly been identified with the atheism of western philosophy.

As early as the Shang Dynasty, there was worship of the spirits of the dead, although wise men still taught that the spirits of the dead do not exist. We mentioned in the previous chapter that Confucius did not believe in life after death, and therefore did not talk about it. However, the most famous advocates of Chinese "nonconsciousness" (無神論) are Wang Chong (王充, 27 - 97 A.D.) and Fang Zhen (范镇, 450 - 510 A.D.).

In his book, *On Balance* (《论衡》), Wang Chong maintained that man's life is dependent on the "Breath of the Spirit" (元氣), and there is no independent soul outside of the body. When Buddhism became popular in China, Fang Zhen wrote the book, *On Consciousness Extinguished* (《神灭论》), against the teachings of karma and reincarnation. Liang Wudi (梁武帝, 464 - 549 A.D.), founder of Liang Dynasty (502 - 555 A.D.), adopted Buddhism as the national religion. When Emperor Liang ordered more than 60 high officials and Buddhist monks to attack his book in 507, Fang Zhen did not bow to pressure, but remained standing firm in truth. His famous claim was:

When one's body is alive, his consciouness exists, when one's body is dead, his consciousness exists no more.[10]

Although many came to believe in a consiousness after death, all except those who held Buddhist beliefs readily accepted the existence of a righteous and loving God of Heaven, and feared Him. When Chinese talk about *You Shen Lun* (有神論) or *Wu Shen Lun* (無神論), it is a discussion on consciousness after death, not on the existence of God. And more surprisingly, *Wu Shen Lun* (belief in nonconsciousness after death) is truth, and *You Shen Lun* (belief in consciousness after death) is error! How sad the fact that today the very truth of Nonconsiousness after death is used to refute belief in the God of Heaven, a belief which preserved China for thousands of years!

So what about judgment? If God's judgment does not occur during one's lifetime, and His judgment does not occur when one enters the sleep of death, when will God prove His justice? It must be, then, that the dead come forth from their graves and receive their reward or punishment! The righteous man, Job, asked this question,

If a man dies, shall he live again? (Job 14: 14).

Without having an answer to this question from the Bible, the ancient Chinese suggested that it was only reasonable for the dead to come alive again if Heaven is just and righteous.

Wan Zi (文子) asked, "If the dead shall come alive, with whom do you think I will come back?"[11]

Su Yu (叔譽) then gave the names of two powerful men. Wan Zi thought these were not wise and were also selfish. Wan Zi did not want to return with these two. Su Yu then gave the name of one who was unselfish, worked for the good of others, and served the king with all his heart. Wan Zi decided he wanted to return with him.[12]

In this statement, Wan Zi not only guessed that the dead would come alive, but also that there would be two resurrections: one for the good, and the other for the bad! How close to the truth did he come? Let us see what Jesus Himself said in the Bible:

> *"Most assuredly, I say to you, he who hears My word and believes in Him who sent Me has everlasting life, and shall not come into judgment, but has passed from death into life. Most assuredly, I say to you, the hour is coming, and now is, when the <u>dead will hear the voice of the Son of God; and those who hear will live</u>. For as the Father has life in Himself, so He has granted the Son to have life in Himself, and has <u>given Him authority to execute judgment also, because He is the Son of Man</u>." (John 5: 24 - 27).*

God the Father has given the Son authority to judge men. Man can therefore feel assured that their Judge understands all the difficulties of human life, since He is the Son of Man and was subject to man's problems. Therefore, man can understand that the judgment will be fair. Jesus continued His statement about the judgment:

> *"Do not marvel at this, for the hour is coming in which all who are in the graves will hear His voice and come forth—<u>those who have done good, to the resurrection of life, and those who have done evil, to the resurrection of condemnation</u>. I can of Myself do nothing. As I hear, I judge, and My judgment is righteous, because I do not seek My own will but the will of the Father who sent Me." (John 5: 28 - 30).*

There will, in fact, be two resurrections—just as Wan Zi surmised. The "first death" (or "sleep") is not the end for man. The good will be resurrected to everlasting life; while the evil are brought back to life for eternal extinction. Wrote the apostle Paul about this event:

> *Behold, I tell you a mystery: We shall not all sleep, but we shall all be changed—in a moment, in the twinkling of*

> *an eye, <u>at the last trumpet. For the trumpet will sound, and the dead will be raised incorruptible, and we shall be changed</u>. For this corruptible must put on incorruption, and this mortal must put on immortality.*
> *(1 Corinthians 15: 51 - 53).*

A great "change" takes place in some of those sleeping as "the trumpet sounds." When is this, according to the Bible?

> *For the Lord Himself will descend from heaven with a shout, with the voice of an archangel, and <u>with the trumpet of God. And the dead in Christ will rise first</u>. Then we who are alive and remain shall be caught up together with them in the clouds to meet the Lord in the air. And thus we shall always be with the Lord. Therefore comfort one another with these words.*
> *(1 Thessalonians 4: 16 - 18).*

It is when Jesus returns to earth a second time that He calls the sleeping righteous ones to life again. This is the first resurrection. *"They lived and reigned with Christ for a thousand years." (Revelation 20: 4).* "But the <u>rest of the dead did not live again until the thousand years were finished</u>." *(Revelation 20: 5).*

The "second resurrection" comes 1,000 years after the first resurrection of the righteous. This is the resurrection of the wicked. *"Then Death and Hades [the grave] were cast into the lake of fire. <u>This is the second death</u>. And anyone not found written in the Book of Life was cast into the lake of fire." (Revelation 20: 14, 15).*

Lao Zi described this judgment of Heaven in a very vivid way when he said:

> **Heaven's net casts wide,**
> **though its meshes are coarse,**
> **nothing slips through.**[13]

Interestingly, Jesus used the same "net" metaphor for the future judgment, when He spoke to a crowd of listeners:

> *"Again the kingdom of heaven is like a dragnet that was cast into the sea and gathered some of every kind, which, when it was full, they drew to shore; and they sat down and gathered the good into vessels, but threw the bad away. So it will be at the end of the age [end of the world, KJV]. The angels will come forth, separate the wicked from among the just, and cast them into the furnace of fire. There will be wailing and gnashing of teeth." (Matthew 13: 47 - 50).*

But God does not judge men without Himself being judged first: *"That You [God] may be justified in Your words, And may overcome when You are judged." (Romans 3: 4).* On the cross it was Jesus Christ, God the Son, not any human sinner, who was judged and crucified before all men and before the entire universe.

By condemning His only begotten Son to die as a substitute for sinners in all the world, God the Father demonstrated His impartiality against sin, and His great love and mercy for mankind. God's works, words, truthfulness, righteousness, mercy and justice were all judged. *"<u>God is not the God of the dead, but of the living</u>." (Matthew 22: 32).* He is love and life. God opened His heart in a great demonstration of mercy, grace, long-suffering, goodness and love for all to see. He proved to the entire universe His trustworthiness—that He is a friend with whom all the righteous could live throughout eternity.

What standard did God use in the judgment which sentenced Jesus to death? What will be God's standard in the final judgment of men? Jesus died for men's sin, which is transgression of the law. (1 John 3: 4). Jesus was judged as a substitute sinner by the law of God. By the same law, every human will be judged. *"So speak and so do as those who will be judged by the law of liberty." (James 2: 12).*

Just as obedience to traffic rules brings safety, so obedience to God's law brings liberty. To break the rules is to lose safety and liberty. But one's natural self cannot obey the law of God. Therefore, the Lord gives one a new heart which is in harmony with God's law.

7-8: 王若曰："诰告尔多方，非天庸释有夏，非天庸释有殷。乃惟尔辟，以尔多方，大淫图天之命，屑有辞。"

"惟圣罔作狂，惟狂克念作圣，天惟五年，须暇之子孙，诞作民主，罔可念听。天惟求尔多方，大动以威，开厥顾天，惟尔多方，罔堪顾之。惟我周王，灵承于旅，克堪用德，惟典神天，天惟式教我用休，简畀殷命，尹尔多方。"《书经多方》
9："顺天者昌，逆天者亡。"《孟子离娄章句上》
10："三代之得天下也以仁，其失天下也以不仁。国之所以废兴存亡亦然。"（《离娄章句上》）。
11："钦崇天道，永保天命。"《尚书仲虺之诰》
12：万章曰："尧以天下与舜，有诸？"孟子曰："否，天子不能以天下与人。""然则舜有天下也，孰与之？"曰："天与之。""天与之者，谆谆然命之乎？"曰："否；天不言，以行与事示之而已矣。"曰："以行与事示之者，如之何？"曰："天子能荐人于天，不能使天与之天下；诸侯能荐人于天子，不能使天子与之诸侯；大夫能荐人于诸侯，不能使诸侯与之大夫。昔者，尧荐舜于天，而天受之；暴之于民，而民受之；故曰，天不言，以行与事示之而已矣。"《孟子万章章句上》
13："予冲子夙夜毖祀。"《书经洛诰》
14："我将我亨，维羊维牛。维天其右之。"《诗经、我将》
15："天聪明，自我民聪明、天明畏，自我民明威、达于上下。敬哉有土。"《书经皋陶谟》
16：既受帝祉，施于孙子。
　　帝谓文王："无然畔援，无然歆羡，诞先登于岸。"
　　帝谓文王："予怀明德，不大声以色，不长夏以革。不识不知，顺帝之则"《诗经皇矣》
17："恭默思道，帝赉予良弼，其代予言。"《书经说命上》
19："天命不僭，卜陈惟若兹。"《书经大诰》
20：天惠民、惟辟奉天。《书经泰誓中》
21："有皇上帝，伊谁云憎？"《诗经正月》
22："且吾所以知天之爱民之厚者矣，曰以磨为日月星辰，以昭道之，制为四时春秋冬夏，以纪纲之，雷降雪霜雨露，以长遂五谷麻丝，使民得而财利之，列为山川峪谷，播赋百事，以临司民之善否，为王公侯伯，使之赏贤而罚暴，贼金木鸟兽，从事乎五谷麻丝，以为民衣食之财，自古及今，未尝不有此也，今有人于此，骐若爱其子，竭力单务以利之，其子长，而无报子求父，故天下君子，与谓之不仁不详。"《墨子》

第六章
1："吾不知其名，名之曰"道"；强名之曰"大"。"《道德经》第二十五章
2："子绝四：毋意，毋必，毋固，毋我。"《论语子罕第九》
3："道可道，非常道。名可名，非常名。"《道德经》第一章

4："吾不知谁之子，象帝之先"。《道德经》第四章
5："视之不见，名曰夷；听之不闻，名曰希；搏之不得，名曰微。此三者不可致诘，故混而为一。其上不明，其下不昧。……执古之道，以御今之有。能知古始，是谓道纪。"《道德经》14章
6："有物混成，先天地生。寂兮寥兮，独立而不改，周行而不殆，可以为天地母。吾不知其名，字之曰道，强为之名曰大。"《道德经》第二十五章
7："人法地，地法天，天法道，道法自然。"《道德经》第二十五章
8："天下万物生于有，有生于无。"《道德经》第四十章
9：道生一，一生二，二生三，三生万物。《道德经》第四十二章

第七章

1："敢问夫子恶乎长？"曰："我知言，我善养吾浩然之气。""敢问何谓浩然之气？"曰："难言也。其为气也，至大至刚，以直养而无害，则塞于天地之间。其为气也，配义与道；无是，馁也。是集义之所生者，非义袭而取之也。行有不慊于心，则馁也。"
《孟子 公孙丑章句上》
2："便使而今天赐洛书，若非天启其心，亦无人理会得，两说不可偏废也。"《朱子全集》
3："气也者，神之盛也。"《礼记祭义》
12："天命玄鸟，降而生商。"《诗经玄鸟》

第八章

4："象曰：雷雨作，解。君子以赦过宥罪。"《易经解第四十》
5："夫大人者，与天地合其德；与日月合其明，与四时合其序，与鬼神合吉凶。先天而天弗违，后天而奉天时。天且弗违，而况于人乎？况于鬼神乎？《易经乾第一》
6："知进退存亡而不失其正者，其唯圣人乎？"《易经乾第一》
7："象曰：（君子）虽磐桓，志行正也；以贵下贱，大得民也。"
8："圣人以神道设教，而天下服矣。"《易经观第二十》

第九章

1："或问帝之说，子曰："不知也。知其说者之于天下也，其如示诸斯乎！"指其掌。《论语八佾第三》
2：子曰："吾十有五志于学，三十而立，四十而不惑，五十而知天命，六十而耳顺，七十而从心所欲，不逾矩。"《论语为政第二》
3："子温而厉，威而不猛，恭而安。"《论语述而第七》
4："卫灵公问陈于孔子，孔子对曰：'俎豆之事，则尝闻之矣；军旅之事，未之学也。'明日遂行。"《论语卫灵公第十五》

5：子畏于匡，曰"文王既没，文不在兹乎？天之将丧斯文也，后死者不得与于斯文也；天之未丧斯文也，匡人其如予何！"
《论语子罕第九》

6：仪封人请见，曰：'君子之至于斯也，吾未尝不得见也。从者见之。出：'二三子，何患丧乎，天下之无道久矣，天将以夫子为木铎。'"《论语八佾第三》

7：夫子曰："君子学道则爱人，小人学道则易使也"
《论语阳货第十七》

8：颜渊喟然叹曰："仰之弥高，钻之弥坚，瞻之在前，忽焉在后。夫子循循然善诱人，博我以文，约我以礼，欲罢不，既竭吾才。如有所立卓尔。虽欲从之，未由也已。"《论语子罕第九》

9："一阴一阳谓之道，...仁者见之谓之仁，知者见之谓之知，百姓日用而不知。"《易经系辞上传》

10："阴阳不测谓之神。"《易经系辞上传》

11："道也者，不可须臾离也；可离，非道也。是故君子戒慎乎其所不睹，恐惧乎其所不闻。"《中庸》

12：子曰："志于道，据于德，依于仁，游于艺。"
《论语述而第七》

13：子曰："君子谋道不谋食。耕也，馁在其中矣；学也，禄在其中矣。君子忧道不忧贫。"《论语卫灵公第十五》

14：子曰："饭疏食，饮水，曲肱而枕之，乐亦在其中矣，不义而富且贵，于我如浮云。"《论语述而第七》

15：子曰："贤哉回也！一箪食，一瓢饮，在陋巷，人不堪其忧，回也不改其乐。贤哉回也！"《论语雍也第六》

16：子曰："道不同，不相为谋。"《论语卫灵公第十五》

17：子曰："天生德于予。"《论语述而第七》

18：子曰："三人行，必有我师焉。择其善者而从之，其不善者而改之。"《论语述而第七》

19：子曰："默而识之，学而不厌，诲人不倦，何有于我哉？"
《论语述而第七》

20：子曰："朝闻道，夕死可矣。"《论语里仁第四》

21：子曰："甚矣，吾衰也！久矣，吾不复梦见周公！"
《论语述而第七》

22：子曰："圣人，吾不得而见之矣；得见君子，斯可矣。"子曰："善人，吾不得而见之矣；得见有恒者，斯可矣。"
《论语述而第七》

23：子曰："莫我知也夫！"子贡曰："何为其莫知子也？"子曰："不怨天，不忧人，下学而上达。知我者，其天乎！"
《论语宪问第十四》

第十章

3："唯酒无量，不及乱。"《论语子罕第九》
4："然则夫子（孟子）既圣矣乎？"曰："恶！是何言也？昔者子贡问于孔子曰：'夫子圣人乎？'孔子曰：'圣则吾不能，我学而不厌而教倦也。'子贡曰：'学不厌，智也；教不倦，仁也。仁且智，夫子既圣矣。'夫圣，孔子不居－是何言也？"
　　　　　　　　　　　《孟子公孙丑章句上》
5："乃所愿，则学孔子也。"《孟子公孙丑章句上》
6："大哉！圣人之道！洋洋乎，发育万物，峻极于天。优优大哉！礼仪三百，威仪三千，待其人而后行。故曰："苟不至德，至道不凝焉。"《中庸》
8："是以圣人处无为之事，行不言之教，万物作而弗始，生而弗有，为而弗恃，功成而弗居。夫唯弗居，是以不去。"
　　　　　　　　　　　《道德经》第二章
9："天地养万物。圣人养贤以及万民，颐之时大矣哉。"
　　　　　　　　　　　《易经颐第二十七》
10："是以圣人之治，虚其心，实其腹。"《道德经》第三章
11：孟子曰："圣人，百世之师也。"《孟子、尽心章句下》
12："自今及古，其名不去，以阅众甫。吾何以知众甫之状哉？以此。"《道德经》第二十一章
13："圣人以神道设教，而天下服矣。"《易经观第二十》
14．"故立天子置三公，虽有拱璧以先驷，不如坐进此道。古之所以贵此道者何？不曰："求以得，有罪以免邪？故为天下贵。"
　　　　　　　　　　　《道德经》第六十二章
14．"道者，万物之奥。善人之宝，不善人之所保。"
　　　　　　　　　　　《道德经》第六十二章
15："知其白，守其黑，为天下式。"《道德经》第二十八章
17　"是以圣人抱一为天下式。不自见，故明；不自是，故彰；不自伐，故有功；不自矜，故长。夫唯不争，故天下莫能与之争。"
　　　　　　　　　　　《道德经》第二十二章
18："善闭，无关楗而不可开；善结，无绳约而不可解。是以圣人常善救人，故无弃人。"《道德经》第二十七章

第十一章

1："舍弃肉身性命去为天下的人，堪为普天下的寄托；舍弃肉身性命去爱天下的人，堪得普天下的信靠。"《道德经》第十三章
3：是以圣人云："受国之垢，是谓社稷主；受国不祥，是为天下王。"　《道德经》第七十八章
4："大学之道，在明明德，在亲民，在止于至善。"《大学》
5：子曰："天生德于予。"《论语述而第七》

7: 子曰 "三军可以夺帅也,匹夫不可夺志也。"《论语子罕第九》
9: "反者道之动也;弱者道之用。"《道德经》第40章
10: 子曰: "如有王者,必世而后仁。"《论语子路第十三》
11: 子曰: "父在观其志,父没观其行,三年无改于父之道,可谓考矣。"《论语学而第一》
13: "故天将降大任于是人也,必先苦其心志,劳其筋骨,饿其体肤,空乏其身,行拂乱其所为,所以动心忍性,增益其所不能。"
《孟子告子章句下》
14: "焉有君子而可以货取乎?"《孟子公孙丑章句下》
15: "富贵不能淫,贫贱不能移,威武不能屈;此之谓大丈夫!"
《孟子滕文公章句下》
16: "是以圣人后其身而身先,外其身而身存。"
《道德经》第七章
17: "知其荣,守其辱。"《道德经》第二十八章
18: "辟以止辟,乃辟。"《书经周官》

第十二章

1: "兹不于我政人得罪,天惟与我民彝大泯。"《书经康诰》
4: "顺天之意者,义之法也。"《墨子天志中》
5: "顺天意者,义政也。反天意者,力政也。"《墨子天志上》
6: "然则天亦何欲何恶?天欲义而恶不义。然则何以知天之欲义而恶不义?曰天下有义则生,无义则死;有义则富,无义则贫;有义则治,无义则乱。然则天欲其生而恶其死,欲其富而恶其贫,欲其治而恶其乱,此我所以知天欲义而恶不义也。"《墨子天志上》
9: "礼者何也?即事之治也。君子有其事,必有其治。治国无礼,譬犹瞽之无相与,伥伥乎其何之?譬如终夜有求于幽室之中,非烛何见?"《礼记仲尼燕居》
10: "礼之于正国也,犹衡之于轻重也,绳墨之于曲直也,规矩之于方圆也。故衡诚悬,不可欺以轻重;绳墨诚陈,不可欺以曲直;规矩诚设,不可欺以方圆;君子审礼,不可诬以奸诈。"《礼记经解》
11: 子曰: "君子怀德,小人怀土;君子怀刑,小人怀惠。"
《论语里仁第四》
13 公孙丑曰: "道则高矣,美矣,宜若登天然,似不可及也;何不使彼为可几何及而日孳孳也?"
孟子曰: "大匠不为拙工改绳墨,羿不为拙射变其彀率。"
《孟子尽心章句上》
14: "夫礼,禁乱之所由生,犹坊止水之所自来也。故以旧坊为无所用而坏之者,必有水败;以旧坊为无所有用而去之者,必有患。"
《礼记经解》

15: "礼之所兴,众之所治也;礼之所废,众之所乱也。"
《礼记仲尼燕居》
16: "故唯圣人为知礼之不可以已也。故坏国、丧家、亡人、必先去其礼。"《礼记礼运》
18: "然今天下之情伪,未可得而识也,故使言有三法。三法者也?有本之者,有原之者,有用之者。"
19: "于其本之也,考之天鬼之志,圣王之事;于其原之也,征以先王之书,用之奈何,发而为刑,此言之三法也。"
20: "且今天下之士君子,中实将欲为仁义,求为上士,上欲中圣王之道,下欲中国家百姓之利者,当天之志,而不可不察也!天之者,义之经也。"《墨子非命中》

第十三章

1: 樊迟问仁,子曰:"爱人。"《论语颜渊第十二》
2: "夫仁,天之尊爵也,人之安宅也。"《孟子公孙丑上》
3: "温温恭人,如集于木。惴惴小心,如临于谷,战战兢兢,如履薄冰。"《诗经小雅小宛》
4: 孔子曰:"不知命,无以为君子也;不知礼,无以立也;不知言,无以知人也。"《论语尧曰第二十》
5: "事亲如事天,事天如事亲。"《礼记哀公问》
6: 子路曰:"人善我,我亦善之;人不善我,我不善之。"子曰:"人善我,我亦善之;人不善我,我则引之,进退而已耳。"颜回曰:"人善我,我亦善之;人不善我,我亦善之。"
7: "三子所持各异,问于夫子,夫子曰:"由之所言,蛮貊之也;赐之所言,朋友之言也;回之所言,亲属之言也。诗曰:"人之无良,我以为兄"。《孔子集语卷八交道七》
8: 子夏曰:"君子敬而无失,与人恭而有礼,四海之内皆兄也。"
《论语颜渊第十二》
9: "己所不欲,勿施于人。"《论语颜渊第十二》
10: 子曰:"夫仁者,己欲立而立于人,己欲达而达于人。能近取譬,可谓仁之方也己。"《论语雍也第六》
11: 孟子曰:"仁者,以其所爱及其所不爱;不仁者,以其所不爱及其所爱。"《孟子尽心章句下》
12: 孟子曰:"夫仁,天之爵也,人之安宅也。《孟子公孙丑上》
13: 孟子曰:"仁,人之安宅也;义,人之正路也。旷安宅而弗居,舍正路而不由,哀哉!"《孟子离娄章句上》
15: "故不爱其亲而爱他人者,谓之悖德。不敬其亲而敬他人者,谓之悖礼。"《孝经》

16: 子曰: "立爱自亲始,教民睦也。立敬自长始,教民顺也。教以慈睦,而民贵有亲;教以敬长,而民贵有命。孝以事亲,顺以命,错诸天下,无所不行。"《礼记祭义》
17: 孟懿子问孝,子曰: "无违。" 樊迟御,子告之曰: "孟孙问孝于我,我对曰,无违。" 樊迟曰: "何谓也?" 子曰: "生,事之以礼;死,葬之以礼,祭之以礼。"《论语为政第二》
18: 子游问孝,子曰: "今之孝者,是谓能养。至于犬马,皆能养。不敬,何以别乎?"《论语为政第二》
19: "夫婚礼,万世之始也。"《礼记郊特性》
20: 颜渊问仁,子曰: "克己复礼为仁。一日克己复礼,天下归焉。为仁由己,而由人乎哉?"
21: 颜渊曰: "请问其目。" 子曰: "非礼勿视,非礼勿听,勿礼勿言,非礼勿动。" 颜渊曰: "回虽不敏,请事斯语矣。"
　　　　　　《论语颜渊第十二》
22: 子曰: "参乎!吾道一以贯之。" 曾子曰: "唯。" 子出,门人问曰: "何谓也?" 曾子曰: "夫子之道,忠恕而已矣。"
　　　　　　《论语里仁第四》
23: 孟子曰: "君子所以异于人者,以其存心也。君子以仁存心,以礼存心。"《孟子离娄章句下》

　　　　　　第十四章

1: 诚者,天之道也;诚之者,人之道也。《中庸》
3: 子贡曰: "夫子之文章可得而闻也,夫子之言性与天道,不可得而闻也。"《论语公冶长第五》
4: "诚者,天之道也;诚之者,人之道也。不勉而中,不思得,从容中道,圣人也。诚之者,择善而固执之者也。"《中庸》
7: "诚则明矣,明则诚矣。"《中庸》
8: "诚者,物之终始;不诚,无物。是故,君子诚之为贵。"
　　　　　　《中庸》
9: "诚者,非自成而已也,所以成物也。成己,仁也;成物,知也。"《中庸》
10: "故至诚无息。"《中庸》
11: "唯天下至诚,为能经纶天下之大经,立天下之大本,知天地之化育。夫焉有所倚?肫肫其仁,渊渊其渊,浩浩其天。苟不固聪明圣知达天德者,其孰能知之?"《中庸》
12: "故至诚无息;无息则久。久则征。征则悠远,悠远则博厚,博厚则高明。博厚所以载物也,高明所以覆物也,悠久所以成物也。博厚配地,高明配天,悠久无疆。如此者,不见而章,不动而变,不为而成。"《中庸》

13: "是以声名溢乎中国，施及蛮貊；舟车所至，人力所通，天之所覆，地之所载，日月所照霜露所队，凡有血气者，莫不尊亲；故曰配天。"《中庸》
15: "格物、致知、诚意、正心、修身、齐家、治国、平天下。"
16: "从天子以至于庶人，壹是皆以修身为本。"《中庸》
17 "心不在焉，视而不见，听而不闻，食而不知其味。"《大学》
18: "非知之难，行之惟难。"《书经、说命》
19: "常德不离，复归于婴儿。"《道德经》第二十八章
20: 孟子曰："大人者，不失其赤子之心者也。"
《孟子离娄章句下》
21: 子曰："朝闻道，夕死可矣。"《论语、里仁第四》
22: "唯天下至诚，为能尽其性；能尽其性，则能尽人之性；能尽人之性，则能尽物之性；能尽物之性，则可以赞天地之化育；可以赞天地之化育，则可以为天地参矣。"《中庸》

第十五章

1: 子曰："加我数年，五十而学易，可以无大过矣。"
《论语述而第七》
2: "易穷则变，变则通，通则久。是以自天佑之，吉无不利。"
《易经系辞下传》
3: "天生蒸民，　　上天降生天下万民，
有物有则，　　为所有事物定下了法则。
民之秉彝，　　百姓秉持永恒之法，
好中懿德。"　　因而切爱那可慕之德。"
《诗经、大雅、蒸民》
4: "天非徒赋命于人，授以形体心识，乃复佑助谐合其居业，使有常生之资。"
5: 子曰"性相近也，习相远也。"《论语阳货第十八》
6: 子曰："已矣乎，吾未见好德如好色者也。"
《论语卫灵公第十五》
7: 子曰："已矣乎！吾未见能见其过而内自讼者也。"
《论语公冶长第五》
9: 曾子曰："吾日三省吾身：为人谋，而不忠乎？与朋友交，而不信乎？传不习乎"《论语学而第一》
10: "见贤思齐焉，见不贤而内自省也。"《论语里仁第四》
11: 子曰："三人行，必有我师焉。择其善者而从之；其不善者而改之。"《论语述而第七》
12: 子曰："德之不修，学而不讲，闻义不能徙，不善不能改，是吾忧也。"《论语述而第七》

13: 子贡曰："君子之过也，如日月之食焉，过也，人皆见之；改也，人皆仰之。"《论语子张第十九》
14: 子曰："主忠信，毋友不如己者，过则勿惮改。《论语子罕九》
15: 子曰："过而不改，是谓过矣。"《论语卫灵公第十五》
17: "其匪正有眚，不利有攸往。无妄之往何之矣？天命不佑，行矣哉？"《易经无妄第二十五》

第十六章

1: 玉不琢，不成器；人不学，不知道。《礼记学记》
2: 子曰："丘之祷久矣。"《论语述而第七》
3: "学问之道无他，求其放心而已矣。"《孟子告子章句上》
4: 子曰："吾尝终日不食，终夜不寝，以思，无益，不如学也。"
《论语卫灵公第十五》
6: "虽有佳肴，弗食，不知其旨也。虽有至道，弗学，不知其善也。"《礼记学记》
7: 子曰："君子博学于文，约之以礼，亦可以弗畔矣夫！"
8: "温故而知新，敦厚而崇礼。"《中庸》
9: 子曰："学如不及，犹恐失之。"《论语泰伯第八》
10: 子曰："学而时习之，不亦乐乎？"《论语学而第一》
11: 子曰："学而不思则罔，思而不学则殆。"《论语为政第二》
12: 子曰："道听而途说，德之弃也。"《论语阳货第十七》
13 子曰："攻乎异端，斯害也已。"《论语为政第二》
14: 孟子曰："孔子登东山而小鲁，登泰山而小天下，故观于海者难为水，游于圣人之门者难为言。"《孟子尽心章句上》
15: 屈原曰："天者，人之始也；父母者，人之本也。人穷则反本，故劳苦倦极，未尝不呼天也，疾痛惨怛，未尝不呼父母也。"
《史记屈原列传》
16: "皇矣上帝！临下有赫。监观四方，求民之莫。"
《诗经皇矣》
17: "我将我享，维羊维牛。维天其右之。"《诗经我将》
18: "凡我造邦，无从匪彝，无即淫，各守尔典，以承天休。尔有善朕弗敢蔽，罪当朕躬，弗敢自赦。惟简在上帝之心，其尔万方有罪在予一人，予一人有罪，无以万方。呜呼，尚克时忱，乃亦有终。"
《书经汤诰》
19: "宅新邑，肆惟王其疾敬德，王其德之用，祈天永命。"
《书经召诰》
20: "渐泯泯棼棼，罔中于信，以覆诅盟，虐威庶戮，方告无辜上，上帝监民，罔有馨香德，刑发闻惟腥。"《书经吕刑》

21：子疾病，子路请祷。子曰："有诸？"子路对曰："有之《诔》曰：'祷于上下神祇。'"子曰："丘之祷久矣。"
　　　　　　　　　　　　　　　　《论语述而第七》

第十七章

3："天垂象，圣人则之。郊祭，天之道也。"
9："也往古之时，四极废，九洲裂，天不兼覆，地不周载。火焰炎而不灭，水浩洋而不息，猛兽食颛民，鸷鸟攫老弱。于是女娲炼五色石，以补苍天。"《淮南子》
13：子贡欲去告朔之饩羊。子曰："赐也！尔爱其羊，我爱其礼。"
　　　　　　　　　　　　　　　　《论语八佾第三》

第十八章

1：季路问事鬼神，子曰："未能事人，焉能事鬼？"曰："敢问死。"曰："未知生，焉知死？"《论语先进第十一》
3：原始反终，故知死生之说。《易经系辞上传》
5："所谓死者，无有所有知，复其未生也。"《吕氏春秋贵生篇》
6：众生必死，死必归土，此之谓鬼。《礼记祭义》
7：魂气归于天，形魄归于地。《礼记郊特性》
12：游于圣人之门者难为言。《孟子尽心章句下》
13：二十四年春，穆叔如晋。范宣子逆之，问焉，曰："古人有言曰：'死而不朽'，何谓也？"穆叔曰：'豹闻之，大上有立德，其次有立功，其次有立言，虽久不废，此之谓不朽。"
　　　　　　　　　　　　　　　　《左传襄公二十四年》

第十九章

1：天网恢恢，疏而不漏。《道德经》第七十三章
2：文子问："死者若可作，吾与谁归？"《礼记檀弓下》
3："天道福善祸淫，降灾于夏，以彰厥罪。"《书经汤诰》
4：王曰："呜呼，敬之哉，官伯族姓，朕言多惧，朕敬于刑有德，惟刑今天相民，作配在下，明清于单辞，民之乱，罔不中听狱之两辞，无或私家于狱之两辞，狱货非宝，惟府辜功报以庶尤，永畏惟罚，非天不中，惟人在命，天罚不极，庶民罔有令政在于天下。"
　　　　　　　　　　　　　　　　《书经吕刑》
6："惟天降灾祥在德。"《书经咸有一德》
7："天命不僭，卜陈惟若兹。"《书经大诰》
8："积善之家 必有馀庆；积不善之家，必有馀殃。"《易乾卦》
9：或曰："天道无亲，常与善人"。若伯夷叔齐，可谓善人者非邪？积仁洁行如此而饿死！且七十子之徒，仲尼独荐颜渊为好学。然回也屡空，糟糠不厌，崦卒早夭。天之所施善人，其何如哉！盗贼日杀不辜，肝人之肉，暴戾瓷睢，聚党数千人横行天下，竟以寿终。是遵何德哉？"《书经蔡仲之命》

10:　"善有善报，恶有恶报。不是不报，时候未到。时候一到，立即全报。"　"善恶到头终有报，只争来早与来迟。"《增广贤文》
11-12：　赵文子与叔誉观乎九原。文子曰："死者如可作也，吾谁与归？"叔誉曰："其阳处父乎？"文子曰："行并植于晋国，不没其身，其知不足称也。""其舅乎？"文子曰："见利不顾其君，其仁不足称也。我则随武子乎。利其君不忘其身，谋其身不遗其友。"
《礼记檀弓下》

第二十章
1：　"朋来无咎。反复其道。"《易经复第二十四》
　"反复其道，七日来复，天行也。"同上。
2：　"假我数年，五十以学易，可以无大过矣。"《论语述而第七》
3：　"孔子晚而喜《易》"。《史记孔子世家》
4：　"五十而知天命"。《论语为政第二》
5：　《复》，德之本也。《复》，小而辨于物。《复》以自知。
6：　"复，其见天地之心乎？"《易经复第二十四》
7：　复：亨。出入无疾，朋来无咎。反复其道，七日来复，利有攸往。同上。
8：　"反复其道，七日来复"，天行也"。同上。
10：　象曰：雷在地中，复。先王以至日闭关，商旅不行，后不省方。同上。

第二十一章
1：　"是故，谋闭而不兴，盗窃乱贼而不作，故外户而不闭，是谓大同。"《礼记、礼运》
2：　"大道之行也，天下为公，选贤与能，讲信修睦。故人不独亲其亲，不独子其子，使老有所终，壮有所用，幼有所长，矜、寡、孤、独、废疾者，皆有所养。男有分，女有归。货恶其弃于地也，不必藏于己；力恶其不出于身也，不必为己。是故，谋闭而不兴，盗窃乱贼而不作，故外户而不闭，是谓大同。"同上。
3：　孟子见梁惠王。王曰："叟，不远千里而来，亦将有以利吾国乎？"孟子对曰："王何必曰利？亦有仁义而己矣。"《梁惠王章句上》
4：　"老吾老，以及人之老；幼吾幼，以及人之幼，天下可运于掌"。《梁惠王章句上》
6：　子贡问于孔子曰："敢问君子贵玉而贱　者何也？玉之寡而碈之多与？"孔子曰："非为碈之多，故贱之也，玉之寡，故贵之也。夫昔者君子比德于玉焉。温润而泽，仁也；缜密以栗，知也；廉而不刿，义也；垂之如坠，礼也；叩之其声清越以长，其终诎然，乐也；瑕不掩瑜，瑜不掩瑕，忠也；孚尹旁达，信也；气如白虹，天也；精神见于山川，地也；圭璋特达，德也。天下莫不贵者，道也。诗曰：'言念君子，温其如玉。'故君子贵之也。"《礼记燕义》
7：　"乾为天，为圜，为君，为父，为玉。"《易经、说卦传》

305